Moonshots

CREATING A WORLD OF ABUNDANCE

How Entrepreneurs
are Enabling Life
Without Limits

NAVEEN JAIN
— With —
John Schroeter

Moonshots
- PRESS -

Published in the United States by Moonshots Press™,
an imprint of John August Media, LLC.

www.moonshotspress.com

Moonshots Press books are available at special discounts
for bulk purchases. For more information, please contact
the Special Markets Department at:
John August Media, PO Box 10174, Bainbridge Island, WA 98110
or email **business@moonshotspress.com**

Book and cover design by Ed Rother, ER Graphics

Printed in the USA

Library of Congress Cataloging-in-Publication Data is available.

ISBN: 978-0-9997364-0-1 (Print)
         978-0-9997364-1-8 (eBook)

LCCN: 2017964189

Entrepreneurship | Technological innovations | Strategic planning | New business enterprises

First Edition

10 9 8 7 6 5 4 3 2 1

Probable impossibilities are to be
preferred to improbable possibilities.

—*Aristotle*

CONTENTS

PART ONE

PART TWO

PART THREE

FOREWORD

PEOPLE OFTEN ASK ME how to go about becoming a millionaire. By now most people know my smart-ass answer: "Start as a billionaire and launch a new airline!"

What most people *don't* get from this little rejoinder is the suggestion that they're actually asking the wrong question. Rather than asking successful people about how to get rich, they ought to ask them about how to do things that are meaningful. Now that would be a good question! And it's one question that my good friend Naveen Jain sets out to answer in this fun book.

My life has never been about anything to do with material wealth. The fact is I've always had just one mission in life, and that is to make people's lives better. Sometimes the efforts fail and flounder, but other times they're wildly successful. Sometimes they're surprisingly easy; other times they're a real moonshot. In all cases, though, across all the Virgin companies, it's our custom to work with crazy ideas and see just how far we can take them. It's an ethos that has taken me from selling vinyl records out of the boot of my car to making commercial space travel as accessible as commercial aviation.

As diverse as the Virgin companies are, there's still one thing that grounds even the craziest of ideas we've pursued: there's no point in starting a business if it's not going to make a dramatic, positive difference in other people's lives.

You make a difference in the world by solving problems, and entrepreneurs are the world's best problem-solvers. To that end—and to what's truly exciting and amazing about all of this—*there are no rules*. If there were, you can be sure we would be breaking every one of them. I'm so thankful I never learned all the conventional "dos and don'ts" of starting and running a business. It's actually been a tremendous advantage for me (as I often say, you don't learn to walk by following rules—you learn by doing and by falling over). It's also the reason we've been able to go in and shake up entire industries. It's because we are "virgins" in every market we take on that we bring a very different mindset to the problems and challenges there. Indeed, we do things very differently. Consequently, industries are changed simply because we have entered them. And that experience has become a great passion in its own right—I can't stop doing it!

I believe there is no greater thing you can do with your life and work than to follow your passions—but in a way that has a purpose beyond profit. And if the object of your pursuit is a "massively transformative purpose," then believe me, you'll never have to worry about the rewards—they will follow in turn. I can also tell you that working in this way requires a different kind of mind—an inquisitive, curious, questioning, and imaginative mind—the kind of mind that puts wind in the entrepreneur's sails. Fortune indeed favors those whose mindset—and creative optimism—drives them to work to make a massive difference in the world. It's a mindset that is equally essential to preparing you for any of the many *possible* futures that might be in store for us—what Naveen calls the "quantum future." And the more audacious your vision for that future, the better.

> **" I have always set for myself huge, seemingly unachievable challenges—*moonshots*. I have found this approach to be the real difference maker in my life. And it can be for yours, as well. "**

I have always set for myself huge, seemingly unachievable challenges—*moonshots*. I have found this approach to be the real difference maker in my life. And it can be for yours, as well. Indeed, if your dreams don't scare you, then they are too small.

Between the covers of this book is the straightest path for anyone who wants to take that huge, audacious, impossible, and scary dream, wrap it in passion and conviction, and then, driven by the entrepreneurial mindset, "just do it." And you *can* do it. Contrary to what I was once told, you're never too old to rock, and you're never too young to fly. So take your best shot—and while you're at it, make it a *moon*shot. Make it count. Make it bold. Because while the brave may not live forever, the cautious do not live at all. To all these ends, every entrepreneur should read this book.

—*Sir Richard Branson*

INTRODUCTION

As I celebrated what was right with the world, I began to build a vision of possibility, not scarcity. Possibility... always another right answer.

—Dewitt Jones

Y OU'D NEVER KNOW IT by watching the news these days, but there is indeed much to celebrate about what is right with the world. And that includes the unprecedented ability we have today to fix what's wrong with it. Empowered by exponential technologies and entrepreneurial creativity, we're beginning to see that there's really nothing we cannot achieve. Just consider, for example, that in biology, we're editing genes inside the human body and regenerating complete organs; in computer science, we're witnessing the advent of quantum computing and the brain-computer interface; in physics, we've finally realized the long-sought metallic hydrogen—a "Holy Grail" room-temperature superconductor that will also enable deep space launches with a single-stage rocket; in space, we've observed gravitational waves, are finding more nearby exoplanets in the "Goldilocks Zone" (just right for supporting life), and, perhaps most interesting of all, discovered that Uranus' atmosphere of hydrogen sulfide, ammonia, methane, and carbon dioxide makes its air smell like a giant fart. How can we not be excited to be living in such times!

Amazing things are indeed happening every day, and each new discovery opens new vistas and possibilities. Never in human history have we enjoyed so many astonishing innovations—and so many new "right answers." Yet curiously, many "wrong answers" persist, kept alive and perpetuated by a news industry that panders to mankind's most primal instincts. Rather than orienting and advancing our thinking toward an abundant future, the media profits by regressing it to primitive modes we've long outlived. Fear, sensationalism—and generally just making the world feel less safe—are their stock in trade. Yet while our survival instincts have evolved to predispose us to a hyper awareness of potential threats, and that programming is stubbornly still with us, we have got considerably more mental bandwidth available for the sunnier side of life. But the media environment seems to keep those positive signals shrouded in noise.

Of course, eons ago, when people lived on the savannas of Africa, they quite necessarily stayed attuned to the hazards of the wild. Indeed, it was a dangerous place and time. In those days, if you missed out on the bad news, you got wiped out of the gene pool. If, on the other hand, you didn't get the *good* news, well, nothing much was lost. Opportunity costs were comparatively low. Today we don't need to fear attack by saber-toothed tigers. We're decidedly at the top of the food chain now, and yet, we remain attuned almost exclusively to the bad news. Sadly, this steady diet of gloom and doom has affected—or shall we say infected—our global consciousness.

> **Empowered by exponential technologies and entrepreneurial creativity, we're beginning to see that there's really nothing we cannot achieve.**

We now need to fundamentally change the software of our mental and instinctual programming from one based on threat and survival to one of promise and prosperity. Otherwise, the programming that ensured our survival all those years ago might just lead to our extinction tomorrow. But let me assure you—the world *is* going to be a better place tomorrow.

It's really not surprising, though, that we haven't progressed much on the "future front." We still face it with more fear and trembling than excitement and anticipation. I've become convinced that the reason for this is twofold. First, we've forgotten how to dream big dreams—the *really* big dreams—the kinds of dreams that show that mankind can reach for, and actually touch, the stars. "Impossible" dreams that truly do come to pass when somebody dares to dream them. Dreams that are so big that when you share them with others, they begin to wonder if you might be crazy.

The second condition holding us back—and perhaps the reason for the first—is a fear of failure. The fear of failure (there's a word for it—*atychiphobia*) is so debilitating and immobilizing that it keeps many people from ever attempting to achieve anything at all. Indeed, the phrase "in your dreams" has come to mean "don't even think about it!"

Both of these conditions, though, are nothing more than mental constructs. They are, quite literally, all in one's head. A mindset ruled by these two modes of thought constitutes a deadly one-two punch, the results of which are manifested in the myriad and systemic crises-inducing paths we find ourselves walking today (and find us still cautiously approaching corners around which saber-toothed tigers might be lurking).

Our mindset is a mind-bogglingly powerful entity. It is entirely responsible for the world we've created, and it will define the world we'll live in tomorrow. In the end, we will realize either the world we *fear* to imagine or the world we *dare* to dream.

> **Today, we need to fundamentally change the software of our mental and instinctual programming from one based on threat and survival to one of promise and prosperity.**

Our fear of the future, though, like any phobia, has an underlying cause. And if we can get at the root cause, then everything—and I mean *everything*—can change. But first, we need to identify and properly frame the nature of the threat that we *actually* face—the true and active menace that simultaneously precludes bold and audacious dreams and forever has us pulling in our horns for fear of failure. Because we all do indeed have something great to fear—even though we may not yet recognize it as such. And I'm guessing that it will surprise you.

○ ☽ ● ☾

What do you believe is the single greatest threat to the survival of humanity? The possibility of artificial intelligence taking over the world? Extreme climate change? Nuclear war? Global pandemic? Asteroid impact? Or is it something that's never occurred to us—perhaps something we might even think of as innocuous, harmless, or even beneficial? Something like ... *sustainability*.

Sustainability? Yes, actually. Sustainability. And the fact that nobody ever guesses this one is precisely why we're all in for a very rude awakening.

Somehow, we have become convinced that sustainability is the answer to responsibly managing our dwindling resources—after all, it's just common sense, right?—when in reality, it actually constitutes our greatest peril. *By far.* Far more than the possibility of climatic disruption, job-killing robots, or even nukes. Here's why.

Every imagined catastrophic event[1] that could spell our collective doom shares a common underlying cause: the ever-growing demand and competition for ever-shrinking resources. In other words, *scarcity*. Think about it. Scarcity is an extraordinarily powerful two-edged force that not only gives rise to wars, but also happens to be a source of tremendous profits. Scarcity is big business, and it is perpetuated—indeed sustained—by the tools of economics. But the global response to the problem of scarcity—well-meaning programs of conservation and sustainability—only ensures its continued dominance in the world. In the end, sustainability serves to reinforce the value of scarce commodities. But there's another problem: *sustainability is actually not sustainable.*

The fact is, we're going to need a whole lot more of everything, and we're going to need it soon. By 2050, we're going to need at least *twice* as much as we consume today. Twice as much water, twice as much food, twice as much energy, twice as much land, twice as much healthcare, twice as much education. No amount of conservation or design for sustainability will ever be sufficient to meet the overwhelming demands that we continue to lay upon Spaceship Earth.

We are rapidly approaching the point on the graph where the demand for resources takes a giant hockey stick turn upward, shooting above and beyond the line that plots the slowing growth rate of available resources. And if demand is growing at an exponential rate against limited, linear supply, then sustainability runs out of gas pretty fast. It doesn't take a rocket scientist—much less an economist—to forecast this obvious outcome and the global crisis it will precipitate. Sustainability and conservation, then, ultimately amount to nothing more than straightening pictures on the wall of a burning building. Worse, the attempts to push out that dreaded point of divergence stall the development of the solutions that can actually solve these looming problems now. Indeed, a sustained mindset of sustainability will only hasten the crisis.

> **We will realize either the world we *fear* to imagine or the world we *dare* to dream.**

We have to create *more of what we need* rather than consume *less of what we have*. And to do that, we're going to have to adopt a fundamentally and radically different way of thinking and operating. For starters, we need to acknowledge that the consequences of a global economy driven by scarcity are not just to be found in some far-off future—we're living with them now. Billions of people are without basic education, safe water, adequate nutrition, or access to healthcare. For many, famine, war, and pestilence are always close at heel. Indeed, the conditions for the bottom billion in this world are already catastrophic.

So how, then, will we get these "nonexistent" resources? The only way we *can* get them—through creative destruction, the massive disruption of the status quo, and a deliberate blowing up of the established means of resource acquisition, production, and allocation. More to the point, they'll come through a historic convergence of three powerful forces:

1) The impending bankruptcy of an unsustainable scarcity-driven economy.
2) Technology that is advancing on an exponential scale.
3) The rise of an entirely new class of entrepreneurs who will be the principal drivers of the coming disruptions.

This convergence—unprecedented in human history—will upend every notion we have about our civilization: how we live, *where* we live, how we work, how we get around, how we interact, even *what we are*. And all of these outcomes will be realized by the ushering in of a previously unknown kind of economy—an economy of *abundance*. An economy whose very basis lies in sharp contrast to everything that's being peddled to and simply taken for granted by a naïve public.

Consider the Unite Nation's (UN) 17 Sustainable Development Goals (SDG), for example. These comprise an ambitious set of objectives that span ending poverty to dealing with climate change to reducing income inequality—and all by the year 2030. Who wouldn't want to see these outcomes realized?! Yet, while more than 90 percent of CEOs fully support the SDG agenda, fewer than 20 percent say they're able to do anything about it. We have a major gap here, which led BlackRock's Larry Fink, noting that many governments are also failing to prepare for the future, to turn up the heat on corporations to pick up the slack. In a famed letter, he told them, "... society increasingly is turning to the private sector and asking that companies respond to broader societal challenges ... Society is demanding that companies, both public and private, serve a social purpose." Well, they can demand all they want, but if the incentives are not aligned—and they are not—then nothing, as we shall continue to see, will ever change. Consequently, the SDGs are really nothing more than a nice to-do list. And while laudable—the SDGs do express a beautiful vision—they offer no blueprint for achieving any of them. Moreover, they do nothing to address the *underlying causes* of the 17 critical challenges they identify. The UN did, however, publish *The Lazy Person's Guide to Saving the World*—an appeal to individuals to do what they can to support the sustainability goals. Consistent with the basic sustainability theme, every one of the points in the guide asks us to *do* less *with* less.

Indeed, both the UN and Mr. Fink are appealing to the wrong constituencies. It is not governments, corporations, or private individuals who will solve the sustainability crisis. Only creative, resourceful entrepreneurs who dare to dream big, audacious dreams can do it. And they *are* doing it. These are entrepreneurs who imagine a world where there is *more* than enough of everything for everybody—and without end. It's a moonshot, to be sure, but let me also assure you that it is entirely possible.

This book is an exercise in extending the frontiers of the possible. But like the nature of our biggest threat, they too are not what you might imagine. The frontiers we must begin to exploit lie entirely within the human *mind*. It is, after all, only the human mind that can resolve to transmute the massive and otherwise intractable problems we face into a world

> **In the end, sustainability serves to reinforce the value of scarce commodities. But there's another problem: *sustainability is actually not sustainable*.**

of abundance and human flourishing. Amazing possibilities truly are as close as a simple interior change—a change of *mindset*—that will bring about massive changes on the exterior—that is, the world.

It happens that the greatest challenges facing humanity are also the biggest untapped opportunities for entrepreneurs. Undeniably, as John W. Gardner put it, "We are continually faced with a series of great opportunities brilliantly disguised as insoluble problems." And make no mistake: these are *trillion* dollar opportunities. But these are also challenges that can only be met with a renewed and empowered mindset of abundance—a mindset that emerges only when built upon a foundation of possibility, fueled by imagination, and fired by curiosity. These are the cardinal points of the moonshot—all of which ultimately converge to orient the entrepreneur to the True North of radical possibility and the abundant world it can yield.

I know these things to be true, because I am deeply and personally engaged with several exciting moonshot initiatives: one called Viome aims to make illness "optional" through the tuning of the gut microbiome—the forgotten but newly rediscovered seat of both health and disease—and another called Moon Express that seeks to solve the world's energy problems by mining the astounding wealth of resources that presently lie untapped in our own backyard—the moon.

My great hope is that the day we land our robotic module on the moon, it will be marked as the seminal event that will inspire every entrepreneur to discover just how unlimited their possibilities really are, and that they will be encouraged to find and take their own moonshots. People will again begin to believe that everything is possible. And if I and my small company of 40 people can accomplish such an audacious dream as mining the moon, so that energy becomes too cheap to meter and humans become a multi-planetary species, then what can *you* do?

Sadly, many people today are given to believe that what was possible for previous generations is not possible for this one. But how can this be? There has never been a time in human history when people have enjoyed access to such resources as we have today, and when a small group of people can do things that, in the past, could only be contemplated by the nation-states. Yet a pessimistic malaise has descended like a fog and somehow captured a generation.

If this dark and fearful mindset is allowed to prevail, then we are in for a collapsing of great ambitions and intellectual and imaginative dreams. We could see a wholesale retreat from possibility and a loss of crucial backbone where, in exchange for an illusion of freedom and security, we surrender everything to a vast but inept bureaucracy that will happily accept the defeat of human initiative. This kind of resignation is nothing short of a disassembling of human potential. But I don't believe we will allow it to happen.

I believe that every person on Earth has a moonshot inside them. If they don't believe it themselves, it is only because they do not realize just how extraordinary they truly are, and how easily potential is tapped when one's mindset is aligned to this truth. The greatest movements in history have always begun with a change of consciousness. And we can see that, despite the generational, widespread malaise mentioned earlier, such a new consciousness is being awakened today in a renaissance of the entrepreneurial spirit. Indeed, I believe that only the rise of the entrepreneurial spirit can overcome this noxious, media-fueled malaise and fashion a new and invigorated vision for the world.

> **These are the cardinal points of the moonshot—all of which ultimately converge to orient the entrepreneur to the True North of radical possibility and the abundant world it can yield.**

Technology has leveled the playing field for anyone who wants to enter the arena. No one needs to give you permission, and no one can stop you from entering it. Once we all realize this, we can deflate the debilitating, scarcity-driven power structures that feed off of human energy. All that is needed is the conviction—and a touch of audacity—to begin. And you don't even have to be wealthy to do it.

"Somehow," says Astro Teller, "society has developed this notion that you have to have a huge amount of money to be audacious. I don't believe that … Taking good, smart risks is something that anyone can do, whether you're on a team of five or in a company of 50,000 … The secret ingredient you need for moonshots doesn't cost a thing."

That secret is the entrepreneurial mindset. It is the key the key to opening previously unimagined frontiers of human prosperity.

It goes without saying that pulling off a moonshot is hard work. And while you might not get there, you have to begin with the assumption that you will. When I cofounded Moon Express in 2010, I said to a group of entrepreneurs that I didn't know exactly how we were going to accomplish our goal. It was indeed an audacious goal, but there was no question in our minds that we were going to accomplish it. I also reminded them that we've all had the experience of watching history being made, but it is only once in a lifetime that one gets a chance to make that history oneself. I asked them, do you simply want to stand by and watch it being made again or do you want to be a part of it? That really is the choice. Being part of making history is a choice that is available to absolutely anyone who will dare to make it.

Here's the irony: launching a moonshot, while certainly challenging, can actually be easier than starting a smaller company based upon a less ambitious goal. And what many people dismiss as "crazy" might actually be well within reach. History is replete with examples. Whether your particular moonshot is a figurative one or a literal one, the same principles—and mindsets—apply, and they will get you well on your way to solving the big problems in the world that you care about and are inspired to meet.

○ ◐ ● ◑

The term "moonshot" has its genesis in the Apollo program—the most audacious endeavor in the history of mankind, involving not only a highly volatile mixture of fuels to get it off the ground, but an equally volatile combination of technologies, engineering, basic science, politics, and economics required to bring it to fruition. Such endeavors are inherently difficult, always unproven, and by nature, risky. But they also carry tremendous potential for changing the world and moving humanity forward.

Google's X, the semi-secret R&D wing, adopted the term to define their *modus operandi* in developing and de-risking early-stage ideas, with a view to parlaying them into solutions that solve real problems. "We look for the intersection of a big problem, a radical solution, and breakthrough technology," their statement begins. "We start with a large problem in the world that if solved, could improve the lives of millions or even billions of people. Then we propose a radical solution that sounds impossible today, almost like science fiction. Lastly, we look for a technology breakthrough that exists today; this gives us the necessary hope that the solution we're looking for is possible, even if its final form is five to 10 years away and obscured over the horizon."

> **Here's the irony: launching a moonshot, while certainly challenging, can actually be easier than starting a smaller company based upon a less ambitious goal.**

Consequently, moonshots occupy a precarious territory between pure possibility and pure science fiction. That's what makes them both rare and special: driven by curiosity, imagination, vision, and a good dose of passion, they set out to massively transform the status quo. But again, because the goal is to achieve something that is an order of magnitude greater than what exists today, it doesn't necessarily follow that it will be an order of magnitude more difficult than, say, aiming for something that is just 10 percent better. That's not a moonshot. If the limits of your vision constrain you to creating something that's merely 10 percent better, 10 percent faster, or 10 percent cheaper, then you're operating in the biggest possible sphere of competition. Moonshots completely obviate competition. Moonshots fundamentally redefine what is actually possible in a given space, which entirely transcends competitive thinking. And that's why they always sound "crazy."

Every breakthrough starts out in life as a crazy, impossible idea—until it is actually done. As Niels Bohr once said to fellow physicist Wolfgang Pauli, "We are all agreed that your theory is crazy. The question that divides us is whether it is crazy enough to have a chance of being correct!" If people don't think your idea is crazy, then that's a clue that you're not operating in the moonshot arena.

People naturally favor the "10 percent better" route only because they believe it is less risky to pursue a smaller goal in a well-understood, high-confidence world. But this is an illusion. Moonshots *appear* to be far riskier simply because they venture into unexplored territory; they aren't an obvious extrapolation of what's happening today. But that is precisely why they play to the entrepreneur's advantage. Moonshots fundamentally move the goalposts; they envision a very different, if not radically different, outcome. They also ultimately require what is perhaps the scarcest resource of all: the audacious, if not eccentric, entrepreneur with an equally audacious dream. That resource has always been scarce. As John Stuart Mill said, "That so few now dare to be eccentric marks the chief danger of our time." And sadly, it marks ours no less today. Though they are rare, an entrepreneur who has a moonshot on his mind is our greatest resource. My hope is to develop more of them.

In the chapters that follow, I take you deep inside the development of the successful entrepreneur's mindset (Part One), and then present a few "eccentric" moonshots that serve to illustrate the power of these principles (Part Two). Each of these "moonshot platforms" addresses territories that are incredibly ripe for profitable, world-changing disruption: energy, healthcare, and education. Finally, I offer a few key insights to help guide the successful launch of your big idea (Part Three).

To such ends—and to reaching such inspiring horizons—the ideas and examples presented in this book are only seeds—seeds in search of fertile ground. When those seeds are properly sown, watered, and exposed to sunlight, they stand a good chance of bearing fruit. But those same seeds—the ideas and elements that make up the entrepreneurial mindset—often lie dormant as mere potential until they are activated. It's the activation part of the equation that we're concerned with here.

As Erasmus said, "Fortune favors the audacious." But here's an even more audacious idea: Aim for the heavens and you will get Earth "thrown in."

---

1. Even the fear of so-called catastrophism can lead to both anarchy and governmental overreach. There is indeed great danger in a widespread mindset of catastrophe. As one pundit put it, "One can construct an apocalyptic scenario from almost any problem." But the odds of Earth getting struck in one's lifetime by even a small asteroid? About one in 300,000—nothing to lose much sleep over. Of course, an asteroid strike does present a potential single point of failure for the planet, as it did for the dinosaurs. I like to joke that had there been just one entrepreneurial dinosaur, perhaps today they wouldn't be swimming in our gas tanks.

PART ONE

The Pillars of the Entrepreneurial Mindset

CHAPTER 1

The Quantum Future

The empires of the future are empires of the mind.

—Winston Churchill

N 1825, IT WAS WIDELY BELIEVED that the human body would not withstand travel at the extraordinary speed of 30 miles per hour—a pace faster than a galloping horse. Surely, it was assumed by medical professionals at the time, passengers would simply *melt* at such a sustained speed. What's more, the train's acceleration would be enough to cause female passengers' uteruses to "fly out of their bodies." So when the Stockton-Darlington Railway set out upon its maiden adventure that year, people feared the worst. As it turned out, happily enough, the railroads did not become littered with either melted carcasses or flying uteruses.

Fast-forward 75 years and we find the introduction of an even more radical development: automatic elevators. And again, people were terrified of the things—they simply refused to ride in a car without an operator at the helm. To help assuage nervous riders, a soothing voice piped into the car greeted them as they entered. "This is an automatic elevator," intoned the disembodied host. "Please press the button for the floor you desire."

If you can put yourself in the shoes of this circa 1900 urbanite, perhaps you can imagine why it would take nearly 50 years—nudged along by an elevator operators' strike in 1945—before the public would come to trust and accept this new mode of transport. Now, of course, the idea of an elevator operator is a quaint throwback.

It seems mankind has always had an uneasy relationship with new technology. Even the introduction of street lights was cause for concern. Upon their introduction, a 19th-century German newspaper actually detailed six "grave consequences" for any township that dared install them. So today, when three-quarters of people surveyed worldwide express serious misgivings about the safety of fully autonomous vehicles, can we blame them?

Trains, automatic elevators, street lights, and now self-driving cars. Technology changes, but human nature, apparently, does not! Nevertheless, just as we did with trains, elevators, and street lights, we'll get past any skepticism about the safety of self-driving cars.[1] And when we inevitably do, the very idea of a steering wheel will be happily relegated to the dustbin of history, right along with buggy whips and elevator operators.

This, of course, begs the question about what else we might expect 10 or 20 years down the road. Aside from sparing anxious parents the prospect of drivers' education for their kids (yes, this rite of passage will also pass with self-driving cars[2]), on the very near horizon, for example, we can already see machine intelligence approximating that of humans in many respects. What will it mean then when we are able to achieve true man-machine symbiosis, where our mental and physical capacities are enhanced in no small way by AI, and our human sensibilities remain? Will we forever feel like Spock and Bones trapped together inside the same body? Indeed, the very nature of our identity will come into question with such man-machine mergers. But there is no question that as we eventually come to transcend our "biological roots," these technologies will also make us better, faster, stronger, and—to take the *Six Million Dollar Man* one step further—smarter, too. Moreover, at the rate that exponential technologies are driving costs down, going bionic won't cost anywhere near six million dollars.

○ ◗ ● ◖

The term *bionic*—coined sixty years ago—is a portmanteau of the words *biology* and *electronic*. In the decades since, we've witnessed a great many examples of bionics at work—from artificial limbs and organs to eye, ear, and brain implants. But the things that will contribute to making us better, faster, stronger, and smarter will also be decidedly organic, as we'll also be able to replace and *enhance* (via 3D printing, CRISPR, and other biotechnologies) diseased, damaged, or tired organs—a development that may have many marketers rethinking the concept of the lifetime guarantee.

In the very near future, we'll be making stronger, more resilient humans with the help of high-performance prosthetics, as well as through the grafting of "smart skin," muscle tissues grown in bioreactors, and entire chains of foreign DNA into our own; we'll be inventing ways that help us to learn faster both naturally and via electronic neural stimulation; we'll improve our senses of sight, hearing, and touch by augmenting our organic capacities with a combination of genetic editing and myriad sensors placed in and on our bodies—enabling razor-sharp acuity as well as the continuous monitoring of all our vital statistics. We'll travel at speeds of 700 miles per hour without getting airborne (or melting), and also be able to appear instantly, anywhere, holographically. And our cars, if there will still be such a thing as private car ownership, definitely won't have steering wheels.

As wild as some of these things seem to our current sensibilities, they are actually all here now or are on the very near horizon. Indeed, as they said when they rebuilt Steve Austin—the Six Million Dollar Man—"We have the technology." And when this exponentially advancing technology is scaled across a critical mass of humanity through the work of creative entrepreneurs, the world will be irreversibly altered.

It's the futurists who are plotting these amazing courses, and to thrive in the life to come, we would all do well to become futurists ourselves. But just what, exactly, does that mean?

More than mere forecasters, futurists immerse themselves in worlds transformed by imagined realities that today might seem implausible, or even impossible. They trade in "nonexistent" technologies, which, in many cases, may really only be a few iterations away from commercialization. They see clearly the emerging developments that will completely disrupt the conventional linear market trends. Indeed, their vision transcends such trends by bringing both wide angle and zoom lenses together in a complex view of a great many moving parts that will ultimately converge and synthesize entirely new realities. In other words, versions of the world made possible by moonshots. What's more, futurism is a skill that anyone can learn—and that the entrepreneur *must* learn.

There's one other important aspect that distinguishes the futurist: he does not view future possibilities as mere intellectual exercises or curiosities, but rather as completely viable, fully realizable visions of a future, that, while perhaps "thousands of tomorrows away," is almost tangible today. And because of his rarefied vision, the futurist will be well positioned to prosper in that world when it actually comes to pass—and some version of it certainly will come to pass.

Surprisingly, though, most people really don't spend much time thinking about what lay ahead. In a survey conducted by the Institute for the Future, for example, researchers found that only about a third of Americans regularly think about their futures even five years out, with the remaining majority reporting that they seldom, if ever, give it a thought. The consequences of this "future gap," of course, will be amplified a hundred-fold in the coming days of mass disruption—a lack of foresight that could prove devastating for those who do not plan for this new and rapidly emerging world. Truly, the less one thinks about his future, the less control he will have over his place in it.

One component of this complacency is a tragic, yet socially conditioned, lack of curiosity—a topic I'll explore more deeply later in the book. For the moment, though, speaking to its importance, Jane McGonigal, a senior researcher at the organization that conducted the survey, explained, "Curiosity about what might happen in the future, the ability to imagine how things could be different, and empathy for our future selves are all necessary if we want to create change in our own lives or the world around us." Fortunately, there's still time to develop that vitally necessary and future-changing curiosity.

In the meantime, consider just one topic that might serve to pique that curiosity now—the advent of artificial intelligence. Today we are witnessing a great proliferation of so-called "narrow" AI, that is, machine learning-driven tasks that are actually quite limited in scope. For example, while Big Blue, Watson, or AlphaGo might defeat world champion players, you could easily beat them in a game of checkers. Artificial "general" intelligence, on the other hand, is the stuff of the *singularity*, where machines attain a level of intelligence sufficient to successfully perform any intellectual task that a human being can carry out. For

> **Our future is not cast in stone. It is a malleable and dynamic fabric of amazing potentialities, possibilities, and probabilities. And every passing moment is an opportunity for our intervention.**

the time being, though, as David Hanson, creator of the Sophia humanoid robot, notes, "There's a certain expression of genius to be able to get up and cross the room and pour yourself a cup of coffee." To be sure, it's still the simple things that separate humans from robots.

So when will this superintelligence arrive? Exactly how much time do we have to prepare for it? There's considerable debate about this—and artificial general intelligence does indeed run up against massively complex computational challenges that must be overcome if it is to comprehend all facets of human intelligence. But what everybody seems to forget is that human minds are designed to think *linearly*. That is, it's hard for the mind to grasp the concept of exponential effects. For example, while it may take 10 years for a technology to progress 10 percent, it won't take another 90 years to complete its development cycle. We forget that since the technology is doubling every year, we are actually less than four years away from completing the remaining 90 percent. This is the power of the exponential curve: we progress rapidly from 10 to 20 to 40 to 80 to completion. (This is precisely what we witnessed with the human genome sequencing project.) And once we add quantum computing to the mix, Moore's Law will start to look downright pessimistic!

All this is to say that tomorrow will come—and singularity or no, it will be substantially different than anything we know today. That much is certain. But it's what we do today that will shape the future, and our place in it, which brings us to a certain philosophy of futurism—a philosophy that undergirds much of what follows in the chapters ahead.

○ ◑ ● ◐

The problems and grand challenges we face today in the world did not suddenly appear out of nowhere; they've been growing gradually—so gradually that they escape notice until they reach a tipping point. In most cases, these are problems that could have been dealt with easily had they been addressed when they first began to emerge. But we routinely neglect such minor problems, especially when we're more concerned with the little problem we neglected yesterday that has reached crisis proportions today! (As the old saying goes, "Hindsight explains the injury that foresight would have prevented.") Indeed, we're far more inclined to reach for the aspirin than the vitamin that could have prevented the headache in the first place.[3] But once that little problem grows up to be a crisis, it can be solved only at great expense. And of course, it often never does get solved, if by then there are too many competing special interests who have gotten themselves too deeply invested in it all.

And so, today we find ourselves living in yesterday's tomorrow—which, as it turns out, was never given much thought. Consequently, it brings with it all its baggage in its various stages of adolescence. The good news, though, is that going forward, our future is not cast in stone. It is a malleable and dynamic fabric of amazing potentialities, possibilities, and probabilities. And every passing moment is an opportunity for our intervention. As such, we can think of the future as a *tabula rasa* upon which we can impose our will, imprint our image, and build, well ... anything we might imagine.

The future really doesn't care what we do with it. Time may have an arrow, but it has no bias, no agenda, no particular preferences at all. And as long as Earth keeps circling the sun, time will just keep flowing no matter what we do, tomorrow after tomorrow—an ever-emerging and rolling reality offering a vast and virtual land grab for anyone who dares to purposefully venture into it. But how will we face this future from where we stand today? What, exactly, are our options?

On one hand, we can passively follow the threads laid down yesterday and watch them as they unfold into a future of others' making. This would be a future thrust upon us. A future that *happens* to us. Or we can jump into the arena and engage the emerging patterns that others are weaving, responding to and making the best of them as they are at any given moment. This would be a future that perhaps anyone can enter into with reasonable effort and awareness. But there's a better option: we can wake up, get out in front of it all, and fashion a future of our *own* design. This would be a future that we consciously and deliberately conceive and give birth to—a future that springs forth from human imagination, creativity, and ingenuity. A future imagined in big, audacious strokes whose execution has the power to transform life as we know it. This is entirely possible! That is, if you believe it—that the future is not some sort of preordained drama in which we are merely actors, passively playing scripted roles on a stage that is nothing but an illusion. Some people, after all, believe we are actually living in a giant simulation.

But if we are not free agents, then there is no basis for ethics; the notions of the good, the true, and the beautiful have no meaning. Nor do words like evil, injustice, guilt, innocence, or personal responsibility. When free will is eliminated, then everything is permissible. Conversely, if we believe that the future is purely random, that everything is beyond our control, then what would be the point in trying to control it or influence it in any way? Grand challenges focused on solving the world's great problems would be futile. Might as well just ride the Earth and try to get a tan.

As an entrepreneur, you know that these things aren't true. But you also know that we cannot take for granted that the future will be better by default. Which means we need to work to bring about that better future, that the future we imagine cannot happen absent our active and purposeful participation.

So, then, will you dare to imagine the world anew? Will you dare to believe, for example, that illnesses can be eradicated, that no one should ever go hungry, that we can eliminate the root causes of war, that a world blessed with an abundance of resources and access to quality education can lead to a grand flourishing of human potential and fulfillment? All these things *are* possible. The enabling technologies to accomplish such visions are already here or close at hand. All that is needed is the will to make them so. But as we've suggested, your vision of the future is not without competing worldviews. Indeed, the future is a precarious thing and very much up for grabs. Which vision of the future will ultimately prevail? Will others prove to be more tenacious? To what lengths will they

> " Every act is an irrevocable selection and exclusion. In other words, by making the deliberate choice—or allowing others to make the choice for us—*we determine the future state!* "

persevere in creating *their* versions of the future, which may well be antithetical to yours? Will you rule your future or be its passenger? Or even its victim?

The point is that all the potentialities "exist" simultaneously in the ether of the undetermined future. Like the interference patterns that appear in the perplexing double-slit experiments of quantum mechanics, the reality that is ultimately actualized from the myriad possible futures depends entirely upon our—*your*—action. And that action is precipitated by a choice—a decided outcome that is not a function of chance but an exercised will. And when we make that choice, we necessarily close out and collapse all other options—*including those of our competitors and other potential futures.* We can't keep the quantum options open forever!

Indeed, every act is an irrevocable selection and exclusion. In other words, by making the deliberate choice—or allowing others to make the choice for us—*we determine the future state!* Scale up this idea and you'll realize that your choices carry more energy than that released by splitting the atom. Recognize this and, with a little competence on the execution side of the equation, you can, like Archimedes, move the world.

Let's look at this another way. In Einstein's cosmology, our world is part of a block universe, a four-dimensional complex of causality (with time as the fourth dimension). But in this world, no moment in time is singled out as "now"—the future and the past don't exist in an absolute sense as they do for us in our everyday experience. While *we* experience life in a world apparently dominated by Newtonian physics and are relentlessly subject to time's arrow, the quantum world is not quite so constrained. The quantum world is time-symmetric, that is, its equations work both forward and backward; they don't care about time. In fact, recent experiments have actually demonstrated that waves can travel *backward* in time, revealing the bizarre condition of *retro-causality*—the effect preceding the cause—yet another inherent contradiction as weird as anything else one encounters in quantum mechanics.

Nevertheless, we experience life in a decidedly temporal flow. And this flow is not merely an abstraction: we all carry memories that guide us into the future in ways of which we are not even conscious. Our temporal nature actually propels us into the future—that blank slate awaiting a hand to write new chapters. But those chapters are preceded by others, each of which imposes its experiences and expectations (and baggage) on the next. We take the fleas with the dog, as it were. But the history—and the fleas—are essential to opening the possibilities ahead.

The popular saying is that life can only be understood backwards, but it must be lived forward. (And as they also say, people always find it easier to be a *re-sult* of the past rather than a *cause* of the future!) Let's think about this for a moment. In most planning exercises, we take a present-forward approach. That is, we begin with assumptions based on today's realities and extrapolate into the future. But let's flip the paradigm, and begin with the imagined future state and work backward to the present. *This* is how we get to moonshot thinking. And this is precisely how John F. Kennedy approached his vision for the first manned moonshot.

First, he imagined space in the context of life right here on Earth—a place where "... there is no strife, no prejudice, no national conflict ..." He then imagined the moon as a resource whose conquest was deserving the best efforts of all mankind and, infusing a sense of urgency, recognized that the opportunity may never come again. "But why, some say, the moon?" he continued. "Why choose *this* as our goal? They may well ask, why climb the highest mountain? Why, 35 years ago, fly the Atlantic?" He answered these rhetorical questions with the operative words of this chapter, "*We choose.*" And we made the choice in spite of the fact that the technologies and know-how required to accomplish the feat did not yet exist.

> **"Let's flip the paradigm, and begin with the imagined future state and work backward to the present. *This* is how we get to moonshot thinking."**

Today, looking back on looking ahead, the Apollo 11 landing—which did, as promised, happen before the end of the decade—seems an unquestionably inevitable outcome, one so inescapable that it appears to have dictated its cause. And why not? After all, as Einstein said, "People like us, who believe in physics, know that the distinction between past, present, and future is only a stubbornly persistent illusion!"

Causality—whether forward or backward looking—is as potent an agent in the "real world" of ordinary experience as it is in the quantum world. The exercise of free choice—your choice—in the face of an undetermined "multiple choice" future is precisely what defines the relationship between the two. And related

> **The collective forces of change are so powerful that over the next decade or so, nearly half of the current Fortune 500 companies will not survive them.**

they must be. As physicist David Layzer puts it, "... every [quantum] measurement necessarily has at least one foot in the world of ordinary experience." In the end, it does take a conscious human observer to collapse the quantum options to a single outcome. In any event, it is the ordinary experience that we seek to change in our collective prospect, which brings us to another operative word in this brief tour of the future: *change*.

○◑●◐

There's no question about it: we are living in the most innovative—and consequently the most disruptive—decade in human history. Over the course of the next 10 years we will experience fundamental and disorienting changes in the trajectory of how humanity lives. For some, those changes portend the worst of times—an ushering in of a dystopian, jobless society ruled by artificial intelligence—a future that will "happen to us." For the enlightened entrepreneur, though, they herald the *best* of times, bringing newfound freedoms enabled by astounding new technologies that will move humanity forward—a future we create. This is the real stuff of growth.

Everyone wants growth, but nobody wants change. Change, though, is what brings growth, and change is the law of life. Consequently, we find ourselves in perpetually unfamiliar terrain. As an entrepreneur, successfully navigating such terrain will require a map of some sort. This book is that map. But unlike the maps we're accustomed to, this one has none of the familiar Cartesian coordinates. What's more, the map itself is constantly changing, updating, and course-correcting—even as it unfolds. It's as dynamic as the age in which we live. It is, however, a map that will take you not only into the future, but deep inside what is perhaps the most mysterious of unexplored territories: *yourself*. What you will discover when you arrive at this extraordinary destination is a heretofore unrealized capacity for *possibility*—a realization of opportunity that will lift your entrepreneurial vision to previously unimagined heights. Perhaps even as high as the moon.

Still, we shrink from change; yet is there anything that can come into being without it? Is it possible for any useful thing to be achieved without change? For many people, change is a horrifying prospect. Contrary to the old McDonald's campaign, given the way our brains are wired, change is *not* good. Humans simply do not cope well with change.

Change is, after all, a departure from what we know and understand. It can mean a loss of control, a loss of autonomy, a loss of direction. How many times have you heard someone complain when asked to change, "But we've *always* done it this way." It's just easier to follow the rules than to rock the boat. And it's not that people need a lot of encouragement to keep their heads down. The fact is while organizations say they want innovation, they consistently reject creativity.

People intrinsically resist change. As a species, we prefer predictability, stability, permanence, security. When those sensibilities are threatened, anxiety ensues. So we—particularly the more timorous among us—start to do what we always do in such situations: we search for patterns. Patterns that help us regain some sense of balance and control, until we find that they, too, are elusive. The search seems increasingly futile as the patterns themselves are ever-shifting and mutating. For many, reality has become a kaleidoscope!

> **The anxious gap that stands between the present reality and an uncertain future is a fountainhead of possibility.**

No one will question that the direct cause of the dislocations experienced in the 20th century was technology. From the automobile to the airplane, radio to space travel, personal computing to mobile phones, no aspect of life was left untouched by the unprecedented explosion of technology we witnessed in the last century. Amazing as it was, though, it was only the warmup act! Today, we're living in an era where an unparalleled number of technologies are developing and converging—and coming together faster

Market Capitalization of the World's Most Valuable Public Companies

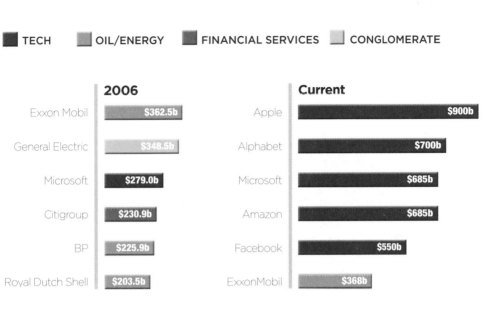

| TECH | OIL/ENERGY | FINANCIAL SERVICES | CONGLOMERATE |

2006

Exxon Mobil	$362.5b
General Electric	$348.5b
Microsoft	$279.0b
Citigroup	$230.9b
BP	$225.9b
Royal Dutch Shell	$203.5b

Current

Apple	$900b
Alphabet	$700b
Microsoft	$685b
Amazon	$685b
Facebook	$550b
ExxonMobil	$368b

Sources: Yahoo! Finance, Forbes

In just over 10 years, the makeup of the world's most valuable companies has undergone a radical shift as the tech sector has surged. How will this graph look in another 10 years?

than ever. That's new. And the effect is exponential. Consequently, every industry is going to be transformed, if not completely dislocated. In fact, the collective forces of change are so powerful that over the next decade or so, nearly half of the current Fortune 500 companies will not survive them.

If you're anxious about any of this, don't worry. Anxiety—"normal anxiety"—is an indispensable asset in one's journey to a thriving future. Anxiety is inescapable. And if used constructively, it can also be a catalyst for amazing creativity. The fact is the anxious gap that stands between the present reality and an uncertain future is a fountainhead of possibility. In possibility comes our freedom. And freedom is the core of the entrepreneurial spirit. Take the edge off that anxiety, and you also attenuate freedom.

It turns out that this is not a new observation. When anti-anxiety drugs were first unleashed on the public in the 1950s, some psychiatrists actually warned about the dangers presented by a society that was *not anxious enough*. "We then face the prospect," one wrote, "of developing a falsely flaccid race of people which might not be too good for our future." Today the United States leads the world in the consumption of anti-anxiety drugs. Yet there has never been as great an opportunity for entrepreneurs to remake this anxious world. And in this world's future, as entrepreneurs figure out how to prevent wars and end disease, famine, and hunger, how to create an abundance of energy and every other resource we need to live abundant lives, anxiety just might evaporate into the ether.

> **Rather than regulating the future, perhaps we should spend more energy deregulating imagination.**

We contrast anxiety, though, with fear. Fear is another matter entirely. Fear is correlated to desire and not to hope. Every desire, as every fear, tends to invent its own techniques. And man is ever at the mercy of his techniques. Alexis de Tocqueville once observed, "I cannot help fearing that men may reach a point where they look on every new theory as a danger, every innovation as a toilsome trouble, every social advance as a first step toward revolution, and that they may absolutely refuse to move at all." That he penned those words in the mid-1800s speaks as much of enduring qualities of human nature as it does to our response to the massive changes that are encroaching upon us today. Again, technology may change, but human nature does not.

As in every age, contemplation of the future requires a certain faith. But in hesitation there is no faith, only *opinion*. This hesitation, I believe, is the death of hope. Indeed, where anxiety can be motivating, fear is debilitating. The fearful do not believe, and therefore, they do not act. They spawn the regressive likes of Evgeny Morozov, who write neo-Luddite screeds against all forms of technology. They dismiss wholesale the untold benefits that technology can leverage to lift billions of people out of poverty, choosing instead to focus solely on its potential for abuse. But technology in and of itself is benign. It can be used by good people or bad people. Notwithstanding, the neo-Luddites believe that technology ought to be reined in by a governmental bureaucracy of ever-increasing size and power. Less innovation and more regulation is their battle cry. In doing so, they exchange an imagined form of tyranny for a real one. There is actually a word for this fear of the future—*chronophobia*. And it seems it's always been with us.

Perhaps we shouldn't be too hard on them, the neo-Luddites. At the heart of their fear is a feeling of powerlessness. But powerlessness, too, is a choice. We are never powerless. And the last thing that should disturb the entrepreneur is a sense of powerlessness about the future. Alan Kay, a pioneer of the personal computer, said, "Don't worry about what anybody else is going to do; the best way to predict the future is to invent it. Really smart people with reasonable funding can do just about anything that doesn't violate too many of Newton's Laws."

To this end, the imagined world is not independent from imagination itself. Rather than regulating the future, perhaps we should spend more energy deregulating imagination—and mustering a little faith in the process! Of course we are not naíve. None of this is to say that faith never admits doubt. Of course it does. After all, we're taking a giant leap in the dark. But if a man chooses to turn his back on the future, no one can prevent him.

In contemplating an uncertain future, it's hard to argue with the old English barrister who wrote, "We stand on a mountain pass in the midst of whirling snow and blinding mist through which we get glimpses now and then of paths which may be deceptive. If we stand still we shall be frozen to death. If we take the wrong road we shall be dashed to pieces. We do not certainly know whether there is any right one. What must we do? 'Be strong and of a good courage.' Act for the best, hope for the best, and take what comes."

Well, I believe we can do better than that. Yes, sometimes the paths are deceptive. Which is why we test, test, and test again. We certainly don't want to freeze to death or be dashed to pieces. Which is why we break big problems down into smaller pieces that are easier to manage and execute. We advance the vision one step at a time with flawless execution and an unwavering eye on the goal. That's how we build the future.

> **The entrepreneur believes in a vision of an unseen future with a conviction that it *could* exist. By virtue of its potential, in some sense it *does* exist. To set it into motion, the entrepreneur simply asks, "What if it could be so?"**

By definition, faith is a belief in something not yet seen. Likewise, the entrepreneur believes in a vision of an unseen future with a conviction that it *could* exist. By virtue of its potential, in some sense it *does* exist. To set it into motion, the entrepreneur simply asks, "What if it could be so?" He casts his pebble of possibility into the pond and initiates the first ripple. And amazing things follow. That's the beauty of the audacious goal: it takes just one person to show others what is possible, to get it going, to create the opportunity for others to visualize it with him. And when it is made visual, we can also project it. If we can project it, we can bring it to fruition.

Uncertainty—the Only Certainty, or Transmuting Uncertainty into Possibility

The future ain't what it used to be. It's actually much, much more. What's more, we can make any future we can imagine, and we can imagine any future we want to create. And whatever uncertainty we may feel about the future we can simply spin into more possibility. In fact, there is great risk in being too certain about anything, for there are always foreseen uncertainties, as well as unforeseen certainties. And let us not forget Donald Rumsfeld's "unknown unknowns." It turns out that certainty can actually be a deadly blind spot in one's view of the future: it can make it all the more difficult to see how things could be otherwise, and consequently, bigger opportunities are often missed. (In fact, as research by Philip Tetlock has shown, those who speak with certainty and spin confident narratives are actually less likely to make accurate predictions.)

Whether known or unknown, certain or uncertain, all future events, by definition, lie in the dimension of possibility, and the entrepreneur's special talent is that he is a "possibility thinker." This, in turn, makes every entrepreneur a futurist. And the greater the uncertainty about the future, the greater the field of possibilities—and the entrepreneurial opportunities awaiting discovery there. In this sense, uncertainty is a synonym for a blank canvas.

This is the very idea that dissolves the seeming paradox between the audacious confidence of the entrepreneur and the need to embrace uncertainty. While not much about the future is always crystal clear, neither is it cloaked in such ambiguity as to preclude any basis for strategic anticipation or foresight. And as we'll see, this strategic anticipation is central to envisioning and developing any moonshot initiative.

Consider another paradox: the more information we are able to access, the more difficult it can be to make sense of it all. In other words, the more information we have, the greater the uncertainty about the ways it might converge to synthesize entirely new possibilities. Up until a hundred years ago, knowledge doubled about every hundred years. By the end of World War II, it was doubling every 25 years. Today it is doubling every 12 months, and the building out of the Internet of Things will see it doubling every 12 hours!

This casts Moore's Law into a very different light. Some believe that Moore's Law ultimately confirms a world of limits and finite resources. But this is an illusion. As the growth of knowledge has transitioned from the linear to the exponential, we see that there are no limits—just greater challenges and opportunities to make sense of it and to connect new and disparate dots—with the help of AI—to create new and exponential opportunities.

Because the future is uncertain, entrepreneurs must think not in terms of certainty, but in terms of *probability*. This requires a certain open-mindedness, essential not only for seeing problems from all angles, but for cultivating the curiosity and imagination we must bring to solving those problems. It is vital, therefore, that one take in information from as many sources as possible and adopt multiple viewpoints when evaluating a problem. This in turn helps to overcome any biases or preconceptions one might have—particularly in the light of new evidence. To this point, Tetlock adds that the best forecasters continuously review their assumptions, update their estimates, and improve their understanding, operating in a "perpetual beta" mode. He identifies this approach as the single most important ingredient in making accurate predictions. "For superforecasters," he explains, "beliefs are hypotheses to be tested, not treasures to be guarded." Meaning, you must learn to change your mind fast and often. Indeed, a mindset of uncertainty can, paradoxically, be the forecaster's best friend.

"I have approximate answers and possible beliefs and different degrees of certainty about different things," said Richard Feynman, "but I'm not absolutely sure about anything." And just look at what his curious uncertainty brought to the world!

Oh, if we could photograph the future. What will the world look like five, 10, 15, or 50 years from now? Forecasting necessarily means engaging in a little *chronesthesia*—mental time travel. An entrepreneur is necessarily a time traveler, who in reckoning his strategies must always "remember the future." Yet it is uncertainty about the future that motivates our action in the first place. Ignorance of the future is actually essential to human progress. Alan Lightman, in his delightful book *Einstein's Dreams*, reveals the paradoxes that arise from glimpsing even brief scenes from the future: "In this world," he writes, "few risks are taken. Those who have seen the future do not need to take risks, and those who have not yet seen the future wait for their vision without taking risks."

One wonders if Ray Kurzweil is one of those rare individuals for whom the curtain on the future has occasionally been drawn back. Ray is famous for the astounding accuracy of his predictions, and we would do well to heed his continuing projections about where technology is leading us. It turns out that his gift, while perhaps more developed than most, is not quite as mystical as it might at first appear. The fact is, Ray follows the exponential trajectories of developments in technologies while presciently connecting adjacent, though not always obvious, dots to bring the future into remarkably sharp relief. Likewise, Peter Diamandis' powerful "Six Ds of Exponential Thinking" helps entrepreneurs to escape the traps of linear thinking and learn how to create maps of the future that one not only can draw, but actually control.

These are skills that entrepreneurs can—and must—develop. In the course of this book, I'll show you how to supercharge these skills through the development of the mindset able to imagine and crystalize amazing visions of the future, to actually empower audacious moonshots—moonshots that only *appear* to be impossible from this side of the looking glass.

But back to the future and our efforts to foresee it.

Forecasting is, to a very large extent, predicting which potential scenarios have the highest probability of actually playing out. Certainly there are correlations between the past and the present that we can predict. But by the same token, looking back is not exactly the best approach to looking forward. Just take a look at the fine print on your next mutual fund statement. The disclaimer usually reads, "Past performance is not indicative of future results." Yet looking back is precisely what many forecasters do, relying, for example, on a fund's track record. Would you be surprised to learn that more than 90 percent of top performers fail to retain that status after two years? This so-called "path dependence" is a particularly dangerous trap simply because the conditions that prevailed yesterday likely won't be relevant tomorrow. And as the pace of developments accelerates, they are becoming less relevant every day. Throw in the myriad new and unforeseen variables that unfold each day with new technological possibilities, and the directions of future choices become even more uncertain. How much more difficult will it be to predict the path of technology as our minds become increasingly augmented by—and merged with—AI? Well, if we factor that question into our trajectory maps, then even more so! In fact, we should count on it.

Beyond these sorts of challenges are the common forecasting gaffes—missed signals, over-predicting, and even under-predicting. Let's start with the perennial favorite, flying cars. First patented in 1910, the aerocar has been maligned nearly as much as the Edsel. Yet even the likes of Henry Ford predicted its arrival. "Mark my word," he said in 1940, "a combination airplane and motorcar is coming. You may smile, but it will come." Well, Ford may have had to wait 77 years, but a production flying car did eventually come to pass.

Let's look at something a bit more recent, and perhaps even more surprising. In the year 2000, I was interviewed by Leslie Walker of the *Washington Post*. "Let's start with Wireless 101," she said to me. "I know there is a stampede underway to put internet content onto wireless networks. But a recent study by the Yankee Group showed most Americans don't have much interest yet in getting info from cellular phones. Weather registered the most interest, yet it drew only a 2 on a scale of 1 to 4. Do you know something most Americans don't?"

Hard to believe, isn't it? I answered, "Cellular phones are likely to be the device for people to get information, conduct commerce, and manage their lives. Most people have not seen the new versions of cellular phones and services that allow them to get access to their calendar, address book, email, stock quotes, etc. They are also able to conduct commerce directly from these devices. Most users do not have vision but tend to use the devices when they see them. It's like any new technology, like the ATM, that will be adopted once users see the benefits of it and see how easy it is to use. We are likely to see over a billion such devices, whether cellular phones or other non-PC devices, that people will use to access information, conduct commerce, and manage their lives. These devices are already very popular in Europe and Japan. InfoSpace is very well positioned to take advantage of these devices today while continuing to provide service on the existing PC/Web format. As I said earlier, we are building the information and commerce operating system for tomorrow and the next century."

> **None of these people were stupid. They were, however, blinkered by a host of factors—lack of imagination, entrenched biases, agendas, success, fear—that prevented a view of what turned out to be very short horizons.**

There are many such stories of extreme nearsightedness—and they're nothing new:

- In 1865, for example, a newspaper editor told his readers, "Well-informed people know that it is impossible to transmit the voice over wires and that, were it possible to do so, the thing would be of no practical value." A decade later, the telephone burst forth from Bell's laboratory, and the world was forever changed.
- DEC's Ken Olson famously declared that there is no reason for any individual to have a computer in their home.

- Apple co-founder Steve Wozniak, who designed the Apple I computer while working at Hewlett-Packard, offered it to HP under their right of first refusal, but they turned him down—*on five separate occasions*.
- Paul Allen, while cobbling together an operating system for the fledgling Microsoft, acquired Seattle Computer Products' OS for a mere $50K. "Why do you want it?" he was asked.
- Even Thomas Edison, in 1913, claimed that the talking motion picture will not supplant the regular silent motion picture. "There is such a tremendous investment to pantomime pictures that it would be absurd to disturb it."
- And then there's PARC. The mouse, removable data storage, networking, the graphical user interface, WYSIWYG printing—all these features were developed and integrated into Xerox's Alto computing platform—in 1973! Then Steve Jobs came to visit. PARC's Larry Tesler, who took part in the technology demonstrations for the small Apple contingent, recalled, "After an hour looking at demos, they understood our technology and what it meant more than any Xerox executive understood after years of showing it to them."

None of these people were stupid. They were, however, blinkered by a host of factors—lack of imagination, entrenched biases, agendas, success, fear—that prevented a view of what turned out to be very short horizons.

As a side note, in the special case of PARC, not only did Xerox executives fail to grasp the import of the technologies embodied in Alto (they viewed them as mere secretarial productivity enhancements—not interesting), Alto's champions failed to inspire a *vision* around the new computing paradigm. This is almost always the outcome when people lead with the technology as opposed to what its benefits can mean to the world. In short, no vision, no zeal, no deal.

More interesting, though, are the trends that emerge from the convergence of completely disparate technologies—otherwise unconnected dots that originate and evolve independently in relatively isolated application spaces. For example, 3D printing was first demonstrated in 1981, but it didn't gain traction until it met up with CAD and the open source movement decades later. Here's an even better example: consider graphics processing units (GPUs), digital cameras, and the Internet of Things, each developing in standalone, application-specific domains spanning gaming consoles to mobile phones to home thermostats. Do you see it yet? Okay, let's throw in LiDAR, machine learning, an array of sensors, and sophisticated actuators. It's probably obvious now. The self-driving car would not be possible without all of these technologies—an almost irreducible complexity—yet none of which foresaw their application in autonomous vehicles at the time they were conceived. *This* is the kind of future event we want to be able to predict. But to do so, the successful entrepreneur must have his feet in multiple technology camps.

And herein lies yet another paradox. Steve Jobs, in his famous Stanford commencement address, said, "Of course it was impossible to connect the dots looking forward when I was in college. But it was very, very clear looking backward 10 years later. Again, you can't connect the dots looking forward; you can only connect them looking backward. So you have to trust that the dots will somehow connect in your future. You have to trust in something—your gut, destiny, life, karma, whatever. This approach has never let me down, and it has made all the difference in my life."

Forecasts are funny things. We can pin a solar eclipse down to the second a hundred years into the future, but we can't get next week's weather right. Sporting events are awash with upsets—and we won't even get into the state of political polling. Nevertheless, as Peter Thiel observed, "We are more fascinated today by statistical predictions of what the country will be thinking in a few weeks' time than by visionary predictions of what the country will look like 10 or 20 years from now."

There you go. Visionary predictions are difficult because they necessarily comprehend ideas *whose time has not yet come*. But the trajectories they'll follow are, to a sufficient extent, still traced out for us. Some of the lines will be dotted, some faint; others will involve a confluence of other lines, while others we'll expect to emerge on faith.

While the task of forecasting has become increasingly complex, in

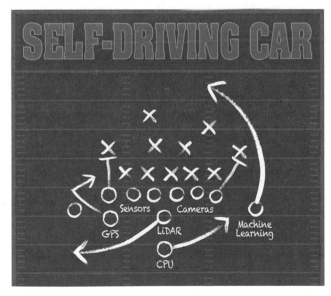

As GPS, GPUs, LiDAR, sensors, and machine learning run their routes and make their blocks, the play unfolds as all the action converges downfield, culminating in the self-driving car.

other ways it has actually gotten easier. In seeing the future, we do, indeed, stand on the shoulders of giants, and thus we are able to see further and with greater clarity than ever before. Today we can make predictions that are based more on data than imagination: the technology roadmaps are already on the drawing boards, and they do reveal clear paths—for those who are able to perceive them. In fact, much of the infrastructure is already in place for enabling technology's next "Cambrian Explosion." The number of block diagrams that include a box labeled "Miracle Happens Here" are far fewer. And, of course, we have a worldwide network (and its myriad graphs) at our disposal.

> " The self-driving car would not be possible without all of these technologies—an almost irreducible complexity—yet none of which foresaw their application in autonomous vehicles at the time they were conceived. "

Ultimately, when you're able to stitch together a view of the future that is, say, 70 percent plausible, then you've also reached a level of confidence that is sufficient to catalyze the venture. It's not unlike the quarterback who releases the ball before the receiver is in position as he runs his route. If all goes well, they'll connect downfield in space and time.

Just as the ball follows the trajectory of the receiver, great athletes play to where the ball is going to be, not to where it is. If you've ever watched a group of third-graders playing soccer, you'll always find them chasing the ball. Professional soccer players never do that; they play to where the ball is going to be passed so they'll be in position to make the goal. It's no different in business—particularly when it involves crucial technologies that are still "in the air."

Consider another take on this idea. Karen Blixen, writing in her memoir, *Out of Africa*, suggests that perhaps the Earth was made round so that we "would not see too far down the road." Well, perhaps Blixen was not familiar with Marconi's famous 1901 transmission of a transatlantic radio signal that did indeed see far down a road—far beyond any straight-line visibility. While the signal was, in fact, headed straight into space, it reflected off the ionosphere and bounced back down toward Earth, effectively skipping along the path to its destination. The ability to "see" around corners, to follow the curvature of the Earth, to see a little further down the road from where we stand today, is precisely the task of the future-oriented entrepreneur. Perhaps it's just a matter of bouncing things off what might at first appear to be barriers. Rather than be thwarted by them, the clever entrepreneur finds a way to harness them to yield the desired advantage. Trajectories are seldom straight lines!

In other aspects, the trajectories we follow not only involve developing technologies, but falling costs, which are equally enabling. At Moon Express, for example, our assumption in 2010 was that a lunar mission would cost a billion dollars. But I believed that the technology curve would bring the cost down to $100M. It turns out that instead of being 10X optimistic, I was actually 10X *pessimistic*. The initial mission will now cost under $10M. That's one reason and illustration of why we are living in such an exciting time: exponential technologies are allowing us to do things that were previously not possible.

Think about this. The cost of the Apollo program, in today's dollars, was well in excess of $100 billion, and it employed some 400,000 people through more than 20,000 industrial firms and universities. In contrast, consider that today's iPhone is more powerful than the computers that landed man on the moon. Now, iPhone technology won't get you to the moon (yet), but the innovations that are making the iPhone cheaper, smarter, and more powerful—and everything that is making the self-driving car possible—are the same kinds of innovations that will make space exploration accessible and affordable. They will, in fact, enable the democratization of space for the benefit of humanity.

Now, to invoke Kennedy's famous speech once again, why do *we*—a small group of entrepreneurs—choose to go to the moon? We choose to go to the moon because it is good business! We're aligning our missions to intercept forecasted technology trajectories that are perhaps 10 to 15 years out. For example, one of the objectives of our lunar initiative is to establish a base and supply chain for the mining and transportation of helium-3—a nonradioactive isotope of helium that, while exceptionally rare on Earth, is in abundance on the moon. Helium-3 is the feedstock for nuclear fusion—a clean form of energy production that can supply the world's energy needs for millennia. There's just one catch. We don't yet have a fusion reactor. In 15 years, though, we will. And by then, we will have built the infrastructure to

> " Much of the infrastructure is already in place for enabling technology's next "Cambrian Explosion." The number of block diagrams that include a box labeled "Miracle Happens Here" are far fewer. "

mine and transport helium-3—and numerous other precious metals—from the moon to Earth. In other words, we're running the route now in order to be in the proper position later to score the goal. Forecasting is not only a matter of recognizing emerging trends and following their respective trajectories, but putting into motion the agents that will harness and combine—and actually enable—those very trends in ways that will synthesize entirely new industries.

We'll leave you with one other inspiring example of aligning business plans to trajectories of future technology developments. Siri was the first AI-driven conversational personal assistant deployed commercially at scale. It was an outgrowth of DARPA's CALO project, which was managed by SRI International (Stanford Research Institute). CALO was defined as a five-year program that launched in 2003 with a total budget of $200M and involved 400 scientists and engineers. The program's chief architect, Adam Cheyer, described the program's goal as an ambitious effort to bring together all the stove-piped aspects of artificial intelligence into an "integrated, human-like system that could learn in the wild." It was so ambitious that he came to think of it as AI's Manhattan Project. In 2008, upon completion of the program, the resulting technology was spun out as Siri with $24M in venture funding. The Siri team had long targeted the smartphone as the preferred platform for the service, but at the time of the company's founding, the smartphone technology was not yet mature enough to support it. But they knew it would be soon enough. And sure enough, the introduction of the iPhone 3GS in June 2009 provided both the requisite processing power *and* the wireless bandwidth to enable Siri to work. A year later Siri was acquired by Apple.

Cheyer adds an important postscript to the story. "Huge progress can be made," he says, "through persistence, creativity, and practicality. Don't get too hung up on the details: just go do it, then iterate and make it better." This is a vital insight, as we'll see in a later chapter. Most entrepreneurs start out spending much of their time focusing on the *how*. "How am I going to do this? How am I going to do that?" This approach invariably leads young companies into the weeds. At this early stage it is far more important to be crystal clear about where it is that you want to go. Rather, ask the *what*, *if*, and *why* questions. When you do, you'll begin to surface the right sets of intermediate goals, tools, and technologies that you'll need to enable the *how*. It's also true that sometimes the needed technologies don't yet exist—but all indications are that they will, perhaps, say, three years down the road. That should only lend urgency to your venture: it might take those three years to build your infrastructure so that you'll be able to intersect the proverbial hockey puck at precisely the right time.

When you can spot trends early enough, you can mature into the emerging spaces much more quickly. Equally important, you can actually shape the directions of the new developments. This affords tremendous competitive advantage because most business leaders, being so married to their own corporate agendas, invariably wait too long. But you, on the other hand, will already be working on the third and fourth iterations. And three or four iterations in just means that many more layers of the "impossible future" peeled back.

Looking Ahead to 2050

Niels Bohr famously quipped, "It's hard to make predictions—especially about the future." In 1950, a group of journalists writing for the Associated Press proved that point when they authored the article "How Experts Think We'll Live in 2000 A.D."

Like most views of the future 50 years on, its visions, some quaint, some profound, ran the gamut from the dystopian to the utopian. There were both hits and misses: while the Earth might still be reeking from a third world war, a housewife will be using an "electronic stove" to prepare roast beef in less time than it takes to set the table. Some of the predictions are eerily prescient. For example, "Civilian scientists will have begun their study of outer space and will be preparing for interplanetary explorations, using methods already understood in mid-century." Forecasts of flying cars alternate with the transformation of the telephone into a portable radio equipped with the "visuality of television." Pretty cool, considering Dick Tracey's radio watch wouldn't be making its debut for another two years!

While achieving the entrepreneurially driven future that we imagine today won't exactly be a cakewalk, it is, without question, very much at hand, being rooted less in science fiction and more in scientific fact. With these thoughts in mind, then, let us look ahead, and see where these developments will take us in the not-too-distant year of 2050.

DISRUPTIONS OF THE WORLD ORDER • I believe that entrepreneurs will emerge as leaders of the new world order, and that the power and influence of the nation-states will wane in comparison. Nevertheless, the nation-states will remain, at least for pragmatic reasons. There will, however, be massive shifts in their respective standings. America, once standing alone at the top of the hill, now shares that ground with China. But not for long. According to Mathew Burrows, a former National Intelligence Council staffer, "By 2030, Asia will have surpassed North America and Europe *combined* in terms of global power, based upon measures of GDP, population size, military spending, and technological investment. China alone looks like it will become the largest economy sometime in the 2020s." Consequently, by 2050, the United States will fall to third place, behind a rapidly ascendant India. Japan, the current No. 4, will fall to eighth place. Mexico, which doesn't even show up in today's top 10 economies, will rise to No. 7—ahead of Japan! Indonesia, currently in eighth place, will rise to No. 4.

Further dinging America's status is Bloomberg's annual Innovation Index that ranks the most innovation-driven countries. For the first time (in 2018), the U.S. fell out of the top 10, its decline marked by a particularly poor showing in STEM education. Meanwhile, other nations—particularly China—are surging with well-funded innovation incentives. We can expect these trends to continue.

Why is this happening? It's happening because capital follows opportunity. And capital builds upon capital. American outsourcing has transformed the American dream into a global dream, and its pace will only accelerate. Consequently, more money will flow into the developing countries; their infrastructures will be modernized, prices for their natural resource exports will rise, and the standard of living—read, buying power—will improve right along with it all. And by 2050, these emerging markets will be huge. According to many analysts, the world economy will double in size by 2050, thanks to innovations and investments in technology. Indeed, the health of the global economy is increasingly linked to how well the developing nations do. Moreover, because by 2050 (also thanks to technology innovations) we will have an abundance of food, energy, water, and land, the political, social, and economic dynamics that have ruled humanity throughout history will have become forever altered. We will see, on every level, the fruits of disruptions of the highest order. The ramifications of this new and developing landscape run deep and wide—and certainly so for entrepreneurs, who must, therefore, adopt a broad, global perspective. But keep in mind that all this jockeying for global power is, at its core, driven by an economy of scarcity.

DISRUPTIONS IN THE NATURE OF OUR HUMANNESS • The same innovations that are starting to transform healthcare will also transform the human body itself—and along with it, every aspect of life and living. By 2050, augmented reality will have given way to augmented humanity. Not only will we be healthier, we'll be better, too. Consider just a few of the technologies that will be fully developed and in the mainstream by 2050:

• Our smartphones will have vanished, replaced by inconspicuous devices we will wear on our clothing and in/on our bodies. Smart contact lenses will project email, text, and images into our field of vision without our having to push or swipe anything. A thought will do it.

• Health monitoring and drug delivery will be transformed through the use of nanobots that will circulate in the body, constantly analyzing our physiology at the molecular level, making illness a thing of the past. This means that we will be able to live as long as we wish, and do so in a healthy body.

- Our brains will be connected directly to the cloud, meaning we will be able to upload our knowledge in a "brain-as-a-service" kind of model. We will be able to buy or exchange knowledge from others to enhance our own capabilities—on demand.
- We will be able to read one another's minds, with explicit permission from participating parties, and without the need to communicate verbally.
- The lines of reality will have become blurred as we will be able to engage the world in a virtual manner, able to appear anywhere holographically. Moreover, with our brains connected in the cloud, all of our experiences and memories will be continually synchronized as though we were actually present in remote locations.
- Language barriers will completely disappear, because our augmented brains will automatically translate one language to another (we're seeing a precursor of this capability today in AI-enabled translation earbuds).
- The ability to write a complete human genome will enable production of designer babies whose "parents" will be computers. As it is, robots are already demonstrating the ability to reproduce.
- We will enjoy augmented capabilities to see and hear across all wavelengths. With the range of human hearing limited to 20 Hz – 20 KHz, and vision restricted to a tiny band of the electromagnetic spectrum, we are, for all practical purposes, deaf and blind. In 2050, we'll be freed from such organic shackles, able to live and operate with vastly higher levels of perception and awareness.
- Every type of screen—phone, laptop, TV—will disappear as we will be able to use augmented reality built into our brains to view and experience every form of content as though it were real.

DISRUPTIONS IN TRANSPORTATION • By 2050, the combination of advances in artificial intelligence and the development of renewable energy sources will have completely transformed the ways we get around and do work on Earth—and beyond.

- By 2050, we will have become a multi-planetary society, with regular commercial flights to the moon, Mars, and other celestial bodies.
- It will be illegal for humans to drive cars on public roads—they'll just be too dangerous.
- You'll be scrapping your car sometime in the 2030s with a phasing out of private ownership, which will completely transform the automotive industry.
- We will have personal drones and personal jetpacks to take us and our goods from one point to another.

- Hyperloops, traveling at 700 mph, will zip us from one point on Earth to another in minutes.
- All modes of transportation will be powered by renewable—or newly plentiful—energy sources, as fossil fuels will have been banned.

DISRUPTIONS IN AI AND NANOTECHNOLOGY · We are presently in the fledgling stages of a fourth industrial revolution. By 2050, much of its promised capabilities will have come to fruition. Cognitive technologies comprising machine/deep learning, natural language processing, speech recognition, and others will have left nothing untouched. And when used to control robotics and nanoscale devices, AI will have taken us places by 2050 that no human has dared imagine, let alone predict.

- Artificial intelligence will have substantially surpassed human intelligence in many application spaces. Consequently, many of today's professions, including lawyers, accountants, primary care doctors, drivers, surgeons, hotel operators, chefs—even musicians—will disappear, having been displaced by superior AI-enabled solutions.
- We will not be working to earn a living, and therefore, we'll be dedicating our energies to creative pursuits that we enjoy.
- Virtually every object in our lives and every component of infrastructure will be smart, connected, and controlled via a combination of the cloud and blindingly fast communications—perhaps even quantum—technologies.
- 5G and its successors will enable not only ever-improving communications bandwidth and throughput, but previously unimagined applications. These advanced communications technologies will be used to transfer physical skills across networks, yielding an "Internet of Skills."[4]
- Through our "embodied" devices, cloud-based AI will constantly monitor all our vital health indicators, including blood pressure, heart rate, blood sugar levels, temperature, and more, averting emergencies and dramatically extending the human lifespan.
- Through the use of fully developed nanotechnologies and metamaterials, we will be able to manipulate and assemble objects at the atomic level, even enabling us to create precious materials—or anything else, for that matter—on demand.
- Metamaterials will allow us to manipulate every aspect of the electromagnetic spectrum, enabling true visual cloaking, noise canceling on a massive scale, the countering of tsunamis—even the ability to view atoms.

We're only scratching the surface with this smattering of the kinds of experiences that will be commonplace in the world of 2050—experiences that will be brought about by entrepreneurs operating right now in history's most disruptive era. Even so, such predictions can be overwhelming to our sensibilities. But if any of these projections give pause, it is because we look at them through the lens of life as we know and experience it today.

As a species, we have always feared the worst, but hoped for the best. And there is much to hope for on our way to 2050. Consider for a moment how much life has changed since 1950—and for the better. In 2050—just three decades down the road—I believe that humanity will look back at the seeds we're sowing today, just as we do of those who envisioned the future in 1950, with the same appreciation for the optimism and sense of wonder that made it all possible. And that's what makes technology entrepreneurship so exciting—and hopeful.

The prophetic Associated Press article from 1950 closes with a compelling observation—one that holds true every bit as much today as we look to our own future. "Today," its authors wrote, "almost alone among men, we have the strength—as we may need to prove—to hold the course we *choose.*"

1. Dr. Gill Pratt, of Toyota Research Institute, reminds us that there are more than 35,000 traffic fatalities every year in the US (1.25 million worldwide). So what if a self-driving car were twice as safe as a human-driven car, cutting fatalities in half to, say, 17,500? "Would we accept such autonomy then?" he asks. "Historically, humans have shown nearly zero-tolerance for injury or death caused by flaws in a machine. And yet we know that the artificial intelligence systems on which our autonomous cars will depend are presently and unavoidably, imperfect. So … how safe is safe enough?" A more fundamental question is, at what point does it become a moral imperative? Like the classic "trolley problem," we're sure to find ourselves facing an increasing number of such tech-inspired conundrums.

2. As will tailgate parties, bumper stickers, bored small town teens cruising Main Street, and other classic elements of car culture. But neither will there be any more parking tickets!

3. Driving this point home, Winston Churchill wisely observed, "Want of foresight, unwillingness to act when action would be simple and effective, lack of clear thinking, confusion of counsel until the emergency comes, until self-preservation strikes its jarring gong—these are the features which constitute the endless repetition of history."

4. Ericsson and King's College London are collaborating to demonstrate novel applications of 5G network infrastructure, including surgical robotics, where an experimental network has created the ability to allow the remote transfer of haptic, tactile, audio, and visual/virtual reality technologies, enabling a surgeon or doctor to perform a diagnosis or even surgery on a patient anywhere in the world. Moreover, the associated data can be stored in a "skills database," ready to be downloaded by medical students anywhere. The research group is even applying the concepts to music performance, where, for example, a pianist could download a musical score from a skills database into an exoskeleton that would move the wearer's fingers until the muscle memory is trained. The aspiring musician could, in effect, "practice" anywhere. How else might entrepreneurs exploit an Internet of Skills?

CHAPTER 2

What If...

*"There's no use trying," she said, "one can't believe impossible things."
"I daresay, you haven't had much practice," said the Queen. "When I
was your age, I always did it for half-an-hour a day. Why, sometimes
I've believed as many as six impossible things before breakfast."*

—**Lewis Carroll, Alice in Wonderland**

S DEVELOPING A MINDSET OF POSSIBILITY really just a matter of practice? Yes, it is! In fact, there's no question about it, particularly when you begin to understand the power of habit. An openness to possibility is perhaps *the* overarching habit that drives the moonshot entrepreneur's thinking. But which comes first, the habit-forming success or the success-forming habit? To answer this riddle, we have to take a short detour into the mechanics of habits—how and why they work, and what you can and cannot do about them.

CULTIVATING A MINDSET OF POSSIBILITY

In every formed habit we find three consistent components: 1) an instigating cue, prompt, triggering event, or other relevant stimulus; 2) the behavioral routine that one performs in response to the stimulus; and 3) the reward that derives from performing the behavioral routine. Cue, routine, reward. Trigger, behavior, satisfaction. However you describe it, every habit formed requires the sequence of these three mechanisms, and every habit performed is exercised because of them. And as to whether the habit is good, bad, or indifferent, the brain does not know—or care; it simply runs the automatic routine associated with a particular stimulus, motivated by the reward the behavior promises to deliver. That's it in a nutshell. Here are two versions of how this can play out:

- "Oh, that's a tough one. I tried that once and it didn't work. See? I told you so."

- "That's an interesting problem. Hmm … You know, if we could solve that … I wonder if … Well, that didn't go the way I expected. Ah, but maybe if we tweak this part just a bit … Yep that did the trick. Cool!"

Do you see the trigger, behavior, and satisfaction bits in each of these examples? They're always there. Now here's the rub: it may be that you cannot completely eradicate a bad habit; once programmed into the brain, it is there to stay.[1] You can, however, change a habitual behavior by manipulating just one of the three habit variables: the middle part—the *routine*. In fact, it's the only component over which you have any direct control.

Behaviorists have found that by identifying the triggers and rewards associated with a particular habit, you can change the routine. And a change in the routine is a change in behavior. Again, the trigger and reward remain unchanged, but in the end, a new habit is formed. In this case, a habit of openness to possibility—a response to a problem that is biased in favor of an optimistic outlook—can transform a scarcity-driven mindset into an abundance-oriented mindset. The scarcity-driven mindset operates by lazy thought habits—the ones that come most naturally, the so-called "paths of least resistance." These are the mindsets that resist change, fear the future, and work to preserve the status quo—no matter how bad it is.

A mindset of abundance is best cultivated by building a foundational habit—a fundamental behavior or practice that, once shifted, has the power to start a chain reaction, transforming many other areas of life and work, thanks to its many ripple effects. And one of those effects is the one that coalesces into *culture*. Imagine a culture of possibility! That's a powerful concept. As Peter Drucker famously quipped, "Culture eats strategy for breakfast."

While your own experience may find you arguing on either side of Drucker's sentiment, what is clear is that the two are very closely related—and that you really can't do without either culture or strategy. The key to leveraging them both for maximum effect lies in aligning the strategic goals with organizational behaviors—behaviors that must be cultivated to form habits. And when organizational habits are aligned with the particulars of business strategy, you've got culture. In the end, culture is really just a series of organizational habits. Purposefully promoting the *right set* of habits in your team ultimately produces a sustainable source of competitive advantage—and your possibility-driven moonshot will exploit every advantage it can muster.

As we'll see in a later chapter, most organizations make choices based on long-held organizational habits, patterns that emerge from thousands of employees' independent decisions over time. They ossify, and become fixed, leaving them vulnerable to disruption, as we see time and time again in large companies. Worse, they become closed to the awesome power and wonder of *unexplored possibility*—the innumerable secrets to discover in one's space, the countless opportunities to make creative, self-sustaining impact in the world. The opportunity costs associated with closed mindsets is incalculable, not only to the organization, but to the human spirit, attenuating the potential of both.

Too many problems are simply dismissed as "too hard." Of course they're hard! But that's why we're here. If the world were perfect, it wouldn't be. Problems are life's essential feedstock. Without problems to solve, there is no motivating tension; without tension, there is no progress; without progress, there is only stagnation. Problems represent our greatest opportunity to elevate every true, good, and beautiful aspect of our humanity. To squander this capacity in a default fixed and lazy mindset is practically a crime against humanity! At minimum, it is a great sin of omission. Humanity is impacted every bit as much by one's inaction as by one's action.

Richard Feynman summed things up this way: "It seems to me that we do think about these [hard] problems from time to time. But we don't put full-time effort on them—the reason being that we know we don't have any magic formula for solving problems, that social problems are much harder than scientific ones, and that we usually don't get anywhere when we do think about them."

> **The scarcity-driven mindset operates by lazy thought habits— the ones that come most naturally, the so-called "paths of least resistance." These are the mindsets that resist change, fear the future, and work to preserve the status quo—no matter how bad it is.**

The bigger problem here is the stunning lack of imagination and initiative in the world that this sentiment exposes. Conquering perceived impossibilities is a walk in the park compared to overcoming inertia. But inertia— root word being "inert"—is the reigning habit we're all up against, and perhaps the entrepreneur's greatest challenge. Or should I say opportunity?

Long ago, William James observed that "the human individual lives usually far within his limits; he possesses powers of various sorts which he *habitually* fails to use. He energizes far below his maximum ..." It's true that we live up or down to what we believe. Enlightened entrepreneurs, though, are audacious enough to actually believe that they can be powerful agents of positive change in the world. Indeed, I believe only the entrepreneur can transcend this state of affairs. And when entrepreneurs demonstrate what is actually possible, then everything becomes possible.

If there is one thing that I've learned time and time again it's that nothing is impossible. A thing only *seems* impossible until someone does it. History is replete with illustrations. Take the four-minute mile, for example. Nobody ran a mile in four minutes because nobody thought it was possible—until one person, Roger Bannister, did it. And when he did, a year later 30 more people did it. Likewise, once you change your mindset from one of scarcity to a mindset of abundance, you begin to think of potentials and possibilities rather than the things that can't be done. You start to see the world in a very different way. And others, thus inspired, will join you.

The big idea behind the XPRIZE Foundation, where I am a trustee of the board, is to encourage this way of thinking. We find the first of these competitions in the amazing story of the Longitude Act of 1714, which offered a substantial reward to anyone who could devise a practical solution to determining a ship's longitude at sea. Comparatively speaking, determining latitude was a piece of cake: just note the altitude of the sun at noon and look up the sun's declination for the day on a table, or, if navigating at night, by the position of guiding stars above the horizon. Finding longitude, however, was an entirely different matter. For that, early navigators had to rely on dead reckoning—not so easy on long voyages and when out of sight of land—a condition that sometimes ended in tragedy.

Galileo, Isaac Newton, and Edmund Halley all lent their considerable intellects to the longitude problem, but even their sophisticated astronomical methods came up short. The problem was so great that in 1714, England's Parliament offered a £20,000 prize to anyone who could solve it. Thus was born the first "grand challenge"—one whose outcome would forever alter the course of global navigation. Interestingly enough, the prize was won by the self-educated English clockmaker John Harrison (1693-1776), who solved the longitude problem with his chronometer—a friction-free timepiece, invulnerable to pitch and roll, temperature, and humidity—that would carry the true time from the home port to any destination.

As for spurring the imagination, the longitude challenge may have overachieved. One proposal called for permanently moored (and manned) barges at optimal intervals in places of established longitude. Rockets would be fired into the air, from which passing ships could, depending on the velocity of sound of the firing of rockets, calculate their longitude. Little thought, however, was put into how these barges would be manned and provisioned.

Sir Kenelm Digby's proposal involved the use of "Powders of Sympathy"—a "magical" substance composed of ferrous sulfate. The idea was to send aboard an intentionally wounded dog as a ship set sail. With the dog's discarded bandage left ashore in London, a timekeeper would dip the bandage into the bowl of sympathy powder each day precisely at noon. The dog would then howl in response to the sympathetically aggravated wound, thereby providing the ship's navigation officer with the needed time cue. The dog's yelp would signal, "The sun is upon the meridian in London," so allowing the difference in time to be immediately determined, giving the longitude. We don't know whether the theory was ever trialed—or how many unfortunate dogs suffered for the cause of science—but bonus points should have been awarded for imagination!

> If the world were perfect, it wouldn't be. Problems are life's essential feedstock. Without problems to solve, there is no motivating tension; without tension, there is no progress; without progress, there is only stagnation.

The remarkable success of the prize inspired a great many other grand challenges, incentivizing innovators to solve many difficult but important problems. You might be unaware, though, that Charles Lindbergh's 1927 solo crossing of the Atlantic was also motivated by a prize—originally offered on May 22, 1919. The challenge was issued by New York City hotel owner Raymond Orteig, who was inspired to create the prize upon hearing WWI ace Eddie Rickenbacker speak of anticipating the day when America and France would be linked by air.

"Gentlemen," Orteig's announcement began, "as a stimulus to the courageous aviators, I desire to offer, through the auspices and regulations of the Aero Club of America, a prize of $25,000 to the first aviator of any Allied Country crossing the Atlantic in one flight, from Paris to New York or New York to Paris, all other details in your care."

Eight years later—*to the very day*—Lindbergh would claim the purse. The effects of the Orteig prize, however, far outreached the crossing of the Atlantic. In the first place, it stimulated a level of investment that was actually 16 times greater than that of the value of the prize itself. And once the ensuing myriad competitive forces were put into motion, an industry was created. The number of US airline passengers skyrocketed from 5,782 to 173,405 in the two years that followed Lindbergh's accomplishment. In 1927 alone, there was a 300 percent increase in applications for pilot's licenses, and a 400 percent increase in licensed aircraft in the United States. Suddenly, global air travel was possible!

Fast forward 77 years to May 1996, when engineer, physician, and entrepreneur Peter Diamandis set out to bring the Orteig prize up-to-date with a $10 million competition for the first civilian organization that could launch a reusable manned spacecraft 100 kilometers into space twice within two weeks. Just as the Orteig prize opened up aviation, the "X PRIZE" aimed to spur the development of another "impossible" industry—civilian space travel. And that it did.

The competition was won by Burt Rutan, whose SpaceShipOne development was backed by Paul Allen and later acquired by Sir Richard Branson, who dubbed his new venture Virgin Galactic—the world's first commercial "spaceline." Dubbed the Ansari XPRIZE, it drew more than 26 teams from seven nations to commit more than $100 million in technology investments in pursuit of the prize. And after the prize was won, a half-dozen new companies entered the nascent market, with nearly $1 billion invested. That's some leverage. More important, the prize made possible world-changing breakthroughs that neither government nor industry seemed able to produce.

So yesterday's impossible has become today's routine. Why, then, are we still so skeptical when it comes to questions of possibility? Imagine the things we could accomplish if we did not think of them as impossible. Perhaps one reason is that there seems to be a great deal of confusion when it comes to discerning the impossible from the merely hard. If you mistake something that's only difficult for something impossible, you'll never attempt to achieve it.

> " The minute you believe something is impossible, it becomes impossible for *you*. I believe that there are very few problems that can't be solved with imagination, innovation, and competent entrepreneurship—provided they don't break too many laws of physics. "

The minute you believe something is impossible, it becomes impossible for *you*. I believe that there are very few problems that can't be solved with imagination, innovation, and competent entrepreneurship—provided they don't break too many laws of physics. But even those are daily being called into question. Consider the recently demonstrated quantum entanglement between the Earth and a low Earth orbit satellite!

Quantum entanglement, which Einstein dismissed as "spooky action at a distance," is a connection between two different particles at the atomic level in which anything affecting one particle also affects the other, even if they are separated by a vast distance. This is much more than just theoretical physics. Quantum entangled particles can be used for encryption purposes, because quantum communications systems can securely exchange encryption keys. If anyone intercepts a quantum message, the interception will change the message, alerting the users to a possible eavesdropper. Researchers from the Chinese Academy of Science and the Austrian Academy of Sciences actually demonstrated the capability. They created entangled pairs of photons and then beamed one of these photons to China's *Micius* satellite, which passed overhead every day at midnight. The other photon remained on Earth (in Vienna). They then measured the photons on the ground and in orbit to confirm that entanglement was present, and that they were, in fact, able to teleport photons in this way. Just imagine how this could revolutionize the very definition of security. And best of all, the method does not appear to involve any yelping dogs.

> **People tend to get caught up in seeing the world only *as it is* and not imagining what the world *could be*. If you focus only on what the world is, then you are resigning yourself to a particular destiny.**

Sometimes you simply have to ask, "What if?" What if it were actually possible? What if it could be done? What, then, would you do?

"Man often becomes what he believes himself to be," wrote Mahatma Gandhi. "If I keep on saying to myself that I cannot do a certain thing, it is possible that I may end by really becoming incapable of doing it. On the contrary, if I have the belief that I can do it, I shall surely acquire the capacity to do it even if I may not have it at the beginning." Indeed, belief in secrets and mysteries—even quantum ones—and your ability to discover and solve them—is a very powerful and effective truth.

While naysayers may still hold sway, we can be thankful that they have not always prevailed. From our perspective today, we can see how amazingly short-sighted many of them have been. For example, in looking forward to the coming century, the 1899 edition of *Punch* magazine presented a dialogue where Genius asks, "Isn't there a clerk who can examine patents?" A boy replies, "Quite unnecessary, sir. Everything that can be invented has been invented." The sentiment even extended to *Scientific American*, which opined, "That the automobile has practically reached the limit of its development is suggested by the fact that during the past year no improvements of a radical nature have been introduced"—the previous year being 1908! In 1895, Lord Kelvin himself declared that heavier-than-air flying machines are impossible. Not to be outdone, in an ultimate twist of irony, Einstein explained in 1932, "There is not the slightest indication that [nuclear energy] will ever be obtainable. It would mean that the atom would have to be shattered at will."

Oddly enough, the skeptics have frequently been considered more credible than other voices. As the conventional wisdom goes, if you're a skeptic, then you're a "good reporter," and if optimistic, then you're clearly someone's puppet. Consequently, you see little else but gloom and doom in the likes of what I like to call the *Crisis News Network*. Indeed, if it bleeds, it leads.

Even formerly optimistic prognosticators have taken their turns for the worse. While his technology predictions made in 1964 proved remarkably prescient, somewhere along the line, even Isaac Asimov lost faith in the future. Consider his comments in this interview in one of the "Plowboy" pieces published in *Mother Earth News*, October 1980:

Plowboy: In your opinion, what are mankind's prospects for the near future?

Asimov: To tell the truth, I don't think the odds are very good that we can solve our immediate problems. I think the chances that civilization will survive more than another 30 years—that it will still be flourishing in 2010—are less than 50 percent.

Plowboy: What sort of disaster do you foresee?

Asimov: I imagine that as population continues to increase—and as the available resources decrease—there will be less energy and food, so we'll all enter a stage of scrounging. The average person's only concerns will be where he or she can get the next meal, the next cigarette, the next means of transportation. In such a universal scramble, the Earth will be just plain desolated, because everyone will be striving merely to survive regardless of the cost to the environment.

Now contrast these sentiments to those of Geoff Woo of the cognitive enhancement company HVMN: "Computers have been the innovation platform of the last decade," he says. "The human body will be the innovation platform of the next decade. Unlocking human potential is such an awesome opportunity. There's so much blue sky to work in. I feel like we're at the very start of the biohacking revolution just like how in the '70s and '80s was the start of the computer revolution. *We get to make the future!"*

People tend to get caught up in seeing the world only *as it is* and not imagining what the world *could be.* If you focus only on what the world is, then you are resigning yourself to a particular destiny—one that is constrained by the familiar—just another version of the anxious world we know today. When you begin to believe that tomorrow is going to be no better than today, that you're helpless, then you are, therefore, also hopeless. Sadly, such attitudes are reaching epidemic proportions. Not only is this tragic, it is completely unnecessary and totally disconnected from the different realities that we can, in fact, bring about—if we have the imagination and will to do so. When fueled by the recognition of our astounding capacities to accomplish great things, we actually can.

○ ◑ ● ◐

"The sun is seen to pour down and expend itself in all directions," Marcus Aurelius wrote, "yet is never exhausted. For this downpouring is but a self-extension; sunbeams, in fact, derive their very name from a word signifying 'to be extended.' To understand the property of a sunbeam, watch the light as it streams into a darkened room through a narrow chink. It prolongs itself forward in a straight line, until it is held up by encountering some solid body which blocks its passage to the air beyond; and then it remains at rest there, without slipping off or falling away. The emission, and the diffusion, of thought should be the counterpart of this: not exhausting, but simply extending itself; not dashing violently or furiously against the obstacles it encounters, or yet falling away in despair; *but holding its ground and lighting up that upon which it rests.* Failure to transmit it is mere self-deprivation of light."

This sunlight is nothing less than the human spirit. It has the power to illuminate the deepest darkness, and imagination is its raw material. Imagination is the infinite, endless combinations of possibilities for envisioning and designing the future we desire. People often say the sky is the limit. The sky is not the limit. There is no such limit. It is an artificial boundary. *Imagination* is our only limit. If we can imagine something then we can accomplish it.

I'd like to digress here for just a moment to shed light on another aspect of possibility—particularly for those to whom this talk of extreme possibility is just an impossible moonshot. What if I were to tell you that there once lived a boy in New Dehli, India, who grew up in the worst poverty you can imagine. Yet through grit and determination, he managed to earn an engineering degree and an MBA before emigrating to the United States—and arriving with just $5 in his pocket. In time, he landed a job at Microsoft, where his work on Windows 95 earned him both patents and accolades for his standout program management work. From there he ventured to found the seminal InfoSpace, which became one of the largest internet businesses in America. He then went on to found a series of other tech companies, including inome, Intelius, TalentWise, and Viome. Along the way, he was awarded the Albert Einstein Technology Medal, named one of the "Most Creative People in Business" by Fast Company, and was presented the Ellis Island Medal of Honor. Today, with Moon Express, he is leading the first private enterprise that will put a lander on the moon, and in the process, open a new era of lunar exploration dedicated to solving the world's energy problems. Impossible as it seems even to me, this is actually *my* story. And I believe that something equally, if not more, audacious, could be your story. If I can do something like this, anyone can.

When you deny people's innate power to dream and imagine big, audacious things, they become slaves to the status quo, a status quo that is preventing real human flourishing. Again, the reason more innovation doesn't happen is because people don't dream; they simply do not take the time to imagine possibilities. Yet the possibilities are inexhaustible. With every solution we are able to create, we generate new prob-

> **People often say the sky is the limit. The sky is not the limit. There is no such limit. It is an artificial boundary. *Imagination* is our only limit.**

lems. There is an overabundance of problems. And every problem comes pre-packaged with opportunities for new solutions.

What does this mean to the entrepreneur? It means the cyclical nature of technology yields a never-ending stream of opportunities—and never-ending reasons for hope and optimism. The technology is available to us *right now* to create, leverage, and deploy the technologies of tomorrow that will solve the world's great problems in innovative ways—multi-billion dollar problems that impact billions of people. Indeed, my fundamental thought pattern is that everything is possible, and the bigger the problem, the bigger the opportunity.

I'll address execution in a later chapter, but for the moment, let me just encourage you to not get too caught up in thinking about what today's technology means in the context of the world's current state. Think instead about the potentials. Forego the *how*, and focus only on what you want to achieve—and why. At this stage, you'll be well-served to be unencumbered by business plans, revenue projections, expert opinions, or other constraints or requirements. Just free your mind to simply imagine, even in a child-like way. It's a liberating and exhilarating experience to indulge in this kind of playful thinking. In fact, it was one of Richard Feynman's great secrets. Likewise, when I start a new company, I don't know how it's going to unfold. I don't know how I'll do it. For whatever "crazy" idea I am contemplating, I simply ask, *what if this were actually possible?* There's simply no better starting point.

The reason imagination is so vital—and why science fiction is so important—is that imagination begets possibility. Equally important, imagination helps you to visualize an idea. If you can't visualize a thing, then it's not likely that you'll ever be able to realize it. This is where science fiction is useful. What if, for example, *Star Trek*'s tricorder could actually be done? You can already visualize it—it's right there in your mind's eye. And when you describe it to others, they see it, too. You then begin to imagine a portable, wireless device in the palm of your hand and whose myriad sensors actively and simultaneously monitor and diagnose a host of potential health conditions. Well, this is the very objective envisioned in the Qualcomm Tricorder XPRIZE that drew 300 teams who competed to develop a solution for providing people with greater choices about when, where, and how they receive healthcare. And *voila!* We now have a tricorder. This really does work.

> **It appears that human performance is optimized to near sea level. But these limitations haven't kept us from venturing to the depths of the ocean or to the heights of the moon. We have, through technology, greatly expanded our sphere of existence.**

I love to start conversations by saying, "Imagine ... Allow yourself to clear your mind and open up to the possibilities that I'm about to describe. And until I tell you, you're not to analyze anything; simply be present and open to everything I say." Then I'll tell them to imagine that this table in front of us doesn't really exist. Invariably they will say, "But wait a minute, we both see the table. How can it not exist?" At this point, they're not ready for every possibility. But it's also the point at which I have the best chance of capturing their curiosity. And hopefully, I've captured yours.

In philosophy, there is always a tension between appearance and reality—between what things *seem* to be and what we can actually *know* about them. These differences get us into trouble all the time. We know, for example, that from a given point of view, the color of the table in front of us will appear to be different under conditions of natural or artificial lighting. To a color-blind person, it will look different still. Or consider the person observing the table through rose-colored glasses, or in candle light. Can anyone say with certainty that the table is in fact brown? You might be tempted to say that such a question is absurd. Of course the table is brown. Any fool can see—and know—that the table not only exists, it is also brown. But no one knows what color the table really is, *in itself.* Under normal daylight conditions we only *perceive* the table to be brown because our eyes are sensitive only to the tiny "visual" portion of the electromagnetic spectrum. But what if our eyes were also able to take in and process ultraviolet light? Not only would the table no longer appear brown, but the trees we once *knew* to be green would be purple! The essence of brownness or greenness is lost in such a world! The point is that whatever we know about the table is only known to us by means of sense-data—and that data can be deceiving. Therefore, we cannot claim that the table or the bottle upon it are the actual equivalents of our sense-data, or that the sense-data reflect the actual properties of the objects. If seeing is believing, then we're going to need a lot more than our eyes! (Likewise, we can consider—or reconsider—the sense of hearing. Given the miniscule range of human hearing—20 Hz to 20 KHz—as mentioned in the previous chapter, we're practically also deaf.)

When I began to think of the company that became Viome, I said to anyone who would listen, "Imagine if there were a world where illness is optional. What if that world could be created? Wouldn't you want to be part of creating that world? I'm not saying that I am doing it, or how I would do it; I'm just suggesting that it's possible." So there's no argument here. You simply ask, could such a world be possible? And if you believe that such a world *is* possible—and that you can actually visualize it—why can't we also create it?

If, on the other hand, I start the conversation from the viewpoint of a specific technology or solution to the problem, people will immediately begin to argue with me—they simply won't believe. But I don't go there. If I ask them only to imagine the possibility, nine times out of 10, they'll come around and agree that yes, it actually *could* be possible. Once we've established that the possibility exists, the only question is how to get there. So I'll suggest bootstrapping some portion of what might become a solution over time. We know it is not going to be the complete solution—not even close—but wouldn't it allow us to get the ball rolling for us to understand what to do next? And people say, you know, you are right. If we can do *this*, then we'll know how to do *that*, and if we know how to do *that*, then we'll know how to do *this*. And step by step, we can actually get there. This way of thinking then becomes a way of being. And it's not hard.

To borrow a line from Feynman, "we're not inventing anti-gravity here." Which, by the way, is possible someday only if the laws of physics are not what we think. But there is a world of possibility even given that the laws *are* what we think. And again, we don't have to violate too many of them!

Taking this cosmological thread a little further, the material stuff of our humanity does, in fact, come from the stars. Why then do we think we can't reach for them? Most people limit their possibility for one reason: they don't believe in what is *actually possible for them to achieve.*

I live in the world of possibilities, and possibility's slow fuse is lit by the imagination. As Galileo put it, "Facts which at first seem improbable will, even on scant explanation, drop the cloak which has hidden them and stand forth in naked and simple beauty."

ADVENTURES IN POSSIBILITY

Let's see how far we can push these concepts with a few thought experiments in possibility. And let's begin with the possibility of writing the entire 24 volumes of the Encyclopedia Britannica on the head of a pin. Absurd? Impossible? Richard Feynman took up this question in his famed 1959 talk, *There's Plenty of Room at the Bottom*, the groundbreaking introduction to the concepts of what came to be known as nanotechnology. "Let's see what would be involved," he began. "The head of a pin is a sixteenth of an inch across. If you magnify it by 25,000 diameters, the area of the head of the pin is then equal to the area of all the pages of the Encyclopedia Britannica. Therefore, all it is necessary to do is to reduce in size all the writing in the Encyclopedia by 25,000 times. Is that possible? The resolving power of the eye is about 1/120 of an inch—that is roughly the diameter of one of the little dots on the fine half-tone reproductions in the Encyclopedia. This, when you demagnify it by 25,000 times, is still 80 angstroms in diameter—32 atoms across, in an ordinary metal. In other words, one of those dots still would contain in its area 1,000 atoms. So, each dot can easily be adjusted in size as required by the photoengraving, and there is no question that there is enough room on the head of a pin to put all of the Encyclopedia Britannica ... and then look through it with an electron microscope!"

With that mental calibration, I'll now ask you to believe much less.

As Elton John sang in *Rocket Man*, "Mars ain't the kind of place to raise your kids." Nonetheless, it's almost impossible to read the news without bumping into a story about Mars and the many plans underway to send humans there. You may think we've got a carbon problem here, but the Martian atmosphere is 96% carbon dioxide. And that's the least of the problems that will be faced by sojourners and emigrants to the Red Planet. Protecting humans from radiation is a chief concern—high-energy particle radiation passes right through the skin, damaging cells and DNA as it goes. Aside from the cancer risks, if the dose is high enough, spacefarers will also suffer acute radiation sickness during their long missions. Remember that a roundtrip to Mars will take at least a year to complete. That's a lot of exposure—and a lot of time to feel really lousy.

> " In many ways, you're actually younger today than you were seven or 10 years ago. Your cells continuously die and are replaced by new ones many times over your lifespan. "

Spaceship Earth, though, is protected from radiation by our magnetosphere, which deflects most of the radiation that would otherwise be incident upon our planet. Our atmosphere takes care of the rest. In the Space Station, which is positioned just within Earth's protective magnetic field, astronauts are still exposed to 10 times the amount of radiation that we get on Earth. Mars, however, has no global magnetic field, and its thin atmosphere doesn't contribute much else.

One of the solutions NASA is investigating involves digging underground habitats, which would protect astronauts from both cosmic radiation and the intense cold. But living underground would be pretty confining, and who would want to go all the way to Mars only to live sequestered in a cave? Maybe there's a better way—a *crazy* way. Could we possibly genetically modify our bodies to make them radiation-proof? What if that were actually possible? With the nascent CRISPR gene-editing technology, this solution appears to be on the horizon. But how? Where would we find radiation-resistant genes to splice into our own, and would they really work?

It turns out that there are microbes that are not only able to survive exposure to radiation, but actually thrive in it, consuming radioactive waste as their energy source! They literally eat radiation for breakfast—just one of our six impossible things to believe today. Among them is the *deinococcus radiodurans*—the world's toughest "extremophile bacterium," at least according to *The Guinness Book of World Records*.

> **So what exactly, then, is *me*-ness if I am both dying and being regenerated every day? What does it mean to me that certain of my genes become expressed with or without my permission, or that they may be altered at will via editing?**

So let's think about this. If you could insert any gene from another organism into your own DNA, what would it be? Well, if you happen to be an astronaut—or aspire to become one—you might want to choose the tardigrade *Dsup* protein. Tardigrades, if you don't recognize them by that name, are also known as water bears—the near-microscopic animals that look like a cross between a flea and a manatee. Tardigrades are tough little critters, surviving temperatures down to near absolute zero. They also exhibit extraordinary tolerance to radiation and other physical extremes. To learn just how tough they are, in 2007, the European Space Agency sent tardigrades into low Earth orbit, where they survived for 12 days—*on the outside of the capsule*. That's tough!

Researchers at the University of Tokyo, using human cells (cultured in a petri dish—not a human subject), have demonstrated that the tardigrade-unique DNA-associating protein—*Dsup*—suppresses and repairs X-ray-induced DNA damage (in both single-strand and double-strand breaks) by about 40 percent, and it improves radiotolerance overall. These remarkable results suggest that tardigrades could be a bountiful source of protective genes for humans in space.

When you consider that NASA accepted only 14 of 18,300 applicants to its latest class of astronauts, you might want to improve your chances with a dose of *Dsup*, and even further with a side of *EPAS1*, the gene that enables Tibetans to get by with less oxygen. Such are the enhancements that would certainly come in handy for a spacefaring people. Crazy? Yes. Possible? Absolutely. *In vivo* gene editing in humans is already happening.

Other concerns for the aspiring spacefarer are the many effects of zero gravity on human physiology. Might there be genetic solutions here as well? The fact is, humans were designed to function and survive within a fairly narrow set of parameters. Without life support devices, we're essentially constrained to a range that spans sea level to an altitude of about 5,000 meters—the practical limit of human acclimation. It appears that human performance is optimized to near sea level. But these limitations haven't kept us from venturing to the depths of the ocean or to the heights of the moon. We have, through technology, greatly expanded our sphere of existence. And as we continue to push beyond our natural physiological limits to explore the solar system, we're learning that additional fortifications to human factors—including genetic ones—will be necessary to adapt to the extreme environments that will be part and parcel of a multi-planetary lifestyle.

Consider, for example, that in a sustained microgravity environment, astronauts suffer bone mass loss at a rate of about 10 times that of osteoporosis in the elderly. While osteoporosis drugs and osteogenic loading exercises have helped a great deal to counter these effects, over long journeys, astronauts will still suffer a net loss. Our bodies really do need gravity to work well. But what if, like countering the effects of radiation, there was a way to solve this problem genetically?

NASA has been asking this question since they discovered that space travel induces dramatic increases in gene expression. The process is called *methylation*—the mechanism by which genes are turned on and off.[2] Dr. Chris Mason, a principal investigator at NASA, described it this way: "Some of the most exciting things that we've seen from looking at gene expression in space is that we really see an explosion, like fireworks taking off, as soon as the human body gets into space."

That may be an exciting discovery for Dr. Mason, but I don't think many of us will be thrilled at the prospect of our genes exploding like fireworks. We'll need to control and/or engineer gene expression in ways that will *augment* and not harm human physiology. Clearly, we need to learn more. In any event, modifications to our genetic code to enhance and extend our capabilities beyond life on this pale blue dot that we call home raise myriad questions about who and what we really are—and what we can become.

> **As science fiction novels are increasingly looking more like everyday user manuals, science fiction writers are going to have to get a lot more imaginative.**

○ ◑ ● ◐

To thine own self be true? Well, sort of. The cells that make up our bodies constitute a dynamic, ever-changing milieu, rife with paradox. The older we get, for example, the younger we get. In many ways, you're actually younger today than you were seven or 10 years ago. Your cells continuously die and are replaced by new ones many times over your lifespan. Your brain, though, is another matter. While neurogenesis occurs in the hippocampus, the striatum, and the amygdala, it appears that we're stuck with all the neurons we'll ever have in the cerebral cortex. It's just about our only original equipment. Because these cells aren't replaced[3], their function diminishes with age. That's a bitch, because the cerebral cortex is responsible for our thinking, perceiving, reasoning, and producing and understanding of language, among other things. Most information processing occurs in the cerebral cortex.

> " If I could transport my memories and my experience to different places at the same time, have I, in effect, teleported myself? The answer may be yes. And if I could actually recollect the memories and experiences associated with the new place, have I really been there? "

It's also true that as we age, our renewal processes—including those that remake our bones—slow down, thanks in large part to the accumulation of senescent cells—so-called zombie cells that are supposed to die off but don't. They tend to squirt out all sorts of inflammation-inducing chemicals that interfere with the health of neighboring healthy cells, including those responsible for bone remodeling, exponentially accelerating the onset of osteoporosis and other age-related diseases. It turns out that grandma didn't fall and break her hip; her hip broke and then she fell. Perhaps there's a way to genetically cause senescent cells to off themselves.

As you might imagine, senescence is a hot research space. The discovery of a new class of drugs called senolytics has demonstrated remarkable potential to reverse the effects of aging by clearing out these zombie cells. The drugs can regenerate bone mass and improve a raft of other age-related conditions, including cardiovascular function. Despite the benefits of eliminating senescence, senescent cells aren't all bad. They actually play a role in healing and scar-tissue formation. Moreover, senescence suppresses the growth of cancer cells. So modulating the senescence effect is a promising development in both cancer therapeutics and aging research. But like many drugs, senolytics may also cause collateral damage. In the meantime, though, you can be sure that old lab mice are enjoying their formerly youthful vigor—including fur regrowth. Oh, to be a mouse!

With CRISPR and Zinc Fingers gene-editing tools, it is now possible to modify, delete, insert, activate, or inactivate any gene—and do so with great precision. So we could, in theory, engineer a kill switch for *selected* senescent cells. If aging is driven in part by changes in gene expression, then the ability to control gene expression using gene-editing technologies could have profound implications. Does this mean we can reset our cells' clocks to zero and further stimulate new cell production even as we age? *What if ...*

But back to another important point about our original equipment. Unlike your cellular molecules that are constantly changing, your core DNA—selective gene expression notwithstanding—remains unchanged from day one. Yet, even this permanency is coming into question.

So what exactly, then, is *me*-ness if I am both dying and being regenerated every day? What does it mean to me that certain of my genes become expressed with or without my permission, or that they may be altered at will via editing? One can argue that my identity—what makes me who and what I am—ultimately boils down to my memory, experiences, beliefs, relationships, talents, personality, and other such attributes. Those are the things that differentiate me from you. But what about the rest of our bodies? Does the number of my toes or the condition of my eyesight matter? Are our organs and limbs really nothing more than replaceable, plug-and-play, or upgradable components?

> **Someone once asked me which science fiction technologies are not likely to become reality. I answered by saying that the question you should be asking is, *what is it that science fiction has not yet imagined?***

"Today," Alvin Toffler wrote in 1970's *Future Shock*, "the man with a pacemaker or a plastic aorta is still recognizably a man. The inanimate part of his body is still relatively unimportant in terms of his personality and consciousness. But as the proportion of machine components rises, what happens to his awareness of self, his inner experience? If we assume that the brain is the seat of consciousness and intelligence, and that no other part of the body affects personality or self very much, then it is possible to conceive of a disembodied brain—a brain without arms, legs, spinal cord or other equipment—as a *self*, a personality, an embodiment of awareness."

Could we then not augment that disembodied brain with an array of sensors and actuators and also call the resulting tangle of wires and plastic a human being? I don't believe that any of us wants to be sporting a robotic body (à la the *Ghost in the Shell*), but look at what's already happening. One day we may replace our knees, the next day, a hip. Some people have prosthetic limbs, while others have an artificial heart. Stephen Hawking "spoke" through a computer interface. For many, dialysis performs kidney functions and respirators do their breathing. And yet all these artificial means notwithstanding, *personal identity is not diminished one whit*. Besides all that, what if I were to tell you that 90 percent of the cells in your body aren't even your own, but a vast community of microbiota that live on and in you in a magically symbiotic way? It's true. More about this later.

So what kinds of possibilities do these insights into the "human body as a platform" open up for the creative entrepreneur? I'm tempted to say the sky's the limit, but we know better! Even if we forego bionics for pure biology, the possibilities are equally, if not more, impressive. For example, instead of replacing organs with mechanical equivalents or transplants, why not 3D-print them using our own stem cells? We could, quite literally, be rebuilding ourselves someday from the ground up, just as we rebuild a car. And, in the spirit of the Ship of Theseus, when you rebuild the car, is it still the same car? These things are no longer the stuff of science fiction. Indeed, as science fiction novels are increasingly looking more like everyday user manuals, science fiction writers are going to have to get a lot more imaginative. And we're just getting started.

The Nature of Identity

As the old saying goes, people want to be unique—just like everybody else. But where, exactly, does our uniqueness lie? Is it in our genome? Somewhere in our brain? How much of our identity is rooted in nature, versus nurture?

I've come to believe that the seat of identity—what makes us unique—lies in the pattern of connections between the brain's neurons. Your 100 billion neurons, each with about 10,000 connections, comprise this pattern called the "connectome"—the intricately interconnected network across which electrical signals conduct and flow to generate your thoughts, feelings, and behaviors. Indeed, the brain starts out in life as a clean slate. It has no "knowledge" until connections are made between neurons. Consequently, these connections hold the key to everything we know, and ultimately, everything we *are*.

If this is true, then what if we could map out those connections, like a circuit schematic? If we could, then perhaps we could also read it in the same way a musician might read a musical score—literally reading one's mind from a printout. Memory, personality, intellect—it would all be encoded there, in the connectome.

That's the idea, anyway, and it's exactly what the Human Connectome Project, sponsored by the National Institutes of Health, has set out to do: map the human brain's neural connections in their entirety.

It's an outrageously ambitious project that is orders of magnitude more complex than mapping the human genome. While there are about three billion base pairs in the human genome, the number of neural connections in the adult human brain are on the order of 300 trillion! That's a lot of wiring—wiring that would stretch for millions of miles if you could lay it all out. Imagine the compute power required to unravel and decipher that much complexity! As it is, researchers spent more than a decade decoding the connectome of a nematode worm—a worm with a mere 302 neurons and just 7,000 connections. So finding the human connectome will prove to be one of the greatest technological feats of all time. But it will also be the first step to understanding and potentially "uploading" one's consciousness in an effort to preserve—or transfer—it.

Think about what this could mean to entrepreneurial endeavors. Just as the decoding of the human genome created entirely new industries, and just as the unfolding understanding of the microbiome is on the cusp of revolutionizing healthcare, when we are able to decode the connectome, well, we can scarcely imagine the possibilities. But just as all these "-omes" are refining our understanding of what we really are, the connectome will take us far beyond ourselves, and indeed, challenge what it really means to "know thyself."

Imagine this: just as we alter the microbiome with diet, completely changing its composition (and therefore controlling gene expression), or edit the genome with CRISPR—inserting whole snippets of code into our DNA—we may someday be able to do the same with the connectome, literally retrofitting, replacing, and augmenting our brains with complete packages of specialized "off-the-shelf" neural networks. Could it also mean that one might erase an entire connectome—the neural equivalent of shaking an Etch A Sketch—and then download an entirely new, ready-made connectome to replace it? Could we, for example, emerge from such a procedure speaking—and thinking—like a French man or woman, complete with memories of strolling down the Champs-Élysées? Could we perpetuate an Einsteinian brain by transplanting it into new hosts—android avatars or biological hosts grown or 3D-printed whole from the DNA of one's choice— where it would accumulate new memories over millennia?

What sorts of intelligent chimeras might we create by transferring such schematics and representations of consciousness and intelligence? Neuroscientists have already managed to graft human brain cells—lab-grown "brain organoids" sourced from human skin stem cells—into the brains of mice. And while these mice didn't stand up on their hind legs and recite Shakespeare, they were, in fact, considerably smarter than their peers, learning far faster and retaining more memory. Imagine reprogramming and up-grading those brains with new and improved connectome "firmware"!

If all of this sounds exciting to you, then you are in for a fun ride. While some of these things are still very much in the realm of hypothesis, scientists are actively pursuing these capabilities. And like most such endeavors, when they mature, they'll likely begin with therapeutic applications. Think, for example, of the insights such connectome-read-ing technology could lend to understanding—and "patching"—a host of mental health issues including autism, bipolar disorder, schizophrenia, addictions, or even Alzheimer's. Could one's lost memories be restored and refreshed via connectome therapy?

Like all advances in the technologies that promise to make us better, stronger, smarter, and longer-living, mucking with the connectome won't come without controversy. Such technologies do indeed pose great and difficult philosophical, logical, and ethical ques-tions. On the other hand, while nature is an amazing innovator, so are we. If we are able to boost and enhance our biology in ways that not only improve quality of life, but make us more productive and healthier, too, then denying such benefits might also present moral dilemmas.

The greatest dilemma involves the nature of identity itself. In Hindu belief, for exam-ple, *Ātman* is the first principle of being. It is defined as "the basic, foundational, self-evi-dent proposition or assumption, the true self of an individual beyond identification with phenomena, the *essence* of an individual," which we can only understand to mean the soul. The real question, then, is does a change in the material equate to a change in the immaterial? The answer is no, it does not; it is "beyond identification with phenomena," meaning the two spheres, while coincident in life, are actually independent.

If we admit the existence of the soul, when we treat the human body as a *platform*, then we're essentially dealing with the body as an "interface apparatus" and not as part of the true nature or essence of the self. That's one way of looking at it, and certainly not all will agree with this premise. Yet, as mentioned previously, we freely and routinely deploy various prosthetics and myriad implanted medical devices—including those in the brain—without concern for impacting personal identity. As Michael Shermer notes in such cases, "Our sense of identity remains intact despite the exchange of body stuff, so our uniqueness appears to be ingrained in the *pattern* more than the material."

Just as our cells are in a continual state of change, the connectome is also a dynamic entity. We change as we grow and age, and so do our connectomes. The mere act of thinking can actually cause neural connections to be altered, and altered again. So what part of our identity remains intact *over time*? Can it be that there is no aspect of *material* identity that is inherent or permanent in any of its forms?

I do not pose these questions to attempt to settle arguments about mind-body dualism nor the difference between philosophical propositions and scientific theories. Instead, I raise these intriguing questions to highlight possibilities and imaginative opportunities about what might lie ahead for humanity over the next few decades. In any event, it is inspired imagination that unlocks the future. And in the hands of entrepreneurs, the technology will most certainly catch up.

I spoke earlier of teleportation in quantum physics. Despite our infantile understanding of the quantum world, there is a sense in which we can do physical teleportation right now. Today we can perform genetic sequencing in one location, electronically transfer the resulting genome data to another location, synthesize that DNA in the new location, and *voilà!*—we've effectively wirelessly teleported bacteria from one place to another.[4] And it is identical to the one you sequenced at the start. Just scale up this idea to *Star Trek*-esque proportions.

Now, assuming that you might get a little queasy at the thought of being de-atomized in one place and hopefully reassembled in proper order at the destination, what if that could be done in a different way—and in a way that doesn't destroy the original you (as the *Star Trek* transporter necessarily does—*Star Trek* does introduce a number of metaphysical conundrums!)? What if it could be done via an ultra-high bandwidth brain-computer interface synced with an organic 3D-printed facsimile at the destination? Imagine that: you'd be experiencing the new location as though you were actually there, because your thoughts would be directly synced with it. Alternatively, your brain could be synced in the cloud, meaning you could be in 10 different places simultaneously, experiencing every one of those places in much the same way that transactions are synchronized—synchronized consciousness. YaaS—you as a service!

Haven't you always wished you could be in more than one place at once? You may soon be able to. Although, you might want to give some thought to just how autonomous those other "yous" might be ...

Let's have some fun with this. If I could transport my memories and my experience to different places at the same time, have I, in effect, teleported myself? The answer may be yes. And if I could actually recollect the memories and experiences associated with the new place, have I really been there?

Think about this in the context of virtual reality, which is, of course, based on illusion. While you may not experience an event with your unaided eyes, your neurons certainly experience it as a real event. If the brain believes that something has happened, did it happen? In a hyper-realistic immersive and virtually enhanced world, how would one know anymore what is real and what's not real? Adding 3D haptics to the mix—imparting the sense of touch to the shapes and contours and sensations of what you see and experience in a virtual world—along with an olfactory display, would stimulate even more sensorial channels, further blurring the line between reality and illusion. These systems are so effective that they are actually capable of producing hallucinations.

So what, exactly, is virtual reality doing to the brain? We don't have all the answers yet, but early research is revealing some fascinating therapeutic benefits, including treating people who suffer from PTSD, as well as aiding the recovery of cognitive function in brain tumor patients and others suffering various forms of cognitive impairment.

As the technology improves and we gain better understanding of its effects, I have no doubt that we'll also learn how to best modulate its application. It's a habit we'll need to acquire as more and more technologies that were previously the province of science fiction become real—and particularly as telepathically controlled mixed reality becomes the norm. These are interesting questions that pose equally interesting possibilities.

Someone once asked me which science fiction technologies are not likely to become reality. I answered by saying that the question you should be asking is, *what is it that science fiction has not yet imagined?* Seriously, who's to say what's going to be possible in a hundred years? Or even 10, for that matter. As a case in point, let's explore the intriguing developments in brain-computer interface technologies a little deeper to discover what sorts of moonshot opportunities these advances present.

○ ◑ ◐ ◑

Most of us who were not born digital natives recall having to remember 20 or more phone numbers. These days, though, can you even remember your own? We don't have to remember phone numbers anymore because we store them in the cloud and access them through a device. I no longer have to remember when Abraham Lincoln was born, because I have on-demand access to that information in the cloud, as well. We have, in fact, been progressively outsourcing many elements of our memory and decision-making to the cloud as we use Google Maps, for example, and other artificial intelligent agents. What is left—the rest of our memory—could also be outsourced to the cloud someday, resulting in powerful new interfaces and interdependencies.

In 1960, psychologist and computing pioneer J.C.R. Licklider looked to cooperative relationships in nature to inspire his seminal ideas about man-computer symbiosis. At the time, though, there were no man-computer symbioses—after all, 1960 was the year of the PDP-1 running the Quicksort algorithm in COBOL. But that didn't prevent him from hoping that "... in not too many years, human brains and computing machines will be coupled together very tightly, and that the resulting partnership will think as no human brain has ever thought and process data in a way not approached by the information-handling machines we know today."

Licklider wasn't content with the merely "mechanically extended man," where the human operator supplied the initiative, the direction, the integration, and the criterion. "These systems certainly did not consist of dissimilar organisms living together," he concluded. "There was only one kind of organism—man—and the rest was there only to help him." What he observed was not so much a mechanical extension, but the replacement of men with automation—hardly the definition of symbiosis. "It seems entirely possible," he continued, "that in due course, electronic or chemical 'machines' will outdo the human brain in most of the functions we now consider exclusively within its province. There will nevertheless be a fairly long interim during which the main intellectual advances will be made by men and computers working together in intimate association." At that time, he estimated that it would be 1980 before developments in artificial intelligence made it possible for machines alone to do much thinking. "That would leave, say, five years to develop man-computer symbiosis and 15 years to use it. The 15 may be 10 or 500, but those years should be intellectually the most creative and exciting in the history of mankind."

> " All the information we need is available on demand as a function of our search. Today that work requires an intermediary—a mobile phone or computer that connects us to information. Tomorrow we may not require the intermediary. "

So the timeline was off a bit—Licklider was indeed an optimist. But his vision could not have been clearer. Interestingly, the term "cyborg" was also coined in 1960. Today we are beginning to merge human and digital intelligence in the very symbiotic way Licklider envisioned. That's actually more ambitious than it sounds—even in this age of artificial intelligence—because achieving anything resembling symbiosis will require uploading one's brain in some respect so that the two entities can communicate effectively in any sort of collaborative way. To this, the moonshot entrepreneur simply asks, "*What if?* What if we could upload human consciousness into the cloud?"

Transcending these ideas, however, are the arguments we all hear that center more on whether the issue is a question of man *and* machine or of man *versus* machine. After all, we've also heard that AI will take everyone's jobs. Just remember that technology always creates more jobs than it displaces. There will always be more than enough room on the planet for robots, AI, and us biological units—even if it means that our bodies become transformed by the technology in the bargain. We're already being primed for this. When you accidentally leave your cellphone behind, do you experience the digital equivalent of missing limb syndrome? The fact is in many ways, we're already cyborgs.[5] The day is coming when that technology will be implanted directly into the body at birth. Imagine our species so transformed! Imagine the myriad ways technology can help humanity solve otherwise intractable problems. Today's crazy "what if" questions will be tomorrow's pragmatic challenges. What's more, as we extend the frontiers of the possible, we'll also learn that intelligent robots won't simply do things better than humans, they'll help humans accomplish things that were previously unimagined.

> " Spanning devices that enable the physically disabled to function more independently, to biofeedback for health and wellbeing, to creating a more immersive gaming environment, to manipulating machinery with little more than a thought, the possibilities are limited only by one's imagination. "

Ray Kurzweil agrees. "My view is not that AI is going to displace us; it's going to *enhance* us. It does already. I mean, who can do their work without these brain extenders we have today? And that's going to continue to be the case."

Chips, implants, electrodes, and various other devices populate the human brain already: retinal electrode implants restore limited sight to the blind; ingestible chips allow patients to monitor their response to medicines via smartphone app, cochlear implants restore hearing to the deaf, and deep brain stimulation treats disorders spanning epilepsy to Parkinson's.

Beyond such therapeutic applications, humans will need to embrace cognitive enhancements in order to stay relevant in an artificially intelligent world. To such ends, entrepreneurs are already working on technologies to explore and push the limits of our human boundaries with new technologies that can help to access, read, and write to and from the most powerful tool on Earth—the human brain. Indeed, understanding the brain and unlocking its potential represents massive opportunities for entrepreneurs.

Then there are the just plain practical aspects of such technologies. The massive avalanche of data, which is accumulating exponentially, serves only to increase our relative ignorance, as we simply can't digest it all. This, too, has the effect of increasing our dependence on technology to provide us with the knowledge we need *when* we need it. The symbiosis is already occurring. Human readers simply cannot keep up, for example, with the number of scientific papers published every day. According to one estimate, it would take 180 hours a week to keep up with the scientific literature in just a single field. Someone else—or *something* else—has to do this for us. All the information we need is available on demand as a function of our search. Today that work requires an intermediary—a mobile phone or computer that connects us to information. Tomorrow we may not require the intermediary.

If this sounds far-fetched, DARPA is already working on this problem, seeking the development of devices that will allow humans to operate machinery and communicate using the power of thought alone. When you think about it, our brains are not the most efficient input/output devices. A good typist, for example, can bang out about 80 words per minute—but maybe only a fifth of that rate when typing on a smartphone. We speak, on average, at a rate of about 130 words per minute (even though we can take in spoken content at about twice that rate). But we *think* somewhere between 1,000 and 3,000 words per minute! Unfortunately, though, the human data transmission apparatus more closely resembles a 1980s modem than anything that might come out of *Star Trek*. Clearly, we have room for improvement. (While the human apparatus is, technologically speaking, as obsolete as a Hayes modem, we would like to think that there is more to life than simply increasing its speed!) But while a high-bandwidth wireless brain-computer interface might seem like a moonshot today, many of the requisite components are already coming together.

MOONSHOTS TO TELEPATHY

Whenever you think a thought—and even when you don't—the more than one hundred billion neurons making up your brain fire through and across an interconnected web of terminals in an elegant electronic interplay. And at just that moment when the sum of input signals into one neuron crosses a certain threshold, that neuron responds by sending an "action potential"—an electrical signal—into the *axon hillock* (the conductive interface that links adjacent neurons), propagating this potential along to the next neuron, and so on through the network, generating your thoughts, invoking memories, producing speech, and the movement of limbs. It's one of nature's truly great wonders.

Like the electronic circuits that they are, neuronal networks work through a recurrent series of on and off signals that can be observed, measured—and tapped—to do work, even beyond our bodies. But also, like the insulation on electrical wire, the brain's neural signal paths are sheathed by a fatty substance called *myelin.* While myelin helps to increase the speed of electrical communications between neurons, it also acts as an insulator. Fortunately, it's not a perfect insulator; some of the electric energy escapes. And it's just those leaky electrical signals that an electroencephalograph (EEG) is able to pick up. But there's another rub: getting at those faint signals is a real challenge.

At the heart of the matter is the mechanical interface between the scalp and the measuring apparatus. But like the myelin that attenuates electrical signals, the skull does a number on them, too. The good news is that the amount of signal that *does* come through is sufficient for detecting the tiny differences in the voltage levels between neurons—the on-off switches—and that's what we're seeking to capture. At this point, it simply becomes a matter of amplifying and filtering those signals for the purposes at hand. And what a world of purposes it is.

Spanning devices that enable the physically disabled to function more independently, to biofeedback for health and wellbeing, to creating a more immersive gaming environment, to manipulating machinery with little more than a thought, the possibilities are limited only by one's imagination.

Where the latter is concerned, just where man ends and machine begins is becoming a little less defined. In this sense, the brain-computer interface—BCI—could open up previously unimagined possibilities. (The folks at OpenBCI are working hard to make this kind of technology inexpensive and available to the masses in order to encourage further exploration.)

Here's one very simple but interesting example. Researchers at Boston University's Guenther Lab and MIT's Distributed Robotics Lab teamed up to investigate how brain signals might be used to control robots, pushing the possibilities of human-robot interaction in more seamless ways. While capturing brain signals is difficult, one signal in particular bears a strong signature and is thus a bit more accessible to headset-based electrode detection.

The error-related potential (ErrP) signal is generated reflexively by the brain when it perceives a mistake, including mistakes made by someone—or something—else. What if this signal could be exploited as human-robot control mechanism? If possible, then humans would be able to supervise robots and immediately communicate, for example, a "stop" command when the robot commits an error. No need to type a command or push a button. In fact, no overtly conscious action would be required at all—the brain's automatic and naturally occurring ErrP would do all the work.

Here's another: *What if* there were a way to communicate with patients who appear to be comatose, are in a persistent vegetative state, or are otherwise unable to communicate verbally or physically?

Locked-in syndrome is caused by damage to certain areas of the lower brain and brainstem (as a result of stroke or other injury), but that spares the upper brain. The consequence is a condition in which a patient is fully conscious and can feel pain, but because of complete paralysis of all or nearly all voluntary muscles, cannot move or communicate. Imagine the nightmare of listening helplessly from your hospital bed as doctors and loved ones discuss turning off your life support. One rare survivor recalls, "The doctors had just finished telling [my wife] that I had a 2 percent chance of survival, and if I should survive I would be a vegetable. I could hear the conversation and in my mind I was screaming, 'No!'"

The good news is that entrepreneurs are exploiting exciting research in restoring communication to those who have lost the capability to communicate. In one case, brain-computer interface technology was able to literally "unlock" a patient

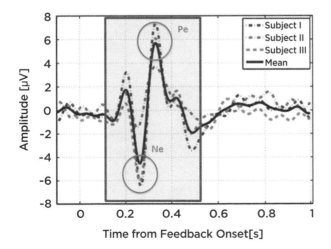

Error-Related Potentials exhibit a characteristic shape across subjects and include a short negative peak, a short positive peak, and a longer negative tail—features easily recognized by deep learning algorithms.

who had spent six years in a locked-in state, allowing him to communicate for the first time since suffering his injury. Imagine six years of solitary confinement inside your head!

Like the ErrP-driven human-machine interaction explored earlier, this technology also relies on thought signals that can be acquired via an EEG headset and then interpreted using machine learning algorithms to control other assistive technologies, whether a communication device or any number of home automation technologies that people then use to interact with their environment.

Mind-powered human-machine interaction. It's no longer science fiction. Licklider would be delighted. Are you imagining the mind-blowing possibilities?!

Amazing as this is, we're only scratching the surface of what's possible in the BCI realm. But when you consider that all mental processes have a neurobiological basis, it really should be possible to "decode" even the visual and audio content of such neural activity, including memory, dreams, music, and other experiences. And it actually is. The ability to do so at economic scale, though, would have massive impact on virtually every field.

To these ends, entrepreneurs are pursuing technologies that will allow people, for example, to telepathically text at 100 words per minute—considerably faster than we can type on a smartphone. Others are seeking to reduce an MRI to a simple headset that would be a thousand times lower in cost and a million times smaller in size. That they're doing it with relatively simple technologies like near-infrared liquid crystal displays and camera chips makes it all the more remarkable. Imagine what this could mean. If MRIs could be reduced to a consumer price point, diseases could be caught much earlier, inexpensive healthcare could be deployed at scale to poor and developing regions, and the brain would be suddenly accessible to an infinite array of telepathic and robotic applications. Indeed, we really have no idea where the hairy edge of physics actually lay.

Other approaches involve injecting the brain with thousands of tiny silicon chips—neural dust—that record and reflect neural information using ultrasound. Like the other players in this nascent field, the end goal is telepathy. But along the way, these technologies can also be exploited as "electroceuticals" for myriad medical applications because they are also able to stimulate nerves and muscles to treat disorders such as epilepsy. In its telepathic context, though, neural dust will not only speed up typing, but enable the control of robots, prosthetics, home automation devices, and any number of other targets of the brain-machine interface.

Such is the exciting stuff of radical possibility.

We could fill a library with examples of the many amazing things that are happening today. We hope, though, this very brief survey will serve to awaken a heightened sense of possibility—possibility fueled by the empowering knowledge that flows from startling new revelations and viewpoints—not to mention another essential feature of the moonshot entrepreneur: *intellectual curiosity.* And curiosity never disappoints.

1. There just might be a shortcut to breaking bad habits. Neuroscientists at Stanford have identified an electrical-activity signature that predicts impulsive actions just before they occur. The signal is generated in the brain's reward circuitry, which reinforces survival-promoting actions by inducing pleasure in anticipation or performance of those actions. A brief electrical pulse delivered at just the right moment can actually prevent them. The intervention might be useful in overcoming destructive impulses or habits, including countering obesity, substance abuse, gambling, sexual addiction, road rage, or other inappropriate or undesirable activities—perhaps even preventing a suicide attempt.

2. Methylation is an epigenetic process that modulates gene activity in response to non-genetic factors including diet, weight, physical activity, and various environmental factors. It turns out that each of these factors is affected by the gut microbiome. Linking these factors in mediating gene expression are the metabolite products of the gut microbiota. New research is helping to tease out the mechanics of how the gut microbiome communicates with the cells of its host to switch genes on and off, but there is much one can do to influence gene expression. Chemical messages produced by bacteria in the gut can kick-start a process that ultimately turns certain genes on or off—simply via diet. It also turns out that epigenetics is reversible. To the extent that we can reverse a gene's state to keep the good while eliminating the bad then perhaps this could cure cancer, slow aging, and potentially much more.

3. It may, in fact, become possible someday to rejuvenate the cells of the cerebral cortex. Stem cells can become any cell in the body, including neurons, with the right biochemical prodding. Madeline Lancaster, of the MRC Laboratory of Molecular Biology, is growing tiny brains with stem cells taken from adult human skin, which she has cultured in her lab. The resulting human brain tissue—a brain organoid—is complete with cerebral cortex. Could this lead to the creation of chimeras? Several labs have grafted these lab-grown organoids into rat brains, connected them to blood vessels, and successfully grown physical links that are, in fact, responsive.

4. Craig Venter's "Digital Biological Converter" receives, via the internet or radio wave, digital biology in the form of DNA sequences, enabling the automatic reconstitution of the components of living systems, without human intervention. Venter views this capability— making a digital copy of an organism's DNA in one place and sending the file to a device somewhere else that can then recreate the original life-form—as akin to teleportation, but in a different way than imagined in the *Star Trek* scenario. Venter insists, though, that this is not fantasy. "The goal," Venter says "isn't to imagine this stuff. We are the scientists actually doing this." While the technology will someday be exploited for filling prescriptions or vaccinations anywhere on demand, Venter is more interested in potential interplanetary applications, spanning the instantaneous provisioning of Martian colonists with the biologics they may need to transmitting the DNA of Martian organisms, should they be found, to Earth for re-creation and study.

5. Mark Stevenson, in his book *An Optimist's Tour of the Future*, brings to this question an interesting perspective. "Transhumanism," he writes, "won't arrive in a revolution, it'll arrive one therapy at a time. Fading eyesight? Try large print. Now these spectacles. Now contact lenses. Now laser eye surgery. Now stem cell therapy to return your eye to its former youth. (In fact, Italian researchers have been using stem cells to cure corneal blindness for more than 10 years.) Bad hearing? Have a large cone to stick in your ear. Now a bulky hearing aid. Now an in-ear hearing bud. Now a cochlear implant. I realize, like it or not, that we're already embracing the transhumanist project; we've just called it 'medicine.' We've inevitably blurred the line between 'therapy' and 'enhancement.'"

CHAPTER 3

Intellectual Curiosity—the Entrepreneur's Superpower

"Curiosity killed the cat," Fesgao remarked, his dark eyes unreadable.
Aly rolled her eyes. Why did everyone say that to her? "People always forget
the rest of the saying," she complained. "And satisfaction brought it back."

—Tamora Pierce, from Trickster's Duet

DESCARTES WROTE, "So blind is the curiosity by which mortals are possessed that they often conduct their minds along unexplored routes, having no reason to hope for success, but merely being *willing to risk the experiment of finding whether the truth they seek lies there*."

The successful moonshot entrepreneur, of course, does hope for success, but there is no denying that a key component of that success is this very innate, intrinsic, inherent, and intoxicating *curiosity*—the species of curiosity that never settles with the surface appearance of things, but rather, like a primal force, compels one to pull back the layers of a mystery in order to lay bare its most fundamental nature. Only then can it be understood and mastered.

Curiosity is not only a vital quality of the entrepreneur, it is the single most important attribute that humans possess. We are, in fact, the only species that asks, "Why?" And *why* is a question that leads to *how*, which is the stuff of innovation.

Curiosity is the light we shine into the dark corners of the world to discover what, just beyond our knowledge, might be concealed there. And when we shine that light into the particularly shadowy recesses we sometimes dare to enter into, we sometimes also emerge from them like Moses descending from the mountain. And the world is changed. Jonas Salk, Alan Turing, the Curies, Barry Marshall, Elsie Widdowson, Mike Stroud, Neil Armstrong, Edward Harrison, and

Isaac Newton are but a few of the people whose moonshot-launching brand of curiosity impacted millions, if not billions.

The idea of the moonshot has come to signify any audacious effort to achieve a seemingly impossible goal. But moonshots appear to be impossible not only for a lack of courage, but of knowledge, as well. Curiosity is our mechanism for bridging the gaps in our understanding of what really is possible. What we don't know, we'll find out, sometimes going to great lengths to do so.

And for tremendously curious people like physicist Richard Feynman, finding out is its own reward—even more rewarding than the Nobel Prize he shared for his fundamental work in quantum electrodynamics. "I don't see that it makes any point that someone in the Swedish academy just decides that this work is noble enough to receive a prize," he said. "I've already gotten the prize. The prize is the pleasure of finding a thing out, the kick in the discovery, the observation that other people use it—those are the real things."

This, as it turns out, is the spirit that differentiates the more curious and creative among us. And just look at the results! Most of the world's great scientists are not necessarily the most talented, but the most compelled by curiosity. Albert Einstein often spoke and wrote of "the enjoyment of seeing and searching." And it is an inexhaustible joy; the thrill returns again and again with every new question that an answer poses. "With more knowledge," Feynman adds, "comes deeper, more wonderful mystery, luring one on to penetrate deeper still. Never concerned that the answer may prove disappointing, but with pleasure and confidence we turn over each new stone to find unimagined strangeness leading on to more wonderful questions and mysteries—certainly a grand adventure!"

> " Curiosity is not only a vital quality of the entrepreneur, it is the single most important attribute that humans possess. We are, in fact, the only species that asks, "Why?" And *why* is a question that leads to *how*, which is the stuff of innovation. "

And what is a moonshot if not a grand adventure! There is absolutely nothing idle about this kind of curiosity. It is unquestionably the most active and powerful force on this planet. It is the entrepreneur's rocket fuel. And yet, for a host of reasons, our world seems hell-bent on eradicating it. It's true. Just listen to the signals we grew up hearing and still tell our children and ourselves: "What you don't know won't hurt you." "Pride and curiosity are the two scourges of our souls." "Curiosity killed the cat." Even Albus Dumbledore got in on the act: "We should exercise *caution* with our curiosity—yes, indeed."

We're born curious—but then we cooperate with a lifelong program to purge ourselves of the capacity, as though it were a horrible malady that can only bring distress. Our education system is particularly complicit in this work, as we'll see later. Some, though, manage to survive the conspiracy. The philosopher Mortimer Adler is one of them. He wrote, "The ability to retain a child's view of the world with at the same time a mature understanding of what it means to retain it, is extremely rare—and a person who has these qualities is likely to be able to contribute something really important to our thinking."

> **Our curiosity doesn't die out, it is *wiped* out. Consequently, as would-be moonshot entrepreneurs, it's likely that we'll have a little rehabilitation to do.**

Adler somehow managed to retain his childlike curiosity for nearly all of his 99 years. But as even he observed, this is an extremely rare condition. Indeed, our curiosity doesn't die out, it is *wiped* out. Consequently, as would-be moonshot entrepreneurs, it's likely that we'll have a little rehabilitation to do. But like a mindset of possibility, curiosity, too, can be cultivated and restored to its full and youthful vigor. Fear, though, often masquerading as sensible conformity, is its greatest enemy. Where our neural responses are concerned, fear and novelty-driven exploration are actually inversely related.

This ties back to something we explored in the first chapter about our human response to the unknown nature of the future. Everybody has some preconceived notions about the world. After all, it's how we make sense of things. But when new information challenges our fundamental assumptions and sense of order, we're suddenly faced with a gap. And gaps are not pleasant. So we work to restore a sense of equilibrium by connecting the emerging dots to create new patterns in an effort to reduce uncertainty, to restore our prior coherence. But the drive to discover these patterns is not curiosity—it is a coping mechanism for dealing with fear. It is, in fact, anti-curiosity. This mode of searching and pattern-making does not seek to discover, but to get everything back into their proper boxes, to make things comfortable again. Curiosity doesn't care about comfort. Curiosity has no fear of the unknown. Curiosity is precisely about being drawn to novel things *because they are new and strange and unknown*. As such, curiosity is, curiously, the best remedy for fear.

Curiosity will conquer fear more than bravery ever will. Indeed, curiosity is a great impelling force that has led many people into dangers from which the merely brave would shrink. So resolve to replace that fear of the unknown with a healthy dose of curiosity. And if a cat dies in the process, then you can know that it died nobly.

I always challenge people to let go of certainty. Certainty only hardens one's mind against possibility. Here's the vital point: certainty's opposite is not uncertainty. It is curiosity. It is possibility. Beware that man who speaks of "settled science"—he is a murderer of possibility, an assassin of curiosity. Settled science is the *end* of science—and of curiosity. Nothing is more oppressive than the suppression of curiosity—the prohibition to think beyond what is regarded as established. *That's* the world the moonshot entrepreneur seeks to overturn. The incurious will never help us here. Rather, we have to help them. They have to be shown what is possible by challenging the very foundations of what they simply take for granted. Only then will their eyes be opened to the wonder of possibility that only curiosity can inspire and reveal.

Daniel Dennett was thinking of chimpanzees' response to human speech when he observed, "They never show any interest. They never apparently get curious about what those sounds are for. They can hear all the speech, but it's like the rustling of the leaves. It just doesn't register on them as worth attention." Sadly he could just as well have been speaking about a lot of people! The astounding, miraculous things that are going on around us in every minute of every day just don't register to them as worth attention; it's just the rustling of the leaves. Feynman, in complaining to an interviewer who was missing this very point, answered, "You come in to me now for an interview, and you ask me about the latest discoveries that are made. Nobody ever asks about a simple, ordinary phe-

> ❝ **Curiosity doesn't care about comfort. Curiosity has no fear of the unknown. Curiosity is precisely about being drawn to novel things *because they are new and strange and unknown.*** ❞

nomenon in the street. What about those colors? We could have a nice interview, and I could explain all about the colors, butterfly wings, the whole big deal. But you don't care about that. You want the big final result ..." It is as though an incuriosity has developed in people's minds, like the buildup of plaque in arteries, hardening them to the wonder that is the everyday world. Indeed, if you haven't come across anything strange during the day, it hasn't been much of a day.

The good news is that curiosity lost can be restored. It begins simply by looking beneath the surface of things—ordinary things. Once you can do this, you'll be well on your way down the rabbit hole. And the further you go into that strange and mysterious place, the more you'll realize that you've caught this "disease"—the disease of curiosity that now is incurable. Fear has given way to fascination as one discovery leads to another mystery which leads to yet another discovery—*ad infinitum*. You become astounded at how connected things are, and yet even more astounded that the universe's small set of rules and laws can yield so many different outcomes and phenomena. It's unbelievable, really. This curiosity can take us from the discovery of infrared light to the reading of a neuron, from the discovery of DNA to editing of the genome, from the discovery of radiation to the fusion of helium-3. And this world of wonder is right outside your front door. Wake up every morning and take it in. Of the smallest detail you encounter, ask *why, how, what if?*

> **Here's the vital point: certainty's opposite is not uncertainty. It is curiosity. It is possibility. Beware that man who speaks of "settled science."**

Think of it: we spin around in space on a pale blue dot, "half of us sticking upside down" as we go round a flaming orb of gas. Consider the myriad and mysterious forces that keep it all going, and that you are a vital part of what keeps it going. How will such a realization reorder your priorities in this life? Resolve, therefore, to become skilled in the art of curiosity! Determine to become a *dilettante*—a promising beginner who always will be one. Fall in love with learning. The curious are never limited by what they know, because they can always increase what they know. Rather, embrace the puzzles—what you *don't* know. That ignorance is your key strength, as we'll soon see. It's what sustains your curiosity; curiosity feeds on the unknown.

○ ☽ ● ☾

Curiosity as a cognitive process is connected directly to motivation—another essential characteristic of the entrepreneur. If you are highly curious, then it follows that you will also be highly motivated. The reverse is also true: the more

INVERTED U-FUNCTION

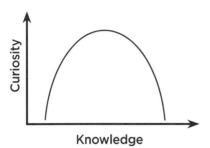

Curiosity

Knowledge

motivated you are, the more you will seek to learn, and the more you learn, the more curious you will become. Curiosity, then, acts like a vortex that sucks you into a giant feedback loop. You can thank your hippocampus for that—it lights up with curiosity-motivated learning. It is also linked to the mechanisms that support the brain's reward system, and interactions between it and the hippocampus put the brain in a state in which you are more likely to learn and retain new information. In other words, curiosity can be habit-forming. Moreover, the curious mind induces a shot of dopamine. Yes, you can get high on high-minded thoughts!

Now, there's an odd phenomenon that affects the state of things like curiosity, and it is reflected in the inverted-U function. As we gain knowledge about a thing, we remain curious—but only up to a point. It appears that curiosity has a sweet spot in the tension between what we know and don't yet know. Once that point is passed, curiosity begins to decline. In other words, your curiosity gets satisfied. There are at least two important takeaways from this. First, we can start the curiosity cycle over again when we apply our curiosity-driven learnings to new or adjacent questions and other abstract intuitions. After all, the more you know, the more you realize how little you know.

The second observation is something we'll take up in greater detail in a later chapter. For the moment, we'll just say the inverted-U, when applied to curiosity and knowledge, is the curse of the expert.

If the genuinely curious person is forever a dilettante, then he never need fear becoming an expert! But certainly, a well-developed sense of curiosity can make him smarter. So is there a connection between IQ and curiosity? Well, there's no question that higher levels of IQ enable those who have it to learn faster and more readily solve problems. But IQ, in and of itself, is passive. IQ has no initiative. It's simply a measure of one's brain's raw horsepower. Curiosity, on the other hand, is an irrepressibly active agent. It is the work of a *hungry* mind.

People with higher levels of curiosity are naturally more inquisitive. Conse-

> **Determine to become a *dilettante*—a promising beginner who always will be one. Fall in love with learning.**

quently, they discover more. They generate more original ideas. What's more, the curious deal better with ambiguity, which is an absolutely essential capacity when navigating an abstract future that holds many different possibilities. So curiosity will beat IQ every time. After all, Albert Einstein himself famously said, "I have no special talents—I am only passionately curious." The important thing he tells us, then, is to not stop questioning. "Curiosity has its own reason for existence. One cannot help but be in awe when he contemplates the mysteries of eternity, of life, of the marvelous structure of reality. It is enough if one tries merely to comprehend a little of this mystery each day."

Curiosity is indeed the catalyst for discovering possibilities and creating opportunities. As you become skilled in the art of curiosity, your ability to identify opportunities and make new connections grows. It all begins with a questioning mind. But what are the questions? As Dr. Seuss observed, "Sometimes the questions are complicated and the answers are simple." Where the future is concerned, it's even more complicated. What are the unknown questions in an unknown future? In such a world, we may not recognize the right answers even if we stumbled on them.

There's a conundrum called "Meno's Paradox," which goes something like this: If you know what you're looking for, then inquiry is unnecessary. If you *don't* know what you're looking for, then inquiry is impossible. Therefore, inquiry is either unnecessary or impossible.

> **The curious deal better with ambiguity, which is an absolutely essential capacity when navigating an abstract future that holds many different possibilities.**

The argument, of course, has a fatal flaw. That's because even when we may not know what we're looking for, the object of our inquiry is not totally unknown. We possess some latent, implicit knowledge of the object which is made explicit by rational inquiry. In other words, we've always got something to go on. We're not completely in the dark, even when it comes to an unknown future. Because we can follow the threads and trajectories of technologies, for example, we can forecast and anticipate their future unfoldings. We have both *a priori* and *a posteriori* knowledge to guide our inquiry into things unknown. Even a little bit of knowledge is sufficient to propel us up the inverted-U.

Earlier we spoke of the curious mind's capacity to deal with ambiguity. Nothing can keep the curious entrepreneur from inquiring into things about which he knows nothing. If you haven't picked up on it yet, this notion will be a recurring theme in this book. Where others abjure ignorance and rely upon experts for clarity, the moonshot entrepreneur embraces ignorance and shuns the expert opinion. Let us be clear: without this element of the mindset, there can be no moonshot. It is prerequisite, and it finds fertile ground only in the mind of the hopelessly curious.

Everything works backward: we don't invent answers, we *reveal* them when we discover the right questions. And we perpetually question our way forward. This matters because we live in a world that is defined by our questions. If you want to create a different kind of world, then you need to ask different kinds of questions. And when these questions find answers—as they ultimately do—

> " Everything works backward: we don't invent answers, we *reveal* them when we discover the right questions. And we perpetually question our way forward. "

they will put us in a new vista, enabling us to see questions unimagined before we got there. The vast landscape—or spacescape—of our ignorance is the great potential difference that pulls lightning down from the clouds.

Instilling a sense of intellectual curiosity, then, is the greatest gift you can offer to people. It not only enables personal growth, but the growth of society as a whole. The minute one stops questioning, things become static. And whatever is static degrades over time. As Ray Kroc said, "As long as you're green, you're growing, and as soon as you ripen, you start to rot."

If one is static in a time of change, then that can only spell irrelevance for that individual. A questioning curiosity is his only hope. If you're predisposed to questioning, then you'll also be comfortable with change. In the eyes of the curious, change is actually a great adventure. In fact, it's the curious who *drive* change. Moreover, intellectual curiosity is what leads non-experts to ask, "Why not?" and then brazenly challenge the status quo or what the experts have simply taken for granted—without question. This is also why they're so easy to disrupt. Curiosity is the accelerant behind the creative destruction that we call disruption. Indeed, as an entrepreneur, curiosity is your superpower.

The old cliché is you can lead a horse to water, but you can't make it drink. Could it be that the damn horse just isn't thirsty? Believe me, when the horse gets thirsty, it'll seek water. As humans, we're born thirsty. Our natural, innate curiosity is that thirst. So drink often, but by all means, stay thirsty.

CHAPTER 4

The Perception is the Reality

If the doors of perception were cleansed everything would appear to man as it is, infinite.

—*William Blake*

NCE UPON A TIME THERE WAS A KING IN INDIA. An astrologer told him: "Whoever shall drink the rain which falls seven days from now shall go mad." So the king covered his well, that none of the water might enter it. All of his subjects, however, drank the water, and went mad, while the king alone remained sane. The king could no longer understand what his subjects thought and did, nor could his subjects understand what he thought and did. All of them shouted "The king is mad! The king is mad!" Thus, seeing no other choice, the king drank the water, too.

• • ◉ • •

Moonshot entrepreneurs are audacious, big-vision-driven people. They dream so big that everyone else thinks they're mad, but they do not feel compelled to "drink the water" to align their perceptions with those of the crowd. If the successful entrepreneurs I know had a nickel for every time they were told that something is impossible or that it won't work, they wouldn't need a dime of venture money. But that's the point of what we're doing—making the impossible possible.

This is a fundamental insight into the mindset of the entrepreneur whose mind is set on achieving a moonshot. In fact, it is the key difference maker. But why does the moonshot entrepreneur believe something is possible when so few others do? What is it that makes their counterintuitive, against-the-grain kind of vision possible in the first place?

Remember my conversation with Leslie Walker of the *Washington Post*? She challenged my vision for the nascent mobile market by asking, "Do you know something most Americans don't?" In the mind of the moonshot entrepreneur, in spite of the questions sometimes being hard, the answers *are* obvious! They're obvious because we have opened our minds to the possibilities of the future. They're obvious because our curiosity has pulled us a little deeper down the rabbit hole or propelled us a little higher into the air. They're obvious because even a small change in perspective brings major changes in perception. Moonshot entrepreneurs simply see the world in a different way. And without these kinds of perceptual skills to help bring audacious visions into focus, there can be no moonshot.

This feature of the moonshot entrepreneur's mindset is a tricky but central aspect of human cognition: perception. Each of us experiences things in individual, subjective ways. What's more, for all of us, perception is influenced by an array of factors that span illusion to conformity to bias. The fact is, we don't see things as they are, we see them as *we* are. Let's take each of these in turn, and discover how entrepreneurs can turn them to advantage.

○◑●◐

Do you recall the viral internet meme about a photo of a dress that some people saw as blue and black, but others saw as white and gold? If you happened to be one of the group who perceived it to be blue and black, the *fact* that it was blue and black could not have been more obvious. That anyone could possibly see it as white and gold was an absurdity. Yet a substantial number of people did—people as diverse as artists and neuroscientists! It seems this particular image pushed a boundary condition in how the brain resolves color. (Incidentally, the dress actually is blue and black. Or so we believe!) The point is that the two radically different ways of perceiving the same object resulted in two very entrenched versions of a single reality.

Here's another. The famous Müller-Lyer illusion that you probably remember from grade school involves two lines that appear to be of different lengths (right).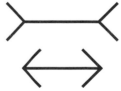

While your eyes might lead you to believe that the top line is longer, a simple measurement will reveal that the shafts of both lines are exactly the same length. Appearances can be deceiving!

For a completely different twist on deception, though, consider the bizarre Asch study (left). In it, participants were asked to verbally state which of the three comparison lines was equal to a reference line, X.

In the first two passes, each with different sets of line

lengths, the group unanimously answered correctly. But on the third set, they all gave the wrong answer. One after another responded that line C appeared to be the same length as line X. What was going on here?

It turns out that all but one of the participants in the study group was in on a secret. Peer influence—not perception—was the actual object of the experiment. And it delivered a big surprise. Faced with overwhelming agreement among a majority, the target went along with that majority *three-quarters of the time!* In other words, he willingly drank the well water.

> " **Welcome to the community of moonshot entrepreneurs—the creatively maladjusted!** "

People have a remarkable capacity to bring themselves into conformity with opinions that are clearly contrary to the evidence, if it reduces social dissonance. To do otherwise would rock the boat, expose the fact that the emperor has no clothes. (As we used to joke, you can fool some of the people all the time—and *that's* our target market!)

Martin Luther King—a moonshot personality if there ever was one—lamented this state of affairs. "Many people," he wrote, "fear nothing more terribly than to take a position which stands out sharply and clearly from prevailing opinion. The tendency of most is to adopt a view that is so ambiguous that it will include everything and so popular that it will include everybody ... The saving of our world from pending doom will come, not through the complacent adjustment of the conforming majority, but through the creative *maladjustment* of a non-conforming minority ... [We are reminded] of the danger of overstressing the well-adjusted life. Everybody passionately seeks to be well-adjusted. We must, of course, be well-adjusted if we are to avoid neurotic and schizophrenic personalities, but there are some things in our world to which men of goodwill must be maladjusted ... Human salvation lies in the hands of the creatively maladjusted."

Welcome to the community of moonshot entrepreneurs—the creatively maladjusted!

None of this is to say that entrepreneurs are free of illusions or strong feelings for belonging. Entrepreneurs are human, too! But we also have a heightened sensitivity to the potential for self-deception—and you are the easiest person to fool.

The difficulty is that so much of what we perceive is subject to interpretation. Consequently, our knowledge always begins with suppositions, assumptions, theories—all of which must be subject to scrutiny. Not only must we grapple with our own perceptions, but the perceptions and subjective interpretations of everyone else!

Some misperceptions are easily corrected, but one species of perceptual interpretation is particularly tenacious: *bias*. To some degree, everyone wears such a set of blinkers. Some biases are cultural. Many are taught in school. Others are insinuated into our thought processes by our various experiences in daily life. Consider confirmation bias—the tendency people have to embrace information that supports the beliefs they already hold, but filter out or ignore contradictory evidence. We tend to see what we *want* to see, we see what we are *prepared* to see, we see what we are *used* to seeing. It's one of the mechanisms by which people construct their particular views of reality and make everything "fit," even when some of the views are known to be in error. So can we blame people when an idea strikes them as crazy? Sometimes, we can. And here's why.

Confirmation bias is seductive precisely because it is easy. It requires very little effort. Most people are pretty vague about what they believe, and so look to pointers that can substantiate what are often half-formed opinions. In other words, theirs is an inherently lazy response. But this laziness is motivated by self-preservation. Part and parcel of confirmation bias is a more insidious feature called denial—not seeing what we *don't* want to see. And it is rooted essentially in the need to preserve one's sense of identity and security—two things people really don't like to see challenged. Reconciling things that might undermine one's worldview is unpleasant work, and we strongly resist having to do it.

From our biased perceptions, we say entrepreneurs pursue "irrational" goals. But where, really, does the "irrational" label stick? What is more irrational than doggedly insisting on what one *believes* to be true rather than examining whether something actually *is* true? If I assert something that you disagree with, you may think it is crazy, not because it is humanly or technologically or scientifically impossible, but quite possibly because it

> **These are illustrations of real paths to possibility, demonstrating that impossibility is just another word for mystery—and mysteries are made to be solved.**

undermines one of your foundational beliefs. It's just easier (and feels safer) to call a radical idea crazy, and not be bothered to do the due diligence to investigate its merits and possibilities.

This is why we spent so much time earlier chasing down "crazy" ideas like editing genes for radiation tolerance and developing mental telepathy using brain-computer interfaces. These are illustrations of real paths to possibility, demonstrating that impossibility is just another word for mystery—and mysteries are made to be solved. One man's crazy is another man's normal.

Moonshot entrepreneurs know that knowledge begins with the awareness of the potential deceptiveness of our perceptions. We also know that knowledge shatters illusions. As Erich Fromm put it, "Knowing means to penetrate through the surface, in order to arrive at the roots, and hence the causes; knowing means to *see* reality in its nakedness."

To this end, when it comes to dealing with bias and perceptual error, the entrepreneur's method is designed to dispatch it quickly and efficiently. But then again, we really all have the capacity to "arrive at the roots." Read the following paragraph to try it for yourself, and be amazed. In this paragraph we have the intriguing "Cambridge Effect," where only the first and last letters of each word are maintained in the right order, while all the other letters are randomly scrambled:

> Aoccdrnig to a rscheearch at Cmabrigde Uinervtisy, it deosn't mttaer in waht oredr the ltteers in a wrod are, the olny iprmoetnt tihng is taht the frist and lsat ltteer be at the rghit pclae. The rset can be a toatl mses and you can sitll raed it wouthit porbelm. Tihs is bcuseae the huamn mnid deos not raed ervey lteter by istlef, but the wrod as a wlohe.

Your brain has no trouble at all making sense of this, scarcely even slowing down the reading. We are indeed remarkably adept at finding the signal in the noise.

In order to challenge our own assumptions and human biases, entrepreneurs not only look at an issue from multiple perspectives, but also test, test, test, and iterate and pivot as necessary—all of which are activities that add to our knowledge. In fact, rather than doggedly hold onto cherished ideas, we actively try to kill them. The truly great ideas will stand up to scrutiny. And those are the only ones we want to advance. At Google's X, they actually reward investigators when they kill an idea—ideas they may have already invested blood, sweat, and tears into over a number of years. It's hard to do. Hence the reward.

This approach is the opposite of arrogance. In conveying our convictions and visions about the possible impossible, we want to show other people the true nature of things as we have discovered them to be. To do so, it is necessary for us to grasp from what point of view others currently approach a matter. Another person's understanding could quite possibly be correct *from their particular point of view*. As such, we must allow them that truth, but also show them the point of view from which it is erroneous or limited.

No one likes to be found wrong. Yet in the sense just described, perception can never really be wrong. If you perceive something in a certain way, then that perception is a fact for you. But what if the world were colorblind, and you were the only person who could perceive this concept called color? Whose perception is wrong, the world's or yours? To everyone else, you'd be as mad as the Indian king! But your *perception* is not wrong. As you go about your life, your perception is *your* reality. It is actualized in your experience and often confirmed by your cohorts. As such, if one seeks to alter people's perception of a thing, then the underlying reality must be revealed—the general understanding of the thing must be changed. This is precisely what the moonshot entrepreneur does when he achieves what everyone else believes is impossible. The truth of the underlying reality is revealed, and with it, everyone's perception is changed. And sometimes it takes time. Let me offer an example.

> **In order to challenge our own assumptions and human biases, entrepreneurs not only look at an issue from multiple perspectives, but also test, test, test, and iterate and pivot as necessary—all of which are activities that add to our knowledge.**

I was speaking recently at an event for women entrepreneurs. They complained to me that women are not being taken seriously, and asked what they could do to change that perception. I answered with a story of my own experience, as an Indian immigrant, of not being taken seriously myself. Twenty years ago, Indians were stereotyped as good, smart, hardworking engineers, but as poor managers. Indians were told that they don't understand American culture, they don't understand how Americans work. They were told that Indians are great individual contributors, but they can never be managers. But here's what happened. Many Indians started to go off to start their own companies. And when those companies were acquired for billions of dollars, suddenly they were good managers. Great managers, in fact! They didn't bother with perceptions—*they revealed the reality*. And now Indians are top-level executives at some of the world's leading companies. Sundar Pichai is the CEO of Google; Satya Nadella is CEO of Microsoft;

Shantanu Narayen is CEO of Adobe; Sanjay Mehrotra is CEO of Micron, Francisco D'Souza is CEO of Cognizant. And the list goes on. None of them started with the generally accepted perception—they got to where they are because they changed how others experienced the fundamental reality.

When I left Microsoft, I was told by someone I admired that I was a great contributor, but he wasn't sure if I would have made a great manager. So when I started my first company, it so happened that I hired him. After a few years, on one occasion he mentioned that he really admired my management style, having completely forgotten what he had said years earlier! As Indians, we had a very different perception of ourselves as managers—it was the "assumed reality" that was the fiction. This self-perception is the starting point, the gateway to the kind of future you imagine. By becoming more consciously and competently attuned to your mindset, you can better direct your way forward.

As with curiosity, we also need to cultivate, broaden, and enrich our powers of perception, to expand the field of vision which enables us to recognize the nonobvious connections, especially beyond the simple cause and effect we so easily default to—and which frequently yields false correlations. The ability to perceive hidden subtleties, then, becomes an acquired trait. "Genius," William James wrote, "means little more than the faculty of perceiving in an *unhabitual* way." And that, again, begins with a change in perspective.

Consider, for example, how the invention of the airplane not only unshackled man from his earthbound condition, it brought him an entirely new perspective on the world. From the air, the first pilots were surprised by the traces of ancient settlements they could make out in the fields below—fields where countless generations had walked and worked without the larger world ever realizing they existed. Even after being shown aerial photographs that clearly revealed the outlines of the sites, the newly discovered features remained, to the people with only a ground-level view, indiscernible.

In the classic Victorian era novella *Flatland*, the story's hero, A Square, is

> **As with curiosity, we also need to cultivate, broaden, and enrich our powers of perception, to expand the field of vision which enables us to recognize the nonobvious connections, especially beyond the simple cause and effect we so easily default to—and which frequently yields false correlations.**

enraptured by an otherworldly and incomprehensible entity named A Sphere, who transports our two-dimensional character (in his world, there is no up or down) into the third dimension. Recalling the experience, A Square cries, "An unspeakable horror seized me. There was a darkness; then a dizzy, sickening sensation of sight that was not like seeing; I saw a Line that was no Line; Space that was not Space: I was myself, and not myself. When I could find voice, I shrieked aloud in agony, '*Either this is madness or it is Hell.*' 'It is neither,' calmly replied the voice of the Sphere, 'it is *Knowledge.*'"

Whether knowledge, madness, or hell, in times of great upheaval, it can be hard to tell. We need to get up into the air in order to see the patterns—existing and emerging—more clearly. The view from the ground, while exacting and detailed, makes it almost impossible to extrapolate any understanding gained there to the larger contexts. (This is the Achilles' heel of the expert.) The insights of Gestalt psychology show us why this is so, that the same objects can be seen in different ways, meaning the same phenomena can also be understood in different ways.

Despite all our technological advances, we continue to live in a kind of two-dimensional Flatland, captive to our respective dimensional biases—biases that inevitably create blind spots. But a radical change in perspective can jolt us into a new consciousness, opening our eyes to a bigger picture that's obscured by the particulars we comprehend at close range. For the entrepreneur, that jolt can also awaken a heightened sense of *radical possibility*—possibility fueled by the empowering knowledge that flows from new viewpoints.

Just as curiosity is more powerful than IQ, the ability to shift your perspective is more powerful than being smart. There is no question that IQ correlates with the ability to see patterns in abstract information. So if you happen to have more of it, then you're lucky. But it is not a prerequisite.[1] It only means that the rest of us have to work at it a little harder. Perception is but a subset of raw intelligence.

○ ◑ ● ◐

Adam Smith may have introduced the idea of the "invisible hand" of capitalism, but the hand of the entrepreneur is all too visible. The moonshot entrepreneur in particular brings to the table different kinds of information that he makes visible in very different ways.

As demonstrated in my conversation with Leslie Walker of the Washington Post, people with different information at their disposal will arrive at very different conclusions, even when operating under the same set of circumstances.

It's the entrepreneur's unique perspective that leads him to conclusions that run counter to the crowd. Moreover, he is convinced that he is correct, while everyone else is wrong. Crazy as it sounds, this is precisely why the entrepreneur is so valuable. If it were not for his radical perspective, things would proceed quite differently. In the end, the entrepreneur bets that he'll profit from this difference in perception when he is ultimately proven correct.

Isaac Newton's experiments in optics provide another fascinating case in point. In his day, it was believed that light was pure and that colors originated from elsewhere in the physical world when matter came into contact with light, most typically from the sun. Newton's experiment, however, showed that light is in fact a compound of many primary colors, which can be separated out and mixed together to form additional colors at will. Newton demonstrated this diffraction, which he called the "inflexion of light," with a prism. In part, due to entrenched biases, his theory of light was met with skepticism from the scientific community. So much so that he actually delayed the publication of his book *Opticks* until the critics were, for the most part, dead.

No one said this was going to be easy! There's a good reason why changing minds is difficult: the world doesn't always want what you want, and there is so much mental programming to overcome.

Research in developmental biology shows that perceptions acquired in early childhood become the fundamental subconscious "programs" that shape one's character. In other words, our perceptions of the world are downloaded directly into the subconscious—and without any filters. We are quite literally programmed.

> I can accept that we acquire many foundational perceptions and beliefs about life long before we've developed a capacity for critical thinking. But I do not accept that these beliefs are in any way permanent.

But let me tell you about the programming I received as a child. Growing up in India, there was "no chance" for me to escape the cycle of poverty that I was born into. I had a different idea about how my life could be, and for this type of thinking, I was called a rebel. I was told that I would be disappointed and frustrated, and would likely get into trouble. "Think smaller," I was advised. My dad, believing he was protecting me, told me the best I could do would be to become an accountant—that would be the ultimate that I could achieve. Any expectation beyond that would only mean disappointment. Engineering? That was out of the question. That kind of education was not available to poor people. "Why aim so high when you know you're going to fail? You're not meant for that, that's not where you come from." In spite of this counsel, I did become an engineer. It turns out that I wasn't any good at it, but that's thankfully not the point! The reason I was considered a rebel was that I didn't follow the rules—*I didn't obey the programming.* My thinking was that if I had followed the rules, I'd still be in India, locked into that same "inescapable" cycle.

I can accept that we acquire many foundational perceptions and beliefs about life long before we've developed a capacity for critical thinking. But I do not accept that these beliefs are in any way permanent, or that we cannot radically alter them at will. No one has to be the victim or slave of their own limiting or sabotaging mindsets or perceptions—or those of others. Whatever has been programmed can be reprogrammed. The human mind is an unimaginably creative and nimble platform capable of defining its reality, infusing perceptions with imagination to generate unlimited possibilities. You could say that my leaving India and becoming an engineer was my first real moonshot. If I could do that, then what else is possible? All it takes is a little imagination—and the right perspective.

○ ◗ ● ◖

Curiosity may be "clever," but wisdom is a wide-angle lens. Cleverness does not always equate with wisdom. Wisdom, in our entrepreneurial sense, comes with the capacity to recognize opportunity in complex possibilities. And that is a defining characteristic of the moonshot entrepreneur. To these ends, you can, as Yogi Berra said, "observe a lot by watching." And the observer matters. Remember how both Relativity and quantum theory so dramatically revised the role that observers play in physics? Not observers as in humans or conscious creatures, but observers as in points of view? Relativity shows that we can't talk about space or time outside a frame of reference, since one observer's time is another's space. Likewise, quantum mechanics taught us that we can't talk about properties of matter without first specifying what we're measuring—its position, for example, or its momentum. In other words, perspective matters. It remains a mystery to us, but one's point of view determines not only how we see things, but how things actually *are.*

So to what lengths can one go to gain greater, more insightful perspective— particularly in a world fraught with paradox and contradiction? What really limits our capacity for seeing? Can our powers of perception be freed from the limits of Flatland? What is it that stands between our consciousness and a geometry of, say, four *spatial* dimensions? What if it were possible to obliterate it?

In the *Brothers Karamazov*, Dostoevsky employs the idea of the fourth dimension to signify that which the Earth-bound human mind cannot grasp. "I have a Euclidean earthly mind," says Ivan Karamazov. "How could I solve problems that are not of this world? ... Such questions are utterly inappropriate for a mind created with an idea of only three dimensions!"

Yet our two-dimensional protagonist from Flatland, A Square, upon grasping that "unattainable" higher dimension, begins to yearn for dimensions higher still. "Shall we stay our upward course?" he asks rhetorically. "In that blessed region of Four Dimensions, shall we linger at the threshold of the Fifth, and not enter therein? Ah, no! Let us rather resolve that our ambition shall soar with our corporal ascent. Then, yielding to our intellectual onset, the gates of the Six Dimension shall fly open; after that a Seventh, and then an Eighth ..."

And then there's the Austrian philosopher Rudolf Steiner, who speculated on the nature of the fourth dimension in this way: "Zero dimension is the point," he explained, "the first dimension is the line, the second dimension is the surface, and the third dimension is the solid body. How do these spatial concepts relate to one another? Imagine that you are a being who can move only along a straight line. What kind of spatial images do one-dimensional beings have? Such beings would be able to perceive only points, and not their own one-dimensionality, because when we attempt to draw something within a line, points are the only option. A two-dimensional being would be able to encounter lines and thus to distinguish one-dimensional beings. A three-dimensional being, such as a cube, would perceive two-dimensional beings. Human beings, however, can perceive three dimensions. If we draw the right conclusions, we must say that just as a one-dimensional being can perceive only points, a two-dimensional being only one dimension, and a three-dimensional being only two dimensions, a being that perceives three dimensions must be a four-dimensional being. Because we can delineate external beings in three dimensions and manipulate three-dimensional spaces, *we must be four-dimensional beings.*"

How's that for perspective?

---

1. Warren Buffet once said, "If I had an IQ of 160, I'd sell 40 points."

CHAPTER 5

Imagine This

You can't depend on your eyes when your imagination is out of focus.

—Mark Twain

WHAT CAN BE MORE REBELLIOUS AGAINST the present reality—or the future—than imagination? What is the future but imagination? The future *is* imagination. It can only be imagined! Imagination is, by definition, the capacity to conceive of what is not. The question is how *you* will imagine the future—because whatever you can imagine, you can create. But how?

That's just it: where the future is concerned, there are no established practices or defined courses of action. Best practices are inherently backward-looking; they won't help us at all in a completely new or redefined landscape. We see time and time again in corporate dynamics a dangerous combination of ignorance and arrogance that believes what was accomplished yesterday will be sufficient for tomorrow. This is also why common management tools such as the S-curve suffer a fatal flaw: they are helpful only as retrospective visualizations, doing nothing to help us clarify possible future developments. While an S-curve can help one understand, for example, the adoption of a new technology like the smartphone, it is blind to the events along the curve, because, as we saw earlier, the components that ultimately converge in such a product are themselves independent vari-

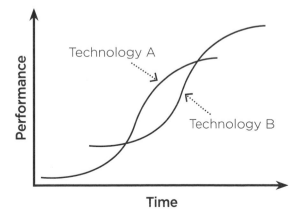

ables—the connections are clear only in hindsight.

Consequently, the future is completely up for grabs. No rules. The wild, wild West. And this introduces a twist to the creative mind. Because if anything goes, then there are no rules to challenge, no expectations to shatter, nothing to subvert. And yet there *is* much to challenge and subvert—and not only with respect to the status quo, but also every competing imagining of the future. Which means you mustn't wait to start creating your version of it. Whatever your designs on the future, now is the time to begin staking out its essential contours and erecting the scaffolding upon which it will be built.

> **Where the future is concerned, there are no established practices or defined courses of action. Best practices are inherently backward-looking; they won't help us at all in a completely new or redefined landscape.**

Archimedes said, "Give me a fulcrum and a place to stand, and with a lever long enough, I will move the world." As a moonshot entrepreneur, this is your only guiding principle: you imagine a world moved; with your creativity you conceive of an original device for effecting that movement; and then through its innovative application, you give the vision *life*.

○ ◗ ● ◖

As we continue to build out our hierarchy of the moonshot entrepreneur's mindset, we have thus far shown that possibility is greater than impossibility and curiosity is greater than intelligence. Now we also see that imagination is greater than knowledge.

Western Union took a pass on the telephone, but not for lack of knowledge. Xerox didn't skip the mouse because of an absence of information. DEC didn't ignore the PC because they didn't see it coming. They all missed these signals for want of imagination. The main thing keeping most companies from creating new and innovative product categories is their inability to see beyond what they're selling—and protecting—today.

"The true sign of intelligence," Einstein said, "is not knowledge but imagination." The store of knowledge in this world is inconceivable. But knowledge hasn't solved the world's problems—it cannot. The vast majority of the problems in this world—and in corporate boardrooms—are caused by failures of imagination.

As such, imagination must have primacy—even over will. Many people believe that a will to act must precede the application of imagination. But imagination must come first. Imagination is the primal force because it requires one to conceive of what does not yet exist. In this sense, imagination is liberating—especially when you don't yet know the solution to the problem at hand. If you can unshackle your mind from all preconceived notions and quite literally let your imagination run wild, you'll be astounded by the outpouring of ideas.

But that unshackling takes work. One must diligently tend to the garden of imagination. Imagination is not some ethereal muse that settles upon your mind like the dew or as seeds sown into just any soil. The mind and the soil must be amended, weeded, and made fertile—a state that requires preparation and attention. Even unexpected "flights of imagination" do not come without certain conditions first being satisfied. There is a certain technique to it all.

Perhaps no one has expressed this idea more eloquently than the British mathematician J.G. Bennett. "Let's take the example of an artist," he wrote. "Without technique, the moment of creative insight can hardly be made fruitful. The same is true for the scientist. This means that one must know the form that will enable one to clothe the moment of insight in some expression. First, one must know the form of thought for oneself, so that the insight may become clear, and afterwards one must know the form of expression so that it may be communicated to others ... If one wants to bring thinking into the sphere of creativity, some preparatory work must first be done."

> " Lateral thinking essentially says you cannot dig a hole in a different place by digging the same hole deeper. That would be vertical thinking, and the bane of nearly every corporate innovation process. Vertical thinking just digs the same hole deeper. "

If it is true that creativity is one part inspiration and 99 parts perspiration, then this is mostly very hard work. But we do have our techniques, one of the most powerful of which is "lateral thinking." Lateral thinking essentially says you cannot dig a hole in a different place by digging the same hole deeper. That would be vertical thinking, and the bane of nearly every corporate innovation process. Vertical thinking just digs the same hole deeper. Lateral thinking is used to dig a hole—even using the same shovel—in a completely different place.

Though it may strike you as counterintuitive, vertical thinking is equivalent to the process of "thinking outside the box." Really? Yes, because this kind of thinking is essentially still concerned with the *same box*! Lateral thinking goes looking for a different box altogether. That means applying the knowledge gained from one industry to a *completely different industry* in order to disrupt it. Otherwise, out-of-the-box thinking can only deliver incrementally better results, and within its own space.

> **The store of knowledge in this world is inconceivable. But knowledge hasn't solved the world's problems—it cannot. The vast majority of the problems in this world—and in corporate boardrooms—are caused by failures of imagination.**

Out-of-the-box thinking is seldom disruptive. Disruption happens when you apply software design techniques to the design of a lunar launch vehicle. Disruption happens when you apply what you learned in space to healthcare. Disruption happens when you apply what you learned in healthcare to education. These are all examples of moving laterally to very different boxes, repurposing knowledge from unrelated fields, transplanting big ideas across industries and disciplines.

Perhaps the original exemplar of lateral thinking was Johann Gutenberg, whose skill with the wine press led to the world's most consequential innovation: the printing press.

Lateral thinking also leverages the power of analogy. Consider actress Hedy Lamarr's WWII-era invention of frequency hopping to protect radio-controlled torpedoes from jamming or interference—inspired by the mechanism used to drive player piano rolls! Her scheme involved switching a carrier among many frequency channels—88, to be exact—using a pseudorandom sequence known to both transmitter and receiver. The principles of her inspired invention are still in use today in CDMA and Wi-Fi. And, more recently, MIT professor Christopher Voigt began exploring how "to pull the tools of electronic circuit design into genetic circuit design." In doing so, Voigt and his team seek to automate the design of genetic modifications, simulating them and generating genetic schematics in much the same way that electronics engineers design circuits. "We think genetic circuits will start appearing in all of the products that touch our lives every day, from foods to clothes to medicines," he predicts.

Lateral thinking even works when composing blues songs! "Now take a knife," said Big Bill Broonzy. "How many things can you do with a knife? You can cut fish, you can cut your toenails; I seen guys shave with it, you can eat beans with it, you can kill a man. There. You name five things you can do with a knife, you got five verses. You got yourself a blues."

Seriously, though, lateral thinking is another important habit of the entrepreneurial mindset, and like all good habits, it too has its own techniques: techniques for tuning one's capacity for cognitive complexity—the ability to see relationships between very different fields of knowledge. Creative innovation comes from connecting disparate and nonobvious dots; it doesn't take place so much within disciplines as it does at the intersections and boundaries between them. Because our brains are naturally associative, it pays to take in wide-ranging material to associate for synthesizing new ideas. Mixing metaphors is another great way to jump-start lateral thinking, as it opens one to possibilities beyond the established patterns that the mind so readily latches onto—especially when considering that the moonshot entrepreneur's objective is to obliterate those patterns.

○ ◑ ◕ ◐

Society always tries to push everyone into the center of the bell curve. Rebels, though, live at the outlying edges. The moonshot entrepreneur is fundamentally a rebel. Not merely a maverick, but a rebel in the full sense of the word. A rebel is not only an independent thinker, but is determined to overthrow every authoritative, self-limiting imposition placed upon his vision—and disposition. He takes his motto from the Royal Society, founded in 1660: *Nullius in Verba*—"Take nothing on authority." The moonshot entrepreneur has no interest in consensus or conventional wisdom.

There's no question that the world's prevailing patterns have served the cause of incrementalism extremely well—and that it has its place and is useful. But incrementalism is also inherently self-limiting. It acts like a governor on an otherwise powerful engine of imagination and possibility. If you try to regulate

> **Creative innovation comes from connecting disparate and nonobvious dots; it doesn't take place so much within disciplines as it does at the intersections and boundaries between them.**

a moonshot, it'll never reach escape velocity. Moonshots, by their very nature, require the throwing off of such encumbrances in order to achieve wholesale, exponential change.

This is the essence of disruption. It is necessarily destructive. But it is a *creative* and imaginative destruction. That said, the word "disruption" has become overused, as has the word innovation. Everybody has disruptive innovation. My concept of disruptive innovation means a complete reimagining of something that everyone takes for granted—again, the keyword being re-imagining.

> **If you try to regulate a moonshot, it'll never reach escape velocity. Moonshots, by their very nature, require the throwing off of such encumbrances in order to achieve wholesale, exponential change.**

Recalling our contempt for the fundamental basis of economics, which is a focus on scarcity, when we engage imagination to move exponentially beyond the status quo into a world of abundance, we also transform the very essence of economic activity. The problem with economists is twofold: 1) they are constrained by linear thinking, and 2) that linear thinking is applied strictly in the context of scarce resources. Thus conditioned, they are unable to imagine a society in which man's basic material needs are completely satisfied. Moreover, because their discipline focuses entirely on the *means* of economic activity—the "how"—they exclude anything to do with the "why."

Economics, like any science, makes no moral judgments in terms of human flourishing. Economics is "values-free." Entrepreneurs, though, are driven entirely by values. And when this values-driven sensibility is amplified in a world where imagination is infinite, then so too are resources—resources that provide for endless combinations of creative and innovative possibilities for moving humanity forward—where human flourishing is not conserved for want of basic needs.

The point we make again and again is that the only truly scarce resources in this world are imagination, curiosity, and creativity. And yet, these are the very assets our society seeks to deplete as early in life as possible. It's why original ideas and world-changing innovations are in such scarce supply. Indeed, imagination, curiosity, and creativity are the very reasons why disruptions can happen at all.

An Exercise in Lateral Thinking

There was a time when you could not get a phone in India. When I was growing up, there was a 20-year waiting list for a phone line. Just one household in our village had a phone, and if you wanted to make a call, you'd make an appointment with them. Little did anyone know what a huge advantage this would turn out to be.

In the US, because of our massive wireline infrastructure, it has actually taken a long time for wireless technology to proliferate. But India, because of the paucity of wireline, or landline service, bypassed wireline completely and adopted wireless at full scale. Nobody has wireline telephones in India! What were once liabilities can actually become great advantages for developing countries. Massive advantages, in fact. I tell entrepreneurs in India that just by virtue of being in India, you don't have the many rules and regulations that are killing us in the US. That means that you have a chance to leapfrog the current innovations.

For example, one of India's biggest problems is the sheer density of the population. What if that could be turned into an advantage? The road infrastructure in India is terrible. The US, of course, has a massive infrastructure for roads, but now, in the new world of delivery technology, the roads are not even needed. What if you could make all deliveries via drones? Given India's population density, drones have only to travel one mile to serve a million people, versus serving perhaps only 10,000 people in the US. The wireless drone-based infrastructure becomes so efficient, then, that the US, even given its less-dense population, will be compelled to import it. Imagine that!

When I speak to entrepreneurs in India, I always ask them why they want to mimic the technologies coming out of the US. These things aren't going to be around in 10 years! They'd be better off creating solutions that are designed for the circumstances and advantages that are unique to India, versus adopting those designed for a distinctly Western paradigm (X's Project Loon being, perhaps, a rare exception). What's more, the resulting innovations will be attractive even to an American market, simply because they must innovate on such a radical scale. India's problems can ultimately yield a massive advantage. It just takes a little imagination.

Education is another area where India's wireless infrastructure could be exploited to far greater effect. With educational programs delivered via smartphones and controlled by AI, they'll end up with a far superior solution than those requiring physical infrastructure. They can bypass the conventional approaches entirely and leapfrog the state of the art for anything coming out of the US. So much so that the last time I spoke at Harvard, I started by saying, "Enjoy it while it lasts!"

CHAPTER 6

Creating the Post-scarcity World—Life without Tradeoffs

We are racing toward a world of abundance, and we are going to be increasing the quality of life for everyone on this planet.

—Peter Diamandis

A MAN WALKING ALONG A ROAD in the countryside comes across a shepherd and a large flock of sheep. He tells the shepherd, "I will bet you $100 against one of your sheep that I can tell you the exact number in this flock." The shepherd thinks it over; it's a big flock so he takes the bet. "973," says the man. The shepherd is astonished, because that is exactly right.

"Okay," he says, "I'm a man of my word. Take an animal." The man picks one up and begins to walk away.

"Wait," cries the shepherd. "Let me have a chance to get even. Double or nothing that I can guess your exact occupation." The man agrees. "You are an economist," declares the shepherd.

"Amazing!" responds the man, "You are right! But tell me, how did you deduce that?"

"Well," says the shepherd, "put down my dog and I will tell you."

• • ◉ • •

Imagine a world in which every resource—energy, water, food, land—was in great abundance. Well, if economics is the science that studies human behavior as a relationship between ends and scarce means, then the economists would have nothing to study—no need to make decisions about how to allocate resources, no tradeoffs to explore, nothing to quantify or forecast. The need to balance butter and guns would be eliminated in favor of all butter and no guns, because there'd be no need to fight over resources. And best of all, we'd have no need of economists!

Is this just a pipe dream? If not, then how, exactly, would we go about creating more energy than we could ever consume? Is it possible? Could we actually create an abundance of food? Of fresh water? Not only do I believe that all these things are possible, I believe we can achieve them in our lifetimes. Moreover, I believe that realizing such possibilities could obviate the prevailing causes of war, enabling mankind to contemplate the real possibility of world peace. Consider what it is that we fight over. We fight over land, we fight over water, and we fight over energy. But all we have to do is look *up*. All those resources are in overwhelming abundance in space.

> " Consider what it is that we fight over. We fight over land, we fight over water, and we fight over energy. But all we have to do is look *up*. All those resources are in overwhelming abundance in space. "

Take Earth's annual production of raw metals, for example. The global market for gold, iron, copper, and a dozen or so other metals is on the order of $600 billion, yet just one near-Earth asteroid is believed to contain more platinum than has ever been mined in the history of the world. The asteroid belt that lies between Mars and Jupiter comprises more than a million such asteroids whose value NASA estimates to be in the hundreds of quintillions of dollars. It's unimaginable.

We are but a tiny pale blue dot, flung out toward the edge of our galaxy—just one of a hundred billion such galaxies "spinning in a heavenly dance" across an ever-expanding universe. So where is this scarcity? We consider resources to be scarce only because in our collective mindset, we believe it is not possible to exploit our celestial neighbors—the moon, Mars, Jupiter, Titan, Europa, the asteroids. But we know that technology changes everything. It *is* changing everything.

◯ ◗ ● ◖

The true scourge of the world is a mindset of scarcity. It is at the root of all the greatest challenges that humanity faces. It is the direct cause of war, poverty, crime, disease, famine, hunger, illiteracy, a sense of hopelessness and helplessness, and nearly every other source of human suffering. And it is big business. So big, in fact, that where there is no actual scarcity, artificial scarcity is created in order to restrict supplies and drive up prices. The concept of scarcity is so deeply entrenched, ingrained, and institutionalized that it has infected the world like a virulent disease that is sucking the very life force out of humanity.

And it has deep psychological effects. When people are pitted against one another for scarce resources, opportunities for common cause take a hit. Those with a scarcity-driven mindset tend to see everything in terms of win-lose. That is, whenever someone else has something, it necessarily means that there is less for everyone else.

> **The true scourge of the world is a mindset of scarcity. It is at the root of all the greatest challenges that humanity faces. It is the direct cause of war, poverty, crime, disease, famine, hunger, illiteracy, a sense of hopelessness and helplessness, and nearly every other source of human suffering. And it is big business.**

The scarcity mindset also sets up yet another insidious series of self-fulfilling prophecies. A mindset that has bought into the scarcity narrative makes everything scarce—including possibility. Scarcity becomes a state of mind, a habit of limits, trade-offs, constraints, and deadly tunnel vision, narrowing both perspective and options. In other words, everything that keeps the economists in business. Everywhere in the world one can see the debilitating effects of scarcity. It kills imagination, fosters short-term thinking at the expense of long-term benefit, breeds a toxic pessimism, and accepts a miserable status quo.

To the mind set on scarcity, everything is a zero-sum game. It produces the worst in humanity. And wherever you find scarcity, you will also find a dearth of mental capacity, as this kind of thinking actually changes the brain. In correlating a mindset of scarcity with poverty, Sendhil Mullainathan, a professor of behavioral economics at Harvard, says, "To put it crudely, poverty—no matter who you are—can make you dumber." As we saw earlier, the poor are paradoxically the least likely to question, challenge, reject, or change their situations, allowing this mindset to set its roots all the deeper.

Scarcity is not only the opposite of abundance, it is the opposite of imagination, possibility, optimism, and every other trait that marks a healthy mindset.

It is, in fact, quite unhealthy. A mindset of scarcity damages the body, mind, and soul, especially as a persistent and pervasive feeling of scarcity conspires with the effects of a media industry fueled by negativity and one's own self-reinforcing thought habits, inducing myriad chronic disorders. We can literally think ourselves sick.

Consider again the workings of the amygdala. To the brain, a sense of scarcity is just as threatening as any other danger signal—perhaps more so, because of scarcity's pervasive nature; it never dissipates in the way that other "ordinary" threats resolve themselves. Normally, when the amygdala starts its chemical chain of events in response to a threat, other mechanisms in the brain shut them down when the danger has passed. The stress hormones are flushed out, and we relax. But if we remain in this hyper-alert state for sustained periods, what was intended to protect us now turns on us. Instead of working to help protect our safety, the constant wash of adrenaline—continuously stimulated by bad news and worry over the many forms of perceived scarcity and other threats that impact daily living—now actually endangers well-being. Anxiety, insomnia, depression, eczema, anorexia, hypertension, diabetes, and a host of other maladies are the common results. When the amygdala is stuck *on*, the stress response spins in an unrelenting feedback loop, and the world forever looks like one big dangerous place.

A dramatic example of the damage caused by a scarcity mindset can be seen in the poor. The scarcity mindset interferes with setting and achieving the kinds of goals that could reverse their condition. Consequently, the impoverished generally don't seek new opportunities. Fear holds them back. This is doubly tragic because it blinds people to the real and substantial progress that is actually being made in this world, where things are getting better day by day—sometimes exponentially so. Just look at our progress over the last 100 years: we've seen a doubling of the average human lifespan and a tripling of average per capita income. Infant mortality has plummeted. We've seen massive cuts in the cost of food, electricity, transportation, and communications. What's more, according to the Flynn effect, we're all getting smarter, too—at a rate of three points per decade.

> **Scarcity is not only the opposite of abundance, it is the opposite of imagination, possibility, optimism, and every other trait that marks a healthy mindset.**

Earlier we mentioned that we really don't have a proper perspective on the true nature of poverty. Not to minimize the conditions of poverty, but in America today, most people living *beneath* the poverty line still enjoy most modern conveniences. Here in Seattle alone, there are 78 different locations, most in the downtown core, where the homeless can get a free meal—and free transportation to get there. As Steve Rhoades, the former Recon Marine who spent 15 years on the street and now works to help homeless veterans, quipped, "You've got to be a moron to go hungry in this country." But the greater point is that even the homeless have access to a higher standard of living than most Americans had just 100 years ago! And yet, an attitude of scarcity and pessimism prevails, setting up a vicious cycle that can be difficult to break. And that difficulty reinforces the scarcity mindset.

> **If you want to eradicate poverty, you must first eradicate the mindset that sustains it. No matter how much financial aid or how many government programs are thrown at this problem, if the mind doesn't accept that things can get better, they won't.**

There is a remarkable passage in the book *Scarcity: Why Having Too Little Means So Much* by Sendhil Mullainathan and Eldar Shafir. It reads, "Dieters can take a break from their diet. The busy can take vacations. One cannot take a vacation from poverty. Simply deciding not to be poor—even for a bit—*is never an option*. There is no equivalent in the world of poverty to the dieter deciding to live with being overweight or the busy person giving up on some of his ambitions. It would be silly to suggest that the rural poor in India should cope with money scarcity by simply moderating their desires."

Now, as someone who did in fact grow up poor in India and who did, in fact, moderate his desires, I take exception to this. It is a debilitating sentiment that brings to mind what Carl Jung considered to be the most important question that anyone can ask themselves: *"What myth am I living?"* But it actually gets worse. Mullainathan and Shafir go on to say, "The failures of the poor are part and parcel of the misfortune of being poor in the first place. Under these conditions, we all would have (and have!) failed."

Do we begin with the chicken or the egg here? Are people poor due to their faulty mindsets, or do they have faulty mindsets because they are poor? Whichever is the cause or the effect, both the reasoning and the outcome are the same and circular—and the faulty mindset persists, generation after generation. And in the end, mindsets dominated by scarcity are tragically closed even to the *possibility* of abundance, thus perpetuating their self-fulfilling prophecies. If you want to eradicate poverty, you must first eradicate the mindset that sustains it. No matter how much financial aid or how many government programs are thrown at this problem, if the mind doesn't accept that things can get better, they won't. And they don't.

There is a Zulu proverb that says abundance does not spread; famine does. For those who believe this, it is absolutely true—life choices springing from such a mindset make it so.

Some suggest that abundance, should we actually attain it, would create a dangerous complacency. While I credit him with an effort to look on the bright side, Dr. Todd May, a professor of philosophy at Clemson University, believes that scarcity is *valuable*, that it contributes to an interesting and meaningful life. "When there is always time for everything," he says, "there is no urgency for anything. A life without limits would lose the beauty of its moments, and it would become *boring*."

Did that statement take your breath away? It should have. First, Professor May assumes that we have any concept of what our limits actually are. Yet, we've not begun to even contemplate what they might be! With an infinite universe to discover, quantum worlds to explore, and ocean depths to plumb—to say nothing of the mystery of our own consciousness—how can we not feel the urgency of our fleeting lives? And how could we not be moved by the possibilities of giving voice to the bottom billion from whom the world has never heard? What contributions might *they* bring if empowered by abundance instead of being crippled by scarcity? What are the possible limits of the good, the true, and the beautiful we have yet to realize—if only we weren't condemned to forever fight over scarce resources? What's "boring" here is the utter lack of imagination that such a sentiment betrays. In any case, I think we can certainly agree that we wouldn't want the bottom billion in this world—the true poor—to be-

> " How could we not be moved by the possibilities of giving voice to the bottom billion from whom the world has never heard? What contributions might *they* bring if empowered by abundance instead of being crippled by scarcity? "

come complacent! The fact is, in times of scarcity or abundance, we will always have the poor—and the complacent—with us. As for the rest, one need only turn to Arthur Schopenhauer, the high priest of pessimism, for the ultimate and logical conclusion of the bankrupt mindset of scarcity:

> All willing springs from a lack, a deficiency and thus from suffering. Fulfillment brings this to an end; yet for one wish that is fulfilled, there remain at least ten that are denied. Further, desiring lasts a long time, its demands and requests go on into infinity; fulfillment is short and is meted out sparingly. All pleasure is simply an illusion designed to give us false hope to make us labor to attain the unattainable. This is the nature of the universe ... If I act, I inflict evil, suffering, and harm on the world, yet if I do not act, evil, suffering, and harm will be inflicted on the world ... Accordingly, happiness lies always in the future, or else in the past, and the present may be compared to a small dark cloud driven by the wind over the sunny plain; in front of and behind the cloud everything is bright, only it itself always casts a shadow. Consequently, the present is always inadequate, but the future is uncertain, and the past irrecoverable. With its misfortunes, small, greater, and great occurring hourly, daily, weekly, and yearly; with its deluded hopes and accidents bringing all calculations to naught, life bears so clearly the stamp of something which ought to disgust us, that it is difficult to conceive how anyone could fail to recognize this, and be persuaded that life is here to be thankfully enjoyed, and that man exists in order to be happy. On the contrary, that continual deception and disillusionment, as well as the general nature of life, present themselves as intended and calculated to awaken the conviction that nothing whatever is worth our exertions, our efforts, and our struggles, that all good things are empty and fleeting, that the world on all sides is bankrupt, and that life is a business that does not cover the costs; so that our will may turn away from it.

And we wonder why we have problems in the world.

○◑●◐

Scarcity, like poverty, is a problem with a poor definition. To understand the true nature of scarcity, we need to look back in history 150 years, when the most valuable metal on Earth was ... *aluminum*. It was so rare—or so it was thought—that Napoleon III broke out the exotic aluminum utensils for his most honored guests. Second-rate guests had to settle for the gold cutlery. The fact is, aluminum is the most common metal on Earth. More common than iron. But because it was so difficult to process, it was, in that day, far more valuable than gold or silver. Technology—and entrepreneurs—changed all that. Engineers Héroult and Hall discovered in 1886—independently and simultaneously—a process for separating aluminum from its ore via electrolysis, thus taking aluminum from rarity to abundance virtually overnight. Today we throw away aluminum cans. You can't pay people to recycle them.

So this wasn't a scarcity problem at all; it was simply a *conversion* problem, which redefines the very nature of the problem itself. Likewise, consider energy. Renewable energy sources comprise a tiny portion of our energy consumption. Ninety percent of our energy is produced from non-renewable sources. Ninety percent! But think of the sun. The Earth's surface receives the average of 164 watts of solar

> **More energy strikes the Earth's surface in 90 minutes than the whole world consumed in the year 2001 from all sources combined. So do we have a scarcity problem or a conversion problem?**

energy per square meter every day—equating to 84 terawatts of power (or 84 billion kWh) per day worldwide. But the worldwide population consumes only about 15 terawatts each day—a mere 17 percent of what is actually available. According to Sandia National Labs, more energy strikes the Earth's surface in 90 minutes than the whole world consumed in the year 2001 from all sources combined.

So do we have a scarcity problem or a conversion problem? Today the state of photovoltaic cells and the batteries to store the captured energy are still relatively inefficient, but the technologies are improving exponentially. Consequently, solar power is growing faster than any other energy source—and the prices are steadily dropping. The same is true of wind power. Offshore wind power is now cheaper than nuclear! If we believe we're running out of energy resources, it's only because we're stuck in a 20th century mindset.

Here's something else to be optimistic about. There's a resource we have in abundance today that we actually wish were a little less abundant—that is, until we are able to fully exploit its economic potential: carbon dioxide. Today we're seeing tremendous advancements in carbon sequestration, the process of atmospheric carbon capture and its long-term storage. In other words, we're actually pulling CO_2 out of the air at its source and converting it into useful products, spanning building materials to carbon-neutral fuel solutions. Indeed, everything is getting better.

The fact is few resources are truly scarce. They may be difficult to access, but that's a different problem—a problem that can be solved with technology. Yet the mindset of scarcity continues to prevail.

> **We have to create more of what we need rather than consume less of what we have. Sustainability is a synonym for conservation of scarce resources, and you cannot achieve sustainability with conservation alone.**

Scarcity manifests only when people believe something is finite. And we have been conditioned to think and act from the standpoint of the finite. But once you change your mindset from one of scarcity to one of abundance, you begin to think of potentials and possibilities rather than the things that can't be done. You'll start to see the world in a very different way.

This is different from the idea of sustainability. We have to create *more* of what we need rather than consume *less* of what we have. Sustainability is a synonym for conservation of scarce resources, and you cannot achieve sustainability with conservation alone. Just consider the definition of economics—"the science which studies human behavior as a relationship between ends and scarce means which have alternative uses." It *begins* with the core assumption of scarcity! Likewise, sustainability operates from the standpoint of scarcity. The problem is that you can never create abundance by conserving resources. If you want more, you have to make more.

Consider the carbon cycle. We'll see, by virtue of how inextricably linked things are, that the domino effects cut both ways, presenting massive opportunities for the imaginative and innovative entrepreneur.

○ ◐ ● ◑

Viewed from space, the most striking feature of our planet is its water. It covers 75 percent of the Earth's surface. As NASA notes, "It fills the sky with clouds. Water is practically everywhere on Earth, from inside the planet's rocky crust to inside the cells of the human body." How, then, can we possibly have a shortage of water? It's a question that recalls the Ancient Mariner's lament, "Water, water everywhere / nor any a drop to drink." And there's the rub. Of all the water on this planet, only 2.5 percent of it is freshwater. And almost all of it is locked up in ice, in the ground, and, as recently discovered, beneath the ocean floor. Scarcely more than 1.2 percent of all freshwater, however, is surface water. So how are we doing with this water, and what are we doing with it?

For starters, would you be surprised to learn that nearly three-quarters of all available freshwater is used for agriculture? It's true—the vast majority of our freshwater is poured directly into agriculture, where, as we will see, it is largely wasted. Worse, it goes to crops that are fed not to people, but to livestock. Astoundingly, 80 percent of all agricultural land in the world is dedicated to grazing and to crops used just for the production of livestock. The seven billion livestock animals in the United States alone consume five times as much grain as is consumed by the entire American population! It turns out that the cattle are doing a lot better than much of the world's poor. That's a big problem in its own right. Seriously, think

> " The 7 billion livestock animals in the United States alone consume five times as much grain as is consumed by the entire American population! It turns out that the cattle are doing a lot better than much of the world's poor. "

WHERE IS EARTH'S WATER?

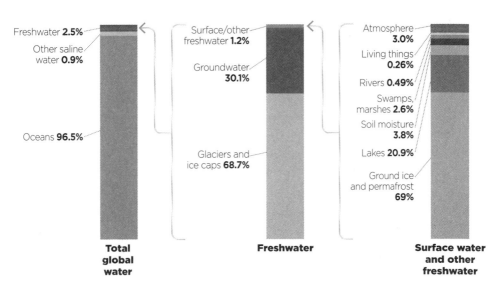

Freshwater **2.5%**
Other saline water **0.9%**
Oceans **96.5%**

Surface/other freshwater **1.2%**
Groundwater **30.1%**
Glaciers and ice caps **68.7%**

Atmosphere **3.0%**
Living things **0.26%**
Rivers **0.49%**
Swamps, marshes **2.6%**
Soil moisture **3.8%**
Lakes **20.9%**
Ground ice and permafrost **69%**

Total global water

Freshwater

Surface water and other freshwater

about the morality of this.

According to the World Health Organization, globally, at least two billion people use a drinking water source contaminated with feces (with much of that being sourced by livestock). Contaminated water can transmit diseases such as diarrhea, cholera, dysentery, typhoid, and polio. Some 842,000 people are estimated to die each year from diarrhea as a result of unsafe drinking water, as well as poor sanitation and hand hygiene. Yet diarrhea is largely preventable, and the deaths of 361,000 children under five years of age could be eliminated each year if these risk factors were addressed. Where water is not readily available, people may decide that handwashing is not a priority, thereby adding to the likelihood of spreading diarrhea and other diseases. Diarrhea is the most widely known disease linked to contaminated food and water, but there are other hazards. Almost 240 million people are affected by schistosomiasis—an acute and chronic disease caused by parasitic worms contracted through exposure to infested water. But again, the cattle are doing just fine.

> **Look at how these "scarce" resources are expended: estimates vary widely, but one conservative calculation shows that it takes 2,500 gallons of water, 12 pounds of grain, 35 pounds of topsoil, and the energy equivalent of one gallon of gasoline to produce *one pound* of feedlot beef.**

Look at how these "scarce" resources are expended: estimates vary widely, but one conservative calculation shows that it takes 2,500 gallons of water, 12 pounds of grain, 35 pounds of topsoil, and the energy equivalent of one gallon of gasoline to produce *one pound* of feedlot beef. By any measure, this is grossly inefficient, if not outright immoral. Put another way, on average, animal protein production in the US requires 28 calories of feed for every one calorie of meat produced. If ever an industry was ripe for disruption, it's this one.

What's more, the unrelenting demand for grazing land is driving continued deforestation, especially in Latin America, where, for example, some 70 percent of former forests in the Amazon have been turned over to grazing, further depleting the ecosystem of its capacity for absorbing carbon and contributing, some say, as much as 25 percent of the increase in atmospheric carbon.

A tremendous amount of environmental damage is done by cattle, which are responsible for a substantial share of greenhouse gas emissions—more than the emissions from all of the world's cars, trains, and planes *combined*. Methane, by the way, traps a whopping 100 times more heat in the atmosphere than carbon dioxide within a five-year period. But cattle raising continues and is growing unabated. The world can't get enough of it. According to the UN Food and Agriculture Organization, global meat production is projected to more than double from 229 million tons in 2000 to 465 million tons in 2050, while milk output is set to climb from 580 to 1043 million tons.

So in the end, the dominant factor modulating the scarcity of freshwater, crop production, and global warming turns out to be ... the demand for beef. The most unsustainable and environmentally damaging industry that civilization has ever seen, oddly enough, is dedicated to keeping those Big Macs flipping on the grill. Yep, McDonald's is the single largest beef purchaser in the world.

McDonald's. And we thought it was cars.

So do we *really* have a freshwater scarcity problem? Until one begins to understand the sequence of consumption cycles, we are constantly only ever solving the symptoms of problems, not the root causes. If we can find a way to reduce cattle raising, for example, we'll not only be able to bring more freshwater and food to the people who desperately need it, but also go a long way toward saving the environment. Indeed, if people really cared about the environment, instead of driving a Prius or a Tesla, all they'd have to do is stop eating beef! Or maybe eat it *just one day less* each week. That will do more for the betterment of the environment—and the world's poor— than driving an electric or hybrid car.

> **" A tremendous amount of environmental damage is done by cattle, which are responsible for a substantial share of greenhouse gas emissions—more than the emissions from all of the world's cars, trains, and planes *combined*. "**

I'm proud to say that while I may drive a Ferrari, as a vegetarian, I'm doing more for the environment than anyone I know. Maybe it's time we look beyond our gas tanks and to our plates. But even though producing alternative protein sources like poultry and soybeans consumes only a fraction of the resources required for the equivalent value in beef-based protein, we know that people are not going to give up their beef. So ... can we have our beef and eat it too?

Well, yes, we can—if we're willing to trade in the dinner plate for a Petri dish. In an effort to solve these massive problems, a cadre of Silicon Valley startups is determined to shift the world's beef production from grass-fed to lab-grown. Could their developments ultimately usher in a post-animal economy? As biology is becoming the new digital (in many respects biology is following the path of the computer industry, but with DNA as the programming language), new possibilities abound. Imagine, for example, producing cow's milk without needing the actual cow. We can now use synthetic biology to create a milk product with the molecular structure identical to real cow's milk. We can even bioengineer that milk to be lactose-free. Likewise, we could produce meat with lower levels of saturated fat, and even cholesterol-free eggs. What's most interesting is that this synthetic biology work is being done by small startups, not large corporations, governments, or institutes. And they are supported by a growing infrastructure of communities, accelerators, and incentive competitions.

So-called "clean meat" is, for all practical purposes, "real" meat, but produced via what I call bio-agriculture—the production of agricultural products from cell cultures—in a lab instead of the slaughterhouse. It's not genetically modified food, but rather "tissue-engineered" food. Products harvested from cell cultures are exactly the same as those harvested from an animal or a plant; they're just grown differently. Stem cells taken from the animal are grown in bioreactors—systems that support a biologically active environment—that will eventually scale in size to increase yields and decrease costs. These biofactories won't be terribly unlike a brewery, but instead of fermenting malted barley, yeast, and hops, they'll be growing muscle cells.

Like the current state of solar energy technologies, synthetic biology is not yet cost-effective, but as the processes develop and scale, lab-grown beef will eventually become cost-competitive with meat sourced from beef on the hoof. This promises to be a truly exponential innovation, as its developers believe they can achieve a 10X improvement in efficiency versus the highest-volume slaughterhouses. In time, a bioreactor half the size of a swimming pool could produce enough beef to feed 20,000 people for a year. And that's without consuming the lion's share of Earth's resources—and without antibiotics. Suddenly our original freshwater and carbon problems become a synthetic biology opportunity. The moonshot

> " Until one begins to understand the sequence of consumption cycles, we are constantly only ever solving the symptoms of problems, not the root causes. "

these companies are pursuing has the truly audacious goal of eliminating all animal slaughter within 30 years.

Where food production is concerned, we can take the concept of abundance even further—as in creating food out of thin air. Literally. A team of researchers at the VTT Technical Research Centre of Finland is developing a process using hydrogen-oxidizing bacteria—that is, bacteria that feed on hydrogen. The bacteria are placed in a bioreactor the size of a coffee cup filled with water. The hydrogen food source is created by an electric water splitter that splits the water into its constituent elements, hydrogen and oxygen. Atmospheric carbon and a dash of ammonia, phosphorous, and salts fertilize the culture, which ultimately produces a dry powder that is 50 percent protein, 25 percent carbohydrate, and 25 percent fats and nucleic acids. In other words, a complete food.

> **A bioreactor half the size of a swimming pool could produce enough beef to feed 20,000 people for a year. And that's without consuming the lion's share of Earth's resources—and without antibiotics. Suddenly our original freshwater and carbon problems become a synthetic biology opportunity.**

Like lab-grown beef, the process is similar to that of brewing beer, but instead of using sugar to feed the yeast, hydrogen is the catalyst. And, like lab-grown beef, if it can be scaled up sufficiently, it could serve as fodder replacement for cattle as we phase out the need for pastureland for feedstock production as an intermediate goal toward eliminating feedlot cattle altogether. Moreover, the protein can be consumed "as is" by humans. The mixture is actually very nutritious. And because the raw materials for the process are available from the air, the technology can be transported to deserts and areas facing famine.[1]

Speaking of deserts and famine, if we can create food out of thin air, can we also make the deserts bloom? We certainly can—if we bring a mindset of abundance to the problem.

For starters, conventional approaches to irrigation waste 60 percent or more of the water to runoff and evaporation. Micro-irrigation technologies, on the other hand, deliver with nearly 95 percent efficiency. And then there's vertical farming, which uses 10 times less water and a hundred times less land than conventional farming—and requires no transportation. Or consider how Israel has raised agricultural water use to an art. Through a combination of desalination, recycling of sewage, drip irrigation (which is vital to keeping the salts at bay), and general water management practices, their farms don't need any rainwater. It turns out, surprisingly, that rain is actually *bad* for desert crops. When rain floods the land, it causes the surface salts to leach into the soil around the plant roots, damaging the rhizosphere—the region of soil that hosts the microorganisms and the vital symbiosis that results. Much of the irrigation water comes from massive desalination plants, which, using current osmosis technologies, yield a freshwater cost of less than $2 per 275 gallons.

> **Pollution is nothing more than resources we are not harvesting. We dispense with them only because we've been ignorant of their value!**

There are problems, of course, with desalination. For one, it turns out that salt forms strong chemical bonds that are difficult to break, and consequently, reverse osmosis is a power-hungry process. But the technology is improving, and I have no doubt that an incentive competition would yield a superior and more cost-effective solution.[2]

The other problem is what to do with all the separated salt waste. The Gulf-area waters are literally brimming with brine as desalination plants dump the salty byproducts back into the sea. This, of course, makes continued desalination costlier, as it is becoming increasingly difficult to process the water if it's saltier to begin with. Perhaps this too is just a matter—and an entrepreneurial opportunity—of converting the otherwise wasted salt into useful products, as we're learning to do now with CO_2.

Chemical engineers have recently managed to streamline the 150-year-old Solvay process for producing sodium carbonate into a highly cost-effective solution that could nearly eliminate the need for brine disposal. One product of the output is sodium bicarbonate—baking soda. Abundance dividend doubled! It turns out that pollution is nothing more than resources we are not harvesting. We dispense with them only because we've been ignorant of their value!

○ ☽ ● ☾

Creating a world of abundance requires foresight and a little imagination. Scarcity, though it produces anxiety about the future, is paradoxically an artifact of the past. We need to view the world—and its future—through a very different set of lenses. When we do, a world of limitless possibility becomes visible. Every day we see new examples of how technologies in the hands of visionary entrepreneurs are turning what were once only fantasies into reality, problems into profitable solutions. Indeed, if you give entrepreneurs a motive to solve problems and create profitable businesses in the process, they will do it.

If anything is truly scarce on this Earth, it is human imagination and ingenuity united with bold entrepreneurs who are willing to take the necessary moonshots. And a mindset of abundance is just the catalyst for imagining what might actually be possible. The greatest discovery of all is that a human being can fundamentally alter his life by altering his mindset. Indeed, if he can do that, he can alter the state of the world.

Exposing the Unequal Economics of Equality

A particularly insidious consequence of the scarcity-driven mindset is the drive for equality. Equality, like all things in an economy based on scarcity, views the conservation of resources as a zero-sum game. In other words, the more I have, the less you must necessarily have. And of course, policies that seek to impose equality only perpetuate the inherent dangers of the scarcity model. Worse, it closes minds to the possibilities of realizing the kinds of abundance that would actually obviate any concern for equality in the first place. Inequality is not the problem. It is an effect. You can never solve a problem by focusing solely on its effects, yet this is exactly what drives for equality do. If one truly cares about equality, he should first embrace the mindset that seeks to produce abundance, rather than fight a scarcity-driven zero-sum game that he can never win.

Equality, like equilibrium, is a form of stasis. As an economic model, because stasis is the opposite of dynamism, it is also fundamentally flawed. The relentless pursuit of equality kills vision and innovation and everything else that flows from a creative imagination. Equality initiatives rely entirely upon the continuance of artificial constraints. Consequently, equality can only *consume* the future; it cannot construct it. It is inherently concerned with the *distribution* of wealth rather than its creation. Because it is a direct result of the scarcity model, it can only yield a future of declining returns for everyone.

Policies that seek to impose equality not only do *not* create equality, they really only affect where innovation and wealth creation will occur—never innovation or wealth itself. This is precisely why we've seen such a wave of outsourcing. Consequently, the pursuit of equality only drives innovation—and its corresponding wealth—away, as it has clearly done over the past few decades. In fact, *trillions* of dollars are being held offshore by US multinational companies, leading with Apple, followed by Microsoft, Cisco, Alphabet, and Oracle.

The bottom line is that neither technology nor wealth can be contained. And it really doesn't matter who is in the White House. Technology has continued to grow through administrations good and bad; it continues apace through recessions, depressions, wars, natural disasters, and other global events—and it continues to do so exponentially. Whenever technological progress is constrained by governmental policies, whether it be stem cell research, the development of CRISPR technologies, or the rolling out of autonomous vehicles, it simply moves to greener pastures. And there are always greener pastures. Once the genie is out of the bottle, technology starts moving, and there is nothing anyone can do to contain or stop it. As such, entrepreneurs are not limited by geographical boundaries—they go to where the opportunities are.

So it matters a great deal how we treat our entrepreneurs. And if they are treated poorly, we should be prepared to watch American wealth flee to other countries. As George Gilder notes, "High tax rates and oppressive regulations do not keep anyone from being rich. *They prevent poor people from becoming rich.* High tax rates do not redistribute incomes or wealth; they redistribute taxpayers—out of productive investment into overseas tax havens and out of offices and factories into beach resorts and municipal bonds. But if the 1 percent and the 0.1 percent are respected and allowed to risk their wealth— *and new rebels are allowed to rise up and challenge them*—America will continue to be the land where the last regularly become the first by serving others."

That said, technology innovation and its attendant wealth creation should not be considered from a purely domestic point of view. As an immigrant and an American, I can attest to the incalculable value of a global perspective. If you allow yourself to be blinkered by a narrow point of view, then you will only bar yourself from massive, global opportunities. Likewise, we must look far and wide and work hard to attract the best and the brightest from the world over, to invite them to help reinvigorate the land of opportunity, and to reward and celebrate their success. By throwing up every obstacle to these ends, we only trigger an exodus of talent, capital, and innovation. China, on the other hand, is gaining tremendous momentum in all three areas. Indeed, we're witnessing the growing trend of "sea turtles"—Chinese talent we've attracted, educated, and hired in America, but who are now returning home, where, believe it or not, there is greater opportunity for them. When people begin to believe that they'll have greater freedom to innovate and advance in China than in America, then everything we're doing must be called into question. When Alibaba, Baidu, and Tencent have become more interesting to global talent than Google, Microsoft, or Amazon, then that is great cause for concern.

Toward resolving this state of affairs, we—and the Chinese—would do well to heed the wisdom of Milton Friedman, who said, "The society that puts equality before freedom will end up with neither. The society that puts freedom before equality will end up with a great measure of both."

....

1. Omar Yaghi, a faculty scientist at Lawrence Berkeley National Laboratory, has created a solar-powered device that pulls water from air—even in extremely arid regions. Based on Yaghi's "metal-organic frameworks," or MOFs, they combine metals like magnesium or aluminum with organic molecules to form rigid, porous structures that efficiently store liquids and gases. Yaghi envisions enabling the sourcing of off-grid water supplied by his device sufficient to satisfy the needs of a household. Other MOFs are able to capture carbon dioxide and even natural gas at their sources.

2. Scientists from the University of Manchester, led by Dr. Rahul Nair, have fabricated a promising graphene oxide filtration device that can produce potable water from seawater or wastewater with higher throughput and less energy than existing polymer-based desalination membranes, highlighting the continuing potential for exponential progress enabled by advancing nanotechnologies and human ingenuity.

CHAPTER 7

Disruption, Wildfires, and the Entrepreneurial Life Cycle

There is nothing more difficult to take in hand, more perilous to conduct, or more uncertain in its success, than to take the lead in the introduction of a new order of things. For the reformer has enemies in all those who profit by the old order, and only lukewarm defenders in all those who would profit by the new order, this lukewarmness arising partly from fear of their adversaries ... and partly from the incredulity of mankind, who do not truly believe in anything new until they have had actual experience of it.

—Niccolo Machiavelli

WILDFIRES ARE A NATURAL AND ESSENTIAL PART of the life cycle of forests. Fires kill diseases and insects that prey on the trees, they clean the forest floor, and nourish the soil. Fire clears the weaker trees and undergrowth, opening it up to sunlight, and restores health to the forest ecosystem. Fire is as disruptive as hell, but it is also vitally important to a healthy forest. It also turns out that the century-old practice of suppressing natural wildfires (not those that threaten life or property) has proven to be nothing less than disastrous for forestry management. The new, enlightened policy? Let 'em burn.

We've also experienced in this country a disastrous policy of protecting businesses deemed "too big to fail." Perhaps we should let them burn, too—clearing the economic ecosystem of "diseases and insects" that prey on consumers, opening the competitive ecosystem to more sunlight, nourishing the entrepreneurial soil, and restoring vigor to the economy.

Just as a healthy forest progresses through its cycles, so too should business. Likewise there is a cycle of entrepreneurship. That life cycle is getting ever shorter, but that also means that there is ever more opportunity. Older companies are dying and new ones keep coming along to replace—or displace—them. This is important to the health of the economy—and to progressing toward a better, more dynamic future. As a company grows and comes to dominate its industry, it also tends to perpetuate the things that made it successful in the first place. Then another company comes along, rethinks the whole arrangement, and challenges the fundamental assumptions of that big incumbent. And suddenly, the incumbent's strongest asset becomes its greatest liability.

Consider Snapchat. It came seemingly out of nowhere. If Facebook could do everything, Snapchat wouldn't exist. But Mark Zuckerberg got caught up in the idea of building a persistent social network. Then somebody came along and asked, what if we had a network that was *ephemeral*—a network where content actually disappears? But Zuckerburg determined that the timeline is what creates the value. Snapchat obliterated the timeline and created a new kind of value in its place. They turned Facebook's strength into a weakness, an asset into a liability. At one point, Google reportedly floated an offer of $30 billion to acquire the upstart, which was declined. Soon, Snapchat will be disrupted, if it hasn't been already. (By the way, Snapchat's market cap, at the time of this writing, is now half that of its value at IPO, which was just what Google had offered. The entrepreneurial life cycle at work.)

To paraphrase Gordon Gekko, disruption is good. Some call it divine demolition. I like the term "creative destruction"—the process of destroying a model from within in order to make room for a new one to emerge. As established businesses are disrupted and displaced, the old structures are necessarily destroyed along with them. The forest renewed through the destructive forces of fire.

> **As a company grows and comes to dominate its industry, it also tends to perpetuate the things that made it successful in the first place. Then another company comes along, rethinks the whole arrangement, and challenges the fundamental assumptions of that big incumbent. And suddenly, the incumbent's strongest asset becomes its greatest liability.**

Some people may wonder if stability isn't a better option. Wildfires are one thing, but wouldn't the economy be better off with a little less chaos? After all, most of the history of economics revolves around the goals of maintaining order and equilibrium. Isn't that the objective? But this is exactly wrong. A capitalist economy is necessarily a complex and *dynamic* system. Order and regularity make for predictability precisely because they are low-information, low-entropy states, devoid of any friction or surprise. They're also devoid of imagination, creativity, or innovation, which are antithetical to stability! That settled old system wants nothing more than a settled, unchallenged future so that it can continue undisturbed. At this stage, the survival of the organism—not the delivery of value—becomes the prime objective. Purpose goes out the window. And this stultifying stability is precisely what needs to be burned out of the ecosystem.

We noted earlier the likelihood that half the current Fortune 500 companies will not survive the coming economic upheavals caused by accelerating convergences of exponential technologies. Consequently, today's Ubers are going to be tomorrow's Kodaks. I cite Uber because it has, in its own right, been a huge disrupter of the status quo. But even a company like Uber, that may have a lead today, will inevitably become obsolete in the near future, because a new set of technologies or market dynamics will arrive to replace it.

We're catching a glimpse of this already. Uber's valuation went from zero to $70 billion in just five years. In the next five years, it may go from $70 billion back to zero. And that may be before it's even had an opportunity to become a public company. In fact, at the time of this writing, SoftBank's recent valuation of its stake in Uber put the company's overall value at just $48 billion. The rapid downward trajectory has begun—a $22 billion reduction in just one year. The reason for this is that the technological shifts that allowed Uber to go from zero to $70 billion are no different from the next seismic shifts that may take it back down to zero: new technologies are emerging and new leaders are going to come along. And anytime a king dies, everybody gets a fair shot at becoming the next king.

◯ ◗ ● ◖

If past is prologue, Jim Collins' book *Good to Great* makes for a fascinating time piece. Published in 2001, it sought to identify the features of companies that enabled them to achieve and sustain market-leading performance. Follow their example, and presumably you could go from good to great, too. But much has changed since 2001. Of the 11 companies that fit the book's good-to-great profile, revenues at two have remained flat, six have been in steady—and in some cases steep—decline, and one went bankrupt. In other words, 82 percent of these erstwhile paragons haven't fared too well. No one is purposely emulating their models now. Perhaps the most remarkable finding of the book's research is the following bit from one of the "key takeaways" sections: "The idea that technological change is the principal cause in the decline of once-great companies (or the perpetual mediocrity of others) is *not supported by the evidence*. Certainly, a company can't remain a laggard and hope to be great, but technology by itself is never a primary root cause of either greatness or decline. Across eighty-four interviews with good-to-great executives, fully 80 percent didn't even mention technology as one of the top five factors in [their] transformation. This is true even in companies famous for their pioneering application of technology, such as Nucor."

Are you astounded by this? In another of the book's "unexpected" findings, "Crawl, walk, run can be a very effective approach, even during times of rapid and radical technological change."

I doubt that Gillette, one of the 11 companies profiled, would agree with either of these sentiments today. In recent years, it has been given a haircut by online shave clubs and watched its revenues get pummeled. Note the startling correlation between the 80 percent who didn't mention technology and the 82 percent whose fortunes have either diminished or tanked—thanks to technology.

It's fun to pick on Gillette, as the company's founder, King Camp Gillette (yes, that was his name), also had ideas about the future, and his were particularly idiosyncratic. Gillette was a utopian socialist. His 1894 book, *The Human Drift*, suggested that all industry should be taken over by a single corporation owned by the public, and that everyone in the US should live in a giant city called Metropolis, which would be powered by Niagara Falls. He went as far as to develop a prospectus for building out this vision, even offering the company's presidency to Theodore Roosevelt. Roosevelt declined the million dollar salary offer. In any case, Gillette's fantasies of a single "World Corporation" promising to eliminate the evils of competition didn't dull his otherwise sharp business sense, which he applied to a more pedestrian objective:

> **Order and regularity make for predictability precisely because they are low-information, low-entropy states, devoid of any friction or surprise. They're also devoid of imagination, creativity, or innovation, which are antithetical to stability!**

revolutionizing the way people shave. No doubt Gillette's current management has thought from time to time about that competition-free utopia.

It fascinates me that the companies doing the disrupting today are getting disrupted themselves before they've even had the opportunity to mature. And that's because innovation is happening now at an exponential pace. By the same token, single companies are disrupting multiple industries at once. Returning for a moment to the example of Uber, the company is not only disrupting the taxi and limo industry, but other forms of delivery logistics as well. But their advantage can also quickly evaporate. The value of Uber's massive driver network may disappear when the self-driving car becomes the dominant paradigm. Instead, car manufacturers will be in the driver's seat—or rather, in control of the driver's seat. If even a couple of these automakers put their heads together, they'll instantly have a bigger driver network than Uber can ever create, and then Uber will be gone.

Tesla could become Uber today. Uber knows this, and actually offered to buy Tesla's entire output of 500,000 cars in 2020. Apparently, Musk didn't return Kalanick's call. What Musk did do, though, was bar Tesla owners from using their cars for ridehailing, taking Uber completely out of the Tesla equation. Musk then announced plans for the Tesla Network—a managed ride-sharing platform that would dramatically slash the cost of Tesla ownership. Most cars sit idle most of the day. Under the program, Tesla owners will be able to exploit the economic utility of their cars, effectively allowing others to pay for them. So while Uber was an early mover in the highly disruptive ridehailing industry, by the time it matures, it'll be that much closer to itself being disrupted. Indeed, the entire auto industry is ripe for disruption, particularly with changing attitudes toward car ownership. That's one reason GM invested $500M in Uber's ridesharing competitor, Lyft. In any event, both Uber and Lyft will become less differentiated over time. And they could both get wiped out when automakers figure out that they can make more money and create higher valuations via ridesharing with autonomous cars than selling the cars outright.

Indeed, all the automakers may need to rethink the nature of car ownership as cars evolve from symbols of independence and identity to mere utilities. In 15 to 20 years, cars will no longer be driven by humans—they will have been legislated off the highways. And this will be necessary because autonomous cars will be able to travel at speeds of 120 mph or more—and tailgate as they go—because they'll all be connected and communicating with one another, operating with a hive-like mind. There's certainly no room for human interlopers in this scenario.

Moreover, the tipping point will come when less than a third of vehicles are fully autonomous, as their safety record will have been established by then. What's more, these autonomous fleets will likely be manufactured, owned, and operated by the automakers, with the market being primed by the Ubers and Lyfts of the world, as well as the trucking and delivery companies. (Why do you suppose Tesla introduced an electric semi?) To those of us who love driving, this prospect has a sad note to it, but digital natives are already taking to the idea. In 20 years, there may be virtually no resistance at all.

In the meantime, imagine how other dominoes will fall with this development. For example, if cars are no longer idle, but circulating with demand, then all the parking lots can be developed into real estate for affordable housing, tipping the real estate domino. And with the rise of telecommuting, people will no longer have to live close to their workplaces. Distance won't matter, because they could be holographically present anywhere. (Holographic telepresence platforms are already proliferating, allowing people to appear in virtually any location without physically being there, speaking and interacting in real time.) These trends are already starting to disrupt the real estate industry. But we're just getting started. We haven't even considered the impact that 100 percent electrified transportation will have on the oil industry—or what it will mean for the electric utilities—to say nothing of the fates of the bumper sticker, meter maids, auto mechanics, and tailgate parties!

> **We're just getting started. We haven't even considered the impact that 100 percent electrified transportation will have on the oil industry—or what it will mean for the electric utilities—to say nothing of the fates of the bumper sticker, meter maids, auto mechanics, and tailgate parties!**

On a more serious note, another not-too-distant goal of self-driving cars is the possibility of a zero-accident future. What happens to the automobile insurance industry when there are no more accidents? How will the auto and life insurance industries be impacted when self-driving cars eliminate the 35,000 road fatalities every year in the US alone—more than 90 percent of which are caused by human error? And with nearly as many patients in the US receiving organ donations—many of which are sourced by road fatalities—how many lives will be lost as a result of those zero-accident cars? Imagine how this might accelerate innovations in organ generation and transplant technologies.[1]

All of these issues are the consequence of just one innovation: the self-driving car. Now, combine a slew of similar technologies, and you can start to see how many other industries will be disrupted in just the same ways.

Again, what this means to the entrepreneur is a never-ending stream of opportunities. Is someone ahead of you? Don't worry—you'll have the chance to overtake them in five years. It doesn't matter which market you choose, you can always disrupt the current market leader.

> **A lot of what passes for disruption today, though, is merely trendy. A disruptive product is not merely better, faster, or cheaper. Competitors can easily respond to such evolutions, and they routinely do.**

None of these changes, though, happens in a vacuum. Every new technology and innovative business model can tip the dominoes across an entire industrial ecosystem. Not even the carwash is safe. On the heels of self-driving cars are self-*cleaning* (and also self-*healing*) cars! It's true! Nissan has developed a novel paint formulated with nanoparticles that generate a layer of air between the coating and anything the road might splash upon it. And should your car ever get a scratch, chitosan-based paint reacts to the UV rays of the sun, stimulating synthetic chains to form and bond with the other materials in the finish, filling in the scratch. Uh, oh, Maaco!

A lot of what passes for disruption today, though, is merely trendy. A disruptive product is not merely better, faster, or cheaper. Competitors can easily respond to such evolutions, and they routinely do. Real disruption is a different matter altogether. A disruption fundamentally changes how something is done, not only in terms of the enabling technology, but also in the innovation of the business model. By this definition, some argue that Tesla is actually not disruptive—the company doesn't offer solutions to problems that consumers can't just as easily satisfy with existing alternatives. Tesla may, however, become disruptive when it redefines the nature of car ownership. And the company has certainly disrupted the way new cars are conceived and manufactured. For example, Musk has approached car design with a radical software-centric development model that enables the company to add or delete features via remote software updates. Consequently, Teslas are the first cars to actually gain value *after* the sale. Besides that, Tesla disrupted the industry simply by virtue of entering it: prior to Tesla, the last domestic company to successfully enter the US market was Chrysler—in

1925! Today, Tesla is ranked as the world's fourth most valuable automaker, surpassing GM, Ford, and BMW.

But while disruption may profoundly alter industries and the companies that operate within them, that's really not the point. Disruption is an *effect*, not an objective. The moonshot entrepreneur's objective is always to create something that is not only new, but radically new—world-changingly new, to invent a term.

Disruption is something that happens to companies when the rules are changed in ways that create new, previously unimagined value for consumers. That said, if your eye is on disrupting the incumbents, then 1) what you're doing likely isn't really new, but a merely competitive or incrementally improved solution to a problem that is already adequately addressed, and 2) if your worldview is filtered through the perspective of the incumbents you're seeking to disrupt, then your vision will be inherently compromised, if not corrupted. Such an orientation will lead you to make very different kinds of decisions—and not necessarily very good ones—and could well blind you to the greater, truly disruptive opportunities.

So let's dispense with the word disruption. That's not the entrepreneur's organizing principle. Rather, let your North Star be a vision of the future that you want to create, irrespective of what anyone else might be doing. Your imagination is infinitely more valuable, important, and powerful than the old guard that may fall by the wayside as a consequence of your vision coming to fruition. Don't worry about them. The incumbents can't go where you're going anyway; they are not geared for it. And if they were to follow your moonshot, it would be at the cost of their legacy business and biggest customers. Anyone familiar with the concept of a quarterly report knows that's not going to happen.

> In my vision of healthcare, there is no need for pharmaceuticals. The pharmaceutical industry obviously can't say that. They are not free to imagine a world that obviates the need for prescription drugs.

When I contemplate a moonshot like making illness optional, for example, I have no baggage in tow, no revenue to protect, no shareholders to satisfy with reports of 10 percent year-over-year growth. This enables me to totally disregard the infrastructure that has grown up around the healthcare industry and reimagine things in a completely different way. In my vision of healthcare, there is no need for pharmaceuticals. The pharmaceutical industry obviously can't say that. They are not free to imagine a world that obviates the need for prescription drugs.

Yet this hasn't kept the pharma industry from taking note of what we're doing at my healthcare company, Viome. Let me explain. Current scientific literature clearly shows that chronic diseases including Parkinson's, Alzheimer's, depression, anxiety, obesity, diabetes, auto-immune diseases, and even cancer are caused by chronic inflammation. It turns out that these diseases are really just symptoms of a deeper underlying cause. Equally surprising is that the same research also establishes the key role played by the gut microbiome in controlling inflammation. But here's the problem: most drug companies focus solely on suppressing the symptoms of the chronic conditions, rather than understanding and treating their root causes. In the prevailing pharma model, they want one drug for each condition. This is why most drugs have an efficacy rate of only about 20 percent. In other words, 80 percent of patients taking the drug receive no benefit at all. Imagine selling a product that doesn't work for 80 percent of the customers, but is still being prescribed to people who are suffering.

Viome simply re-imagined this problem and decided to create one drug for each *person*, rather than one drug per disease. Our "drug" is nothing more than food and nutrition, which is easily personalized. Viome focuses on analyzing each person's gut microbiome, and modulating inflammation responses with precise and personalized nutrition to reduce its effects. And consistent with the findings of the scientific literature, our customers do indeed experience significant reduction and even reversal in chronic conditions. The point, in the context of disruption, is that I don't need to think of the pharma industry as a competitor in any way, shape, or form. If I do my job well, they will become irrelevant.

That, and maybe a match, is really all one needs.

---

1. There are more than 116,000 people on the national transplant waiting list at the time of this writing—considerably more than there are organs available. Consequently, 20 people die each day waiting for a transplant. In an effort to make up this gap, researchers recently created the first human-pig hybrids. The proof-of-concept work, published in the journal *Cell*, details how "human" organs could be grown inside non-human hosts, which could benefit hundreds of thousands of people waiting for organ transplants.

CHAPTER 8

You Don't Have to be a Rocket Scientist to Launch Your Moonshot

In the beginner's mind there are many possibilities, but in the expert's there are few.

—Shunryū Suzuki

"**N**EURALINK IS DEVELOPING ultra-high bandwidth brain-machine interfaces to connect humans and computers. We are looking for exceptional engineers and scientists. No neuroscience experience is required: talent and drive matter far more. We expect most of our team to come from other areas and industries ..."

So reads the homepage of Elon Musk's new neuroscience company, Neuralink. If there is one thing Musk knows, it's that if he is to achieve a moonshot in something as complex as invasive "brain-machine interfaces," the last thing he's going to need is experts in neuroscience.

While this may strike you as completely counterintuitive, as a member of the Board of Trustees at the XPRIZE Foundation, I can tell you that Musk knows what he is talking about. If there's one thing I've learned, it's that XPRIZEs—moonshots by definition—are almost always won by people and teams who have little or no expertise in a prize's domain. Why is that? It's because they don't know what *not* to try. These people attempt amazing things that everyone else in a particular industry assumes will *not* work.

Domain experts are very good at two things: 1) telling you why some things won't work, and 2) coming up with solutions to problems that are only incrementally better than the current state of the art. Worse, as their expertise grows, they begin to assume a mantle of conceit—"an iron gate" that admits no new knowledge or potentially expansive possibilities. And in the process, real, exponential, and entirely possible progress is stalled. As Max Planck lamented, "A new scientific truth does not triumph by convincing its opponents and making them see the light, but rather because its opponents eventually die." Science thus advances one funeral at a time. As we have seen, this was quite literally the case with Isaac Newton's discoveries in optics. It is no different today.

In short, don't ever look to an industry expert for a disruptive solution. Disruptive ideas come from outsiders. If you happen to be an expert, unless you believe that maintaining a marginally better status quo is the best and highest use of your intellect, you may find it difficult to achieve anything noteworthy in your field. If you are such an expert, do yourself and others in the world a great favor by going out and applying your expertise in a completely different area—a field where you have no domain-specific knowledge. Elon Musk and other moonshot entrepreneurs are waiting for you.

Following the disastrous Deepwater Horizon oil spill that spewed millions of barrels of oil into the Gulf of Mexico, BP was hit with a $20 billion settlement with the US Justice Department—a settlement that included a massive cleanup and restoration effort. To that end, BP employed the same oil spill recovery technology and techniques that Exxon used on the Valdez spill more than 20 years earlier. It wasn't very efficient then, and it certainly wasn't going to be any better on this exponentially larger disaster.

Several of us at XPRIZE wondered if there might be a better way to clean it up. It seemed we should be able to come up with something that would be at least twice as good as the existing approach. That conversation led to the Wendy Schmidt Oil Cleanup XCHALLENGE—a one million dollar competition designed to inspire innovative solutions to speed the pace of seawater surface oil recovery resulting from platform, tanker, and other industry spillage. The winning team ended up quadrupling the rate of surface oil recovery, and it was 99 percent efficient. But there's an even better story here.

One of the competing teams that made the finals comprised a tattoo artist, a mechanic, and a dentist. I know, this sounds like the start of a really bad joke. It turns out that one day the mechanic was getting a tattoo on his arm. The tattoo artist, making conversation, asked the mechanic if he had heard about this prize, wondering if he might be able to build a machine that could clean up an oil spill. The mechanic thought it over and said, "You know, oil involves a lot of drilling. I have a dentist who does a lot of drilling—I should go ask him what he thinks." The three of them actually got together on this, and the machine they built was, in fact, twice as good as the existing solution.

Likewise, I am not a rocket scientist, but that didn't keep me from founding Moon Express. Or Viome, with no credentials or training whatsoever in physiology, genetics, or healthcare. My status as a nonexpert has actually been my greatest asset as an entrepreneur. This is why I have never started two companies in the same industry, ever. Infospace, Viome, Intelius, TalentWise, BlueDot, and Moon Express are quite dissimilar. Every company I have started was not only in a different industry from the last, but an industry that was completely new to me. My belief is that once you become competent in a particular domain, you can only improve it incrementally—you can never disrupt it. Disruption happens when someone who has no idea about your industry begins to challenge the very foundations of everything that the experts have taken for granted.

The moonshot entrepreneur wants to demolish the prevailing systems and recreate them without all the accumulated baggage that invariably attends those systems. Moonshots are possible only because audacious entrepreneurs are able to look at a problem from a perspective that the experts have never considered. Thinking in the abstract is something the industry expert can no longer do. And they have their expert brain to thank for that.

> " Once you become competent in a particular domain, you can only improve it incrementally—you can never disrupt it. Disruption happens when someone who has no idea about your industry begins to challenge the very foundations of everything that the experts have taken for granted. "

The brain is the best pattern-matching machine ever created. When an expert is faced with a problem in his domain, he finds an exact match in his historical pattern-matching repository, and perhaps modifies it a bit to fit the situation at hand. The nonexpert, on the other hand, lacks that pattern-matching repository. Consequently, the nonexpert brain will not find a match, and it will be forced to move further up in its hierarchy, becoming increasingly abstract as it goes. In the process, with a little help from imagination, it begins connecting different dots and other possibilities that have never before been combined, and *voilà!*—a radically new and creative idea is born. And the expert said it couldn't be done.

It turns out that qualities like imagination and creativity have life cycles of their own. As people accumulate knowledge in their respective fields, they become increasingly constrained by that knowledge, as well as by their practices and thought habits. They develop a "way of doing things" that may or may not be amendable to new problems that require completely different thought processes and approaches.

I am admittedly painting a picture of experts here with a very broad brush. Not all experts are alike. That said, experts do tend to fall into one of two camps: those who approach problems *conceptually* and those who approach them *experimentally*.

Conceptual thinkers ask very *specific* questions and then *quickly* solve them deductively, that is, by making reasoned inferences. The experimenters, on the other hand, ask *general* questions, which they solve inductively *over time* by amassing evidence that supports their conclusions and serves new generalizations. What do these differences mean to the moonshot entrepreneur as he builds his team? In short, the world.

First, to be fair to the experts, let's clarify one important detail. Conceptualizers and experimenters peak at very different points in their careers, particularly when evaluated within a single discipline. When Einstein quipped, "A person who has not made his great contribution to science before the age of 30 will never do so," it was with a decided bias toward the conceptual thinker. On this score, he, too, was painting with a very broad brush.

> As people accumulate knowledge in their respective fields, they become increasingly constrained by that knowledge, as well as by their practices and thought habits. They develop a "way of doing things" that may or may not be amendable to new problems that require completely different thought processes and approaches.

It is true that for conceptual thinkers, breakthroughs tend to come early in their careers. This is natural, considering that conceptual or theoretical work can proceed apace, unburdened as it is by years of painstaking empirical research. Youth, however, does confer a kind of advantage upon the conceptual thinker: the younger he is, the less knowledge he has accumulated, and thus the more likely he is to challenge the norms and assumptions of his field. In other words, he still doesn't know what "can't be done." But herein lies a trap: having now made his "great contribution," he is instantly transported across the divide. He is now an expert, and therefore, an incrementalist. He now knows too much—he has eaten the fruit of the tree of knowledge, and his knowledge is now more a hindrance than a help. His exponential mindset has become a linear one. No more radical new abstract ideations that are key to breakthrough innovations will be forthcoming. Having thus been exposed to the kryptonite of his expertise, his best work is now behind him, like the old athlete who lives on the mental reruns of his game-winning shot in the final seconds of the homecoming game.

Moonshots happen when curious ignorance meets inspired imagination— qualities the expert now lacks. He is now on the downslope side of the inverted-U curve, where knowledge has extinguished inquisitiveness and, with it, his taste for discovery. But it doesn't have to end like this. Our expert will suffer this horrible fate *only if he remains within his field of expertise!*

Indeed, there is nothing like "knowing it all" to kill one's imagination. That's nothing more than a shortcut to closed-mindedness. Why keep looking when you've already seen it all? Sadly this also comes at a great cost to one's sense of wonder and curiosity—of being an awe-struck beginner.

Steve Jobs realized in retrospect that getting fired from Apple was the best thing that ever happened to him. "The heaviness of being successful," he said, "was replaced by the lightness of being a beginner again, less sure about everything. It freed me to enter one of the most creative periods of my life."

It's true that experts tend to have very narrow points of view. They actually know surprisingly little outside their areas of expertise. Astrophysicist Martin Rees calls out his peers on this point, characterizing them as "depressingly lay outside their specialties." Being so focused, they never build the essential capacity for cross-pollination that comes with cross-discipline collaboration that in turn gives rise to novel and potentially exponential ideas. They are so far down their respective rabbit holes that they never see the light of day.

This is precisely why conceptual thinkers, once having made a significant breakthrough in one field, need to come out of those holes or down from their silos (or ivory towers) and jump into fresh fields where they can once again engage their natural propensities for imagining extreme departures from existing conventions—where they can once again become that unencumbered upstart brimming with big ideas. Or they can stick with their cronies, grow long, grey beards, and become cynics in academia, like their fellow extinct volcanoes.

But what about the experimenters? Are they a horse of a different color? It turns out that unlike the conceptual thinkers who outlive their creative shelf lives, experimenters are just getting started *because* they have accumulated a critical mass of knowledge in their fields. In fact, the more knowledge they gain, the more creative they become! Their tentative but methodical trial-and-error processes work to yield increasing levels of clarity, ultimately delivering the long-sought epiphanies. The downside to this process, in times of rapid change, is the long gestation period that experimenters have historically required. But new practices enabled by high-throughput experimentation techniques can dramatically compress these otherwise long timescales, perhaps even making experimenters temporally competitive with their conceptually driven peers.

While experts are busy generating new knowledge, this is not where the real value lies. Conventional wisdom says that knowledge is power, but this is no longer true. Knowledge has become commoditized, and is increasingly so. There's so much of it, in fact, that it can scarcely be digested—even when it concerns a given expert's domain. The moonshot entrepreneur's concern is the service to which that knowledge can be put in pursuit of a larger goal—an audacious goal whose objective was originally framed by a question—a big "what if" kind of question. Today, the ability to conceive substantive *questions* is power. We are drowning in knowledge but thirsting for questions. Can we count on the experts, conceptual, experimental, or otherwise, to ask the right questions? I don't think so. And the reason goes to the heart of what's wrong in science.

○ ◐ ● ◑

Scientific, technical, and medical (STM) journal publishing is a $10 billion industry trapped in a 17th-century mindset. And the entire STM community is complicit. They continue to buy into this antiquated model because they have been led to believe that there is no other viable option for getting published in a way that can help them advance their careers, gain tenure, or obtain funding for their research. *Even though they know that science is ultimately harmed by it.*

As for authors who have been denied entry into the top journals (and with a rejection rate greater than 90 percent, there are more than a few of them), many cite that the failures were not due to the shortcomings of their science, but rather entrenched editorial boards who are nearly always appointed for life, editorial members who have extraordinary personal biases for what they want published, and other editors who have agendas, often involving favors or *quid pro quo* favoritism to other scientists or special interests. What's more, they routinely marginalize anything that smacks of radical thinking or disruptive concepts.

This is borne out by the fact that no small number of jilted authors went on to win Nobel Prizes, thanks to their persistence in breaking through that artificial barrier. Famous examples include Enrico Fermi's seminal paper on weak interaction, Hans Krebs' paper on the citric acid cycle (aka, the Krebs cycle), Murray Gell-Mann's work on classifying the elementary particles, Peter Higgs' paper on what came to be called "the Higgs model," T. Maiman's report of the first operating laser, Richard Ernst's application of Fourier transform spectroscopy to magnetic resonance, and Donald Rubin's model for inference and missing data, which is of particular interest to artificial intelligence.

> **We are drowning in knowledge but thirsting for questions. Can we count on the experts, conceptual, experimental, or otherwise, to ask the right questions? I don't think so.**

This is a state of affairs that dates even prior to John Harrison's brilliant but nearly blocked solution to finding longitude at sea. Thankfully, he also persevered and ultimately prevailed against the tyranny of the scientific salon of his age. Sadly, the situation persists to this day. Something is wrong with the peer-review system when an expert reviewer considers a manuscript to be "not of sufficient interest" and that manuscript later becomes a classic in its discipline. Contrary to reports by the American Association for the Advancement of Science and the National Academy of Sciences, publication in a peer-reviewed journal is not necessarily the best means of identifying valid research. Indeed, the process is under assault from many critics who say it is ineffective at filtering out poor research, while it perpetuates predictable work at the expense of more imaginative thinking. In the long run we all suffer, argues Don Braben of University College London, because "economic growth depends on unpredictable scientific advances."

For these reasons, Randy Schekman, the American biologist who won the Nobel Prize in Physiology or Medicine, declared, "I have now committed my lab to avoiding luxury journals [e.g., *Nature*, *Cell*, *Science*, etc.], and I encourage others to do likewise. Just as Wall Street needs to break the hold of the bonus culture, which drives risk-taking that is rational for individuals but damaging to the financial system, so science must break the tyranny of the luxury journals. The result will be better research that better serves science and society."

The problem is exacerbated by editors who are not active scientists, but professionals who favor studies that are likely to make a splash. Consequently, the journals artificially restrict the number of papers they accept, a policy that Schekman says drives demand "like fashion designers who create limited-edition handbags."

I don't fault the journal publishers—they have developed an extremely effective and profitable business model. Because the publishers benefit from the *pro bono* labor of authors and the "obligation" of peers to review "without compensation," it's a brilliant business model. And if you've ever had to pay the exorbitant costs of these journals, it makes for an even better revenue model. Notwithstanding, the academics and working scientists who freely contribute their work to the journal publishers continue to support a severely compromised method for disseminating important scientific discoveries. Remarkably, scientists have little to no interest in popularizing their science. For them, it's *Nature*, *Cell*, and *Science* or bust. It's a locked-in, play-by-the-rules cycle that by its very nature precludes anything that hints of potentially disruptive or exponential breakthroughs. Scientists have been well-trained to color within the lines.

In any event, STM content is certainly not easily accessible to lay readers and entrepreneurs who may actually be able to apply scientific findings in solutions to real problems. Sifting through this content requires a suite of sophisticated search strategies and content management tools just to be able to surface articles of interest to your moonshot. You've got to dig them out and make the connections yourself. AI, of course, is starting to change this.

○ ☽ ● ◖

As we pointed out earlier, XPRIZEs tend to be won by nonexperts. It is astounding how far a little incentivizing will go to drive creative and innovative solutions to difficult problems. The XPRIZE Foundation believes that you get exactly what you incentivize—and that without a target, you will miss it every time. Leveraging these two core tenets, the XPRIZE team designs and manages competitions directed toward solving the world's grand challenges. With prizes directed toward finding solutions in health, energy, education, the environment, and other areas, the Foundation casts their invitations to all comers. In other words, the crowd. No credentials of any kind are required to participate. In fact, challenges are framed in a way that don't require any specific domain knowledge. It is an approach that is radically disrupting the nature of R&D, and it is catching on.

When crowds engage with incentive challenges they bring with them unencumbered imagination, a wide variety of skills, a diversity of perspectives, a desire to explore and learn, and a competitive spirit as they work to develop innovative solutions to problems they care about. The deepest motivations are intrinsic. What's more, this motivation is available on-demand, immediately scalable, and incredibly productive.

Incentive contests are particularly helpful when a truly innovative solution might call for a combination of different disciplines, approaches, or thought processes. The more perspectives you can bring to your particular challenge, the better. As I've learned time and time again from my experience with the XPRIZE Foundation, it's often the case that the best ideas come from the most unlikely sources. Imagine running a hundred independent experiments in parallel, literally scaling up an army of innovative thinkers from a variety of fields around the world. Not only is this a powerful approach to R&D, it's amazingly cheap. And while you may end up awarding only a single solution, you'll also have the benefit of evaluating the many submissions, which can provide additional insights, particularly if the ideas are trending in certain directions.

There are numerous platforms available for managing such contests, including Topcoder (programmers), Kaggle (data science), and InnoCentive (innovation). They do the heavy lifting for you in recruiting participants and all the other logistical considerations that go along with such a service, including the transfer of intellectual property rights. But again, it is the diversity of brain power that they bring to bear on your problem. No need to choose between conceptual thinkers or experimenters; you've got the best of both worlds. More important, you get the perspectives of people who are outside your field, which may be just what you need to arrive at a breakthrough solution.

So enlist the crowd as surrogates for your experts. Who knows? You just might get better answers from a tattoo artist, a mechanic, and a dentist.

CHAPTER 9

Sailing True North

Whatever you can do or dream you can, begin it.
Boldness has genius, and magic and power in it. Begin it now.

—Goethe

ALL OUR KNOWLEDGE NOTWITHSTANDING, we would do well to know the great value of what Feynman called a "satisfactory philosophy of ignorance." Not only because ignorance creates the vacuum that impels our intellectual curiosity, but because we really don't have as many answers as we did a few years ago. The more we learn, the more we realize how very little we know. The frontiers of human inquiry are thus without limit, and they invite equally limitless freedom of thought. How then will we respond in a world of such unfettered freedom? Are there any paths that are barred to us? Is there any problem on God's green Earth that we cannot solve?

As entrepreneurs, we have a responsibility to push past the limits of our present experience, to expand the frontiers beyond those that we can see from our current vantage. Indeed, this is exactly what a moonshot accomplishes. For every impossibility it domesticates, new ones step up to take its place. Every attained end is at the same time the beginning of a new course. And one by one, we split the atoms of our unrealized human potential, releasing boundless energy to remake this world in a very different image.

We have billions of years of future ahead of us, but only one brief lifetime in which to leave our mark. Will we leave future generations an equally free hand to shape their worlds? I believe that we have both the power and the charge to do so. And we cannot leave that vital work to invisible hands or other forces to magically bring about that free and prosperous future while we passively or actively abet or hinder it.

Life is short, but not so short that it does not afford sufficiently generous measure to allow us to accomplish many great things—but only if that time is well invested.

Virtually every resource we need to run this world is either in abundance now, or soon will be. But the one thing we cannot renew, extend, or expand is time. Consequently I sleep less. I want to make the best use of every hour I have. There will be plenty of time to sleep when I die. In the meantime, what a way to live! Life is an amazing string of purpose-fueled experiences, yet many people lead lives of quiet—and not so quiet—desperation. For some, life is a burden; they hate their jobs, they are unhappy in their circumstances, there is no passion to light their way. But to what extent have they resigned themselves? How much time do they fritter away watching reality TV or chasing a little white ball around a course?

We all have exactly 24 hours a day to do with what we will. A day is a finite resource and it is distributed with perfect equality. Jeff Bezos or Bill Gates or Elon Musk do not have one minute more in their days than any of us. Is your time any less precious? The truth is that we dissipate so much of it on trivial pursuits and distractions, and then are surprised that it has passed away before we've awakened to the possibilities we've squandered. Indeed, unless we seize the day, it flees. As such, you should take nothing in hand without deliberate purpose—your very unique purpose. To this end, Marcus Aurelius wrote, "A man's true delight is to do the things he was made for. He was made to show goodwill to his kind, to rise above the promptings of his senses, to distinguish appearances from realities, and to pursue the study of universal Nature and her works."

What, then, were you made for? What is it that gives you the strongest sense of sailing True North? If it is something that resonates strongly with that sense, then it is a good thing and may in fact be *your* thing, a calling—the calling you answer with your life. Do you know what it is?

> " Life is short, but not so short that it does not afford sufficiently generous measure to allow us to accomplish many great things—but only if that time is well invested. "

If you are unable to answer that question just now, don't worry. All it means is that you have an exciting time of discovery ahead of you. But you do need to be deliberate about it. To be on this journey is really the greatest thing you can do for yourself and others.

If you find yourself casting about for this sense of purpose, here's a thought experiment that might help get you on your way. Imagine that you have everything you want—whatever it is—a billion dollars, a great house, the car you always wanted, a beautiful family. If you had all that, what would you do? The thing that you would do then is the thing that you ought to do now. If you would do that today, then there will be no need to be anxious for anything else—everything you'll need will come in due course.

To ask another way, what cause or dream or vision would you be willing to die for? If you would be willing to die for it, would you also be willing to live for it? Why is that the harder question?! *That* is what you ought to be doing now. And if that cause or dream or vision is big and audacious, then so much the better; it'll actually be easier to accomplish. We'll address this truth later, but trust me for the moment: the ambitious moonshot is actually easier to pull off than launching a small business.

For anything that you set out to do, then, ask yourself, if it succeeds, will it move the needle? If it doesn't move the needle, then it doesn't really matter. Just walk away from it. Elon Musk has put this question into a simple equation: "For anything you are trying to create," he explains, "what would be the utility delta compared to the current state of the art times how many people it would affect? Something that makes a big difference but affects a small to moderate number of people is great versus something that makes a small difference but affects a vast number of people. The area under the curve would be similar for those two things." What is the area under the curve that you want to affect with your moonshot? What part of the future state of the world do you want to own now? And what will be the future state of that world if you do *not* act? Either way, as we have seen, your decision will impact the future. So what will it take for you to flip the switch that sets the dream in motion?

> **Passion is never a static state, but rather is in constant need of renewal and rededication. Without this understanding one can fall into despair at the first affliction. And there will be affliction.**

Sadly, too many great ideas are spent dammed up against that critical switching threshold, never fully overcoming the many resistances they encounter. In other words, they never really "turn on," and consequently, they are powerless.

The power we're talking about here is passion. Dreams are all well and good, but without passion, that great idea will forever be stuck this side of the energy barrier. It is inert. Current doesn't flow, the concept isn't actualized, the purpose isn't realized, the big idea never sees the light of day—and many people will continue to suffer as a consequence. But if passion is lacking, then what? What is a life without passion to those who will not bother to discover and seize it?

We can no more explain a passion to a person who has never experienced it than we can explain color to the blind. Indeed, to not *will* deeply and sincerely and passionately is the mother of all sins—against yourself and others. It is the squandering of the unspeakable beauty of life and the untold potential it carries within to do a massive good in the world.

One cannot even begin to contemplate the idea of a moonshot without passion driving it. Without passion, you'll simply never stick it out. Without passion, no rational person would see it through. If you are not in love with your vision, you will fail for the simple reason that you will give up. But it is equally important to appreciate that passion is both a direction and a *becoming*. Passion is dynamic. Passion is never a static state, but rather is in constant need of renewal and rededication. Without this understanding one can fall into despair at the first affliction. And there will be affliction. But it is always easier to accept and withstand setbacks when you believe in your vision.

> If you can help other people to become successful, then you too will become successful. You cannot conquer the world, you can only serve the world. And if you do that, then you will have conquered something far more daring, bold, and audacious than the most ambitious of moonshots—you will have conquered yourself.

Moreover, no one does passion—or moonshots—without courage, the strong desire to live but with a readiness to die. As Chesterton wrote, "'He that will lose his life, the same shall save it,' is not a piece of mysticism for saints and heroes. It is a piece of everyday advice for sailors or mountaineers ... This paradox is the whole principle of courage; even of quite earthly or quite brutal courage. A man cut off by the sea may save his life if he will risk it on the precipice."

No doubt you're familiar with Teddy Roosevelt's *Man in the Arena*. It bears frequent reviewing. "It is not the critic who counts," he said, "not the man who points out how the strong man stumbles, or where the doer of deeds could have done them better. The credit belongs to the man who is actually in the arena, whose face is marred by dust and sweat and blood; who strives valiantly; who errs, who comes short again and again, because there is no effort without error and shortcoming; but who does actually strive to do the deeds; who knows great enthusiasms, the great devotions; who spends himself in a worthy cause; who at the best knows in the end the triumph of high achievement, and who at the worst, if he fails, at least fails while daring greatly, so that his place shall never be with those cold and timid souls who neither know victory nor defeat."

> **If, in executing your moonshot, you want to create a massive company, then you'll need to serve a massive market. If you want to create a billion dollar company, it's actually quite easy: solve a 10 billion dollar problem.**

That cold and timid soul who knows neither victory nor defeat is, for all practical purposes, dead to himself and to the world. This is a man who is without passion, and consequently dying in the most tragic of human conditions. Passion is the greatest gift of self-discovery, and ultimately the gift of service to others. If you've not yet found your passion, keep striving for it. Finding your life's passion is the result of relentless pursuit, exploration, discovery, development, and continual formation.[1]

Curiosity and interest may be the sparks that ignite your passion. But then you'll need to fan those sparks for them to catch fire. You'll need to engage them fully and in community with others. You won't discover your interests by navel gazing. But neither can you force the process. The best discoveries always seem to be made by experimenting, engaging with others, and being actively involved with the world and the wonders it offers. It's not something you can predict, but I can assure you that if you will place yourself in the stream of life, your passion will present itself.

This is far more than mere intention, it is *existential*. Nor is what we're talking about merely being goal-oriented. It's about how your passion is strapped to the cause of helping other people. In the end, if your passion is not ultimately directed toward serving others, then it's back to the drawing board. If only selfishly motivated, the rewards will be short-lived, and you will have cheated yourself and others.

There is a massive difference between becoming successful and becoming significant. Moonshots are about significance. And to this end, you've actually got the wind at your back. Our DNA is designed for us to be generous, altruistic, charitable. If you really want to work for yourself, work for the benefit of others. If you can help other people to become successful, then you too will become successful. You cannot conquer the world, you can only serve the world. And if you do that, then you will have conquered something far more daring, bold, and audacious than the most ambitious of moonshots—you will have conquered yourself.

◯◗●◖

A great idea is only an idea if it's not ultimately coupled to a plan for executing it. The moonshot entrepreneur may be audacious, but he's also pragmatic. So in the context of enabling the greatest good for the greatest number of people, how will you begin to think about the design of your moonshot?

Whatever it is that you seek to accomplish, you must begin with the end goal in mind and work backward as you build your plan. You create the future *from* the future, not the past. Knowing that your criteria may be completely different than mine, there are a few things I always look for in a moonshot opportunity. One point, though, on which there is no question, is that there is no shortage of big problems in desperate need of big solutions.

It is a perennial observation that we live in revolutionary times. When has the human race ever *not* been in some form of upheaval, boiling over with contradictions and chaotic forces running amok? Peruse the literature of any age and you will read the same refrain: a world in profound crisis manifested in desperation, cynicism, violence, conflict, fear, and doubt alternating with hope and belief, the yin and yang, the good together with the

> **"** **Everything begins with imagining the world *not as it is, but as you want it to be*. This is your vision—the "what" of your moonshot. Figuring out how to get there from here is your mission—the "how" of your moonshot. Fulfilling the promise is your purpose—the "why" of your moonshot. "**

evil—all are so entwined at times that it is difficult to distinguish the demons from the angels. So what is one to attack first? Disease? Pestilence? Hunger? Illiteracy? Substance abuse? Environmental crises? Economic opportunity? Clean water? Safety, security, and wellbeing? Corruption? Poverty? Each and every one of these issues impacts billions of people globally each and every day.

Indeed, the biggest problems in this world are social problems. If, in executing your moonshot, you want to create a massive company, then you'll need to serve a massive market. If you want to create a billion dollar company, it's actually quite easy: solve a 10 billion dollar problem. Take your pick! Many massive market opportunities are simply waiting for someone like you to wake up one day and make a decision that you'll do *something* about just one of them—any one of which constitutes moonshots worth dying for—and worth even more to live for.

When I wake up at 4:30 every morning, I know why I am awake. If I knew that I had only one year of life left, *this* is what I would be doing. It is what I *am* doing. And I certainly hope I have more than a year left of life to build it out. A little later in this book, we'll tour a few examples of moonshots that are underway right now—examples that can serve as models for your own moonshots. For the moment, though, bringing the previous chapters together to cohere on this one point, everything begins with imagining the world *not as it is, but as you want it to be*. This is your vision—the "what" of your moonshot. Figuring out how to get there from here is your mission—the "how" of your moonshot. Fulfilling the promise is your purpose—the "why" of your moonshot.

I can tell you that the promise will never be fulfilled with short-sighted visions, linear thinking, or incremental solutions. Again, starting with the end and working backward, it will become painfully clear that what is called for are solutions that are not only bigger, but *exponentially* bigger. Entrepreneurs easily fall into the trap of incrementalism when they focus on what is going on today—seeing the world *as it is*. Opportunities abound to contribute some small good through small, additive improvements to existing solutions. And so you are distracted. But because you quickly acquire so much knowledge about these various matters, you fall prey to the same kryptonite that neutered our experts.

Rather, look to this day as the singular, golden, and evanescent moment when you can be simultaneously fired by passion and unencumbered by knowledge. No history, no precedents, no biases, no evidence to the contrary—just wide open imagination and possibility. Ignorance in all its blissful glory. This is where you will find the seeds of the moonshot!

What's more, all the technology you need to start right now is available right now. New and emerging technologies are also being developed that you will intersect as they mature, and just when you need them—if you start today. Why start today if all the pieces may not yet be in place? Because you'll have no small number of intermediate goals to achieve along the way. You have infrastructure to build, data to collect, alliances to make, partnerships to forge, logistics to solve, agreements to negotiate, a team to assemble. When the missing pieces do come together—missing pieces whose trajectories you'll be tracking—you'll be ready for them, and able to receive and exploit them to the greatest degree possible.

This brings us to one of the key reasons why moonshots are easier to execute than conventional endeavors. When you can articulate a grand vision for something that others care about, you attract them to your cause. When you make that vision truly *visual*—that is, conveyed in a way that allows others to visualize in their own minds the world you're describing—then you also *inspire*. When they, too, can imagine this world *with* you, they'll also want to help you create it. When you share the secret, they become your enthusiastic co-conspirators.

Consider this, for example. What if your loved ones would never have to be sick again? Ever. We're talking about an end to cancer, Alzheimer's, Parkinson's—all chronic diseases—forever banished. Isn't that a world we'd want to create? Wouldn't it be lovely if we *could* create that world? An impossible moonshot? Maybe, maybe not. Maybe I have a secret. But it doesn't matter: everyone can imagine and certainly desire a world where their spouse or child or parent would always be in good health. Who wouldn't want to create such a world? It's a world anyone can visualize. And if it were possible—even remotely possible—it would be transformative. Wouldn't it just be cool?

This is the irresistibly attractive quality of a transformative purpose. It's not simply about another great idea, but a mission that others can believe in and get excited about—so excited that they'll be compelled to support the vision. And you, as a moonshot entrepreneur, would be the catalyst to make it happen.

Here's another secret. When you are able to inspire others with the vision for your mission, you stimulate the release of oxytocin in your listeners. The so-called "love molecule," oxytocin is triggered by such positive and stirring encounters, building trust and empathy, and motivating people to want to join you, to work together with you for common cause.

---

1. That said, Mark Cuban warns that the exhortation to follow one's passions is misguided advice. "It is one of the great lies of life," he says, simply because you might not be particularly good at the thing for which you have a passion. Rather, he advises, "Pay attention to those things that you devote time to; double down your investment there. The things I ended up being really good at were the things I found myself putting effort into ... Where you put in your time, where you put in your effort, those tend to be the things that you are good at." This topic is explored further in Chapter 12.

CHAPTER 10

Optimism and Other Self-fulfilling Prophecies

Today is cruel. Tomorrow is crueler. And the day after tomorrow is beautiful.

—Jack Ma

THE SELF-FULFILLING PROPHECY is defined as a prediction that directly or indirectly causes itself to become true—*by the very terms of the prophecy itself.* Self-fulfilling prophecies cut two ways, which serves to demonstrate the remarkable power of one's mindset, whether it is fundamentally optimistic or pessimistic. A self-fulfilling prophecy is powerful precisely because it is its own cause—bringing about its own realization via the positive feedback loop between a belief—even if that belief is false—and the resulting behavior. In the end, the belief, the behavior, and the ultimate realization are all part of the same cloth. We can see this clearly enough in hindsight, but the causal nature of the prophecy blurs the factor of time, which, rather than being linear, is circular.

Earlier we spoke of forecasting the future. The self-fulfilling prophecy, though, is not merely a prediction, it is a *cause.* A forecast is merely an opinion. But the self-fulfilling prophecy, like the collapsing of quantum options, is active and deterministic.

When people make self-fulfilling prophecies that are pessimistic in nature, they are based on the belief they have little to no control over the events in their lives. Not only is this dreadfully ironic (their expectation of having no control ensures that they'll have none), it is a deception. Every decision you make reverberates far and wide into the future—not only your future, but others' futures as well. The effects of your decisions are very real and powerful singularities. By your decisions you define, in a very fractal way, the very trajectories that your life—and the lives of others—will take.

The pessimist takes himself out of that future as a proactive agent. He surrenders himself to what he believes is the randomness of all events that are now completely out of his control or ability to influence. The pessimist surveys his past and, extrapolating to the future, concludes, "I've never seen things get better for me; why suddenly should that change?" And if he is unhappy with the state of that future, depression and despair follow. Pessimism, then, is both the cause and the result of resigning oneself to the belief that tomorrow will be no better than today—the belief makes it so. And it is disturbingly widespread.

People come to believe that human beings are too trapped by one element or another of embodiment to ever transcend their situations and arrive at a truth beyond the borders of their own lives. They conclude that their thought is so shaped by their culture, race, gender, and social and economic position that objectivity becomes nothing more than an elusive dream.

We see this thinking play out in entire communities that share a common set of expectations. Again, this cuts both ways. Like the snake that eats its own tail, the self-fulfilling prophecy also feeds on itself.

But prophecies that perpetuate negative or destructive cycles—poverty, single-parent homes, poor education, lack of opportunity, crime—are never cast in stone. They, too, are ultimately mental constructs, and as such, they are utterly at the mercy of one's will. A community, if it has the desire and will to do so, can graft a completely different narrative into its prophecy and thereby realize a very different future.

Indeed, identity is nothing but a nested set of narratives—narratives of who you are, what you can or cannot do. In the end, whatever it is that you think you can, or think you can't—you're right!

This is why the stakes of one's mindset are so unimaginably high. Infinitely high. Because, whether we realize it or not, we live on this planet like any other organism—with tremendous mutual dependence. Your mindset really isn't just your own business. Consequently, when you withhold a good, something vital is unfulfilled in the world. If people really understood their power and influence in this world, they would be quaking. But they don't, and they are not.

"We are all sad," said Richard Feynman, "when we think of the wondrous potentialities human beings seem to have, as contrasted with their small accomplishments. Again and again people have thought that we could do much better. They of the past saw in the nightmare of their times a dream for the future. We, of their future, see that their dreams, in certain ways surpassed, have in many ways remained dreams. The hopes for the future today are, in good share, those of yesterday."

Most people in this country have a disconcertingly pessimistic outlook on the future. According to the annual Rasmussen poll, a majority believes our best days are behind us. A WSJ/NBC poll asked the perennial question, "Will life for your children's generation be better than it has been for us?" Seventy-six percent answered no—the worst response ever recorded by the poll.

> "A community, if it has the desire and will to do so, can graft a completely different narrative into its prophecy and thereby realize a very different future."

But how does the level of optimism in America rank internationally? Surely, Americans must have a brighter outlook when compared with other countries. The answer? Just 6 percent of Americans believe the world is getting better. Chinese optimism, though, is comparatively off the scale! Meanwhile, the Europeans are the most pessimistic of all. What's going on here? What sorts of self-fulfilling prophecies are we in for?

Our institutions, from education to the media, promulgate and reinforce a mindset of pessimism each and every day. It's been going on for some time and is now well past the tipping point. Herman Kahn, writing in 1982, observed, "Almost every child is told that we are running out of resources; that we are robbing future generations when we use these scarce, irreplaceable, or nonrenewable resources in silly, frivolous, and wasteful ways; that we are callously polluting the environment beyond control; that we are recklessly destroying the ecology beyond repair; that we are knowingly distributing foods which give people cancer and other ailments but continue to do so in order to make a profit." In the end, people are discouraged, demoralized, more heavily regulated, and, well, resigned. Forget a dystopian future—by this standard, we're living in a dystopian present!

No one is disputing that we have problems and challenges. We do indeed have "many miles to go before we sleep." But are we also condemned to a culture of pervasive and corrosive pessimism and decline? Or can we resolve to create a very different narrative for our prophecy? What could possibly be a more important question for the sake of our children? Will we consign them to a world directed by false beliefs and hopelessness? Is our national philosophy now one that despairs of the possibilities *that could exist* by virtue of any human quality which a human being has ever exhibited?

The moonshot entrepreneur believes that such a dark worldview is not only entirely optional, but completely unfounded. It is simply not supported by reality. The fact is that by every objective measure, the world *is* getting better. Much better. The number of people living in poverty has never been lower. There are far more democracies in the world. Literacy has reached an all-time high. Higher food production and lower costs have put a massive dent in world hunger. Infant mortality rates have plummeted. We're on an accelerated path to electric cars and far less consumption of fossil fuels. Sanitation standards, life expectancy, air quality—it's all improving. Heck, even the giant panda is no longer endangered.

What passes for poverty in this country is actually a higher standard of living than the *vast* majority of Americans enjoyed less than a hundred years ago. The poor in this country have indoor plumbing, internet connectivity, access to massive numbers of services, free mobile phones, free healthcare, all the food they can eat. No one in this country ever has to go hungry. In every major city, the homeless can eat tens of meals a day.

There is simply no disputing that we are living in the best times in the history of humanity. And it's getting better. We have *far* more reason to believe in the power of human ingenuity to make it so than to believe we're headed for a massive fail. (Perhaps our perspective is distorted by virtue of living so high up in Maslow's hierarchy?)

We can blame the media for this universally gloomy outlook. We fall for it because we are wired to pay more attention to bad news than good news. Yet goodness, thanks to exponential technologies, is accelerating at a far greater pace. We just don't hear much

> " Our institutions, from education to the media, promulgate and reinforce a mindset of pessimism each and every day. It's been going on for some time and is now well past the tipping point. "

about it. When an airplane doesn't crash, you don't read about it in the papers. But you can be sure that just one incident involving a self-driving car—out of millions of incident-free miles driven—is sure to make front page news.

There is a common feature of these news reports: *experts*. As we've seen, experts tend to be pessimistic. Their knowledge of things as they *are* has closed them to the vast possibilities of what *could be*. Unfortunately, experts are also credible—particularly to an audience that has lost its capacity for critical thinking. While everything else has improved, intellectual honesty—along with curious inquiry—has really taken a hit. But this is really nothing new. John Stuart Mill lamented this state of affairs 150 years ago when he wrote, "I have observed that not the man who hopes when others despair, but the man who despairs when others hope, is admired by a large class of persons as a sage." What could be more pathetic?

Yet here's another paradox. We actually tend to compartmentalize the continuous barrage of negative news. We might grow more pessimistic collectively, but individually, we somehow believe we'll remain above the fray. And this "private optimism"—even in the context of public despair—is surprisingly robust.

This assumes, of course, that we have an optimistic disposition to begin with. Still, this private sunny outlook in the face of a world going to hell in a handbasket is counterintuitive. It turns out it's a fascinating function of an inherent human quality called *optimism bias*—our tendency to overestimate the likelihood of positive outcomes while underestimating the negative ones. Optimism bias explains life in Lake Wobegon, that mythical place where the women are strong, the men are good looking, and all the children are above average.

> **It is precisely because entrepreneurs see the opportunity in every difficulty that they are motivated to reach for the upper branches of possibility, to bring that otherwise unreachable fruit down to Earth.**

The reason for this apparent dichotomy comes down to a question of control. We naturally believe that we have more control over our individual, private lives than the collective, public state of the world. And that is unfortunate, because the state of the world is actually no less in our hands. But if we believe we are helpless when it comes to solving the world's great challenges, then we certainly won't be optimistic about anything getting better. Happily, as we've seen, the reality that the world *is* improving defies what would otherwise be a self-fulfilling prophesy. Human ingenuity and innovation have the power to overcome even the most entrenched of the doom mongers—those "nattering nabobs of negativism." The pessimists may not be aware of it, but the optimists are winning.

Clearly, things could be a lot better. And they will be. Much better. Exponentially better. But it won't be because the pessimists have a hand in bringing about that better future. Their concern is only to protect what they have or know—to keep the future at bay. They must, because as far as they are concerned, things are only going to get worse. And for them—in spite of the exponential improvements—it will be another prophecy fulfilled. Thus unprepared for this exponential future, they will indeed be marginalized. Try as we might, we cannot will the freedom of others who seek to hide from themselves the voluntary nature of their existence.

Of course problems will persist. The moonshot entrepreneur is not indifferent to the many evils in the world—both natural and unnatural. And there certainly is a distinction between being optimistic and being delusional. The optimist believes things will get better, but it's delusional to deny the existence of real suffering. As the old saying goes, the optimist believes that we live in the best of all possible worlds; the pessimist fears this is true.

It is precisely because entrepreneurs see the opportunity in every difficulty that they are motivated to reach for the upper branches of possibility, to bring that otherwise unreachable fruit down to Earth. This is the moonshot entrepreneur's journey, to navigate the convoluted and challenging terrain between hope and despair. It's *because* the moonshot entrepreneur is hopelessly optimistic that he ventures it. It is the core, enabling element. To him, optimism is the only rational response to the exponential possibilities that are now at hand.

If it weren't for the optimists, all the pessimists' worst fears of societal collapse—and worse—would surely come to pass. "So come!" says the old saint. "Never mind weariness, illness, lack of feeling, irritability, exhaustion, the snares of the devil and of men, with all that they create of distrust, jealousy, prejudice, and evil imaginings. Let us soar like an eagle above these clouds, with our eyes fixed on the sun and its rays, *which are our duties.*"

○ ☽ ● ☾

Humans have another fascinating capacity—one even more interesting than the optimism bias: from the comfort of our own living rooms, we can step into the time machine of our minds and walk the streets of the future we imagine—a future that begins simply by visualizing it. But if we're to overcome the pessimists' imaginings of the future, we'd do well to make our version of it easy for them to visualize as well.

In his paper *The Future of Humanity*, Nick Bostrom says, "We need realistic pictures of what the future might bring in order to make sound decisions." Well, there's the rub. What, exactly, constitutes a "realistic" picture of the future? Who will win the competition for it? Which version will prevail? The apocalyptic one or the utopian one? The one that meets the two extremes in the middle? What sorts of "sound decisions" would each of these entail?

Even Schopenhauer noted, "Every man takes the limits of his own field of vision for the limits of the world." These limits are precisely what the moonshot entrepreneur seeks to transcend. This arguing between optimists and pessimists over what invariably turns out to be different takes on conventional worldviews is like a gridlocked congress that accomplishes nothing. All the energy is lost in heat. We need to get up above these clouds, "eyes fixed on the sun and its rays." The moonshot entrepreneur believes we can escape the Flatland of linearity to obliterate the limits of our collective field of vision. The exponential thinking of the moonshot entrepreneur sets out to do nothing less than change all the ground rules. And that is the point. His vision works to hang a question mark on everything we have long taken for granted.

Some people claim that one's rational reason is taken hostage by optimism, that optimists act without sufficient evidence to support their conclusions. At question here is the word evidence, defined as "the available body of facts or information indicating whether a belief or proposition is true or valid." In the course of this chapter alone, we've laid out more than a dozen proof points on how the world is improving. Demonstrably so. The bigger question is what evidence are these naysayers willfully ignoring? Optimism isn't blind faith, but an embracing of hope driven by action and a refusal to acquiesce to the prevailing opinion that we, as a species, are on the slippery slope. To the extent that we are, optimists and entrepreneurs are actually doing something about it.

> The moonshot entrepreneur believes we can escape the Flatland of linearity to obliterate the limits of our collective field of vision. The exponential thinking of the moonshot entrepreneur sets out to do nothing less than change all the ground rules.

Pessimists, on the other hand, contribute nothing to improving outcomes. Their rational reason is actually taken hostage by irrational anxiety. In case anyone needs evidence on this point, research conducted at the University of Cincinnati showed that 85 percent of what subjects worried about never happened. Moreover, of the 15 percent of feared events that did come to pass, 79 percent of subjects discovered that the outcome wasn't so bad after all, and many even learned something worthwhile from the "dreaded" experience.

Pessimism is easy. It requires no effort or imagination. And the pessimist takes it as a pass. If he believes nothing can be done to solve big problems, then why even try? All he can do is wait for the other shoe to drop, so in the meantime, he might as well eat, drink, and be merry. The pessimist then absolves himself of any personal responsibility by assigning blame to someone or something else.

> **" Optimism isn't blind faith, but an embracing of hope driven by action and a refusal to acquiesce to the prevailing opinion that we, as a species, are on the slippery slope. To the extent that we are, optimists and entrepreneurs are actually doing something about it. "**

Take these points to their logical conclusions. Technological innovation is the driver of long-term economic growth. No innovation, no growth. No growth translates to stagnation. Our future prosperity is utterly dependent upon the innovations harnessed by forward-looking—and optimistic—entrepreneurs. Maintaining the status quo—or even worse, retreat—means certain death, the unsustainable consumption of resources, and ultimately, economic collapse. Where self-fulfilling prophecies are concerned, pessimism is nothing short of nihilism.

At least the pessimist can console himself: pessimists are never disappointed.

The foregoing notwithstanding, there is one species of pessimist that bears closer inspection—the so-called "defensive pessimist." In short, by anticipating everything that *might* go wrong and planning accordingly in order to avoid potential pitfalls, the defensive pessimist transforms fearful thoughts into positive action. Like garden-variety pessimists, they lower their expectations to help prepare themselves for the worst—but with one major difference: a positive purpose. Thus armed, defensive pessimists take proactive steps to avoid the potential negative outcomes.

This leads me to believe that the defensive pessimist is really just an anxious optimist. And in a way, the best kind of optimist—the kind you might actually want on your team. In the mind of the defensive pessimist, failure is a highly probable outcome, *and yet* because he has courage, convictions, and purpose, he proceeds anyway. And nine times out of 10, he succeeds.

Fools rush in where angels fear to tread. No wise optimist shuns this maxim. The greatly perpetuated myth is that entrepreneurs are risk-takers. This is nonsense. Entrepreneurs are risk-averse. The first order of any entrepreneurial venture is to de-risk it to the greatest extent possible. In this age of high-throughput experiments, rapid prototyping, sophisticated market testing techniques, crowdfunding community feedback, and other means of market validation, the failure to de-risk is nothing short of negligence. And the moonshot entrepreneur is the most risk-averse of them all, staging the execution of his vision across a series of intermediate goals, laying the pipeline, raising the scaffolding, building a critical mass of data, establishing channels, and reducing costs as he progresses toward the ultimate goal. He has, then, every reason for continued optimism. To all these ends, the defensive pessimist—I still prefer to call him an anxious optimist—can play a vital role. His innate skepticism ought not to be considered the enemy of optimism. Quite the contrary. It is optimism's ideal partner, as it serves to expose hidden potential. It helps to overcome the hardest parts in even the craziest of ideas.

> **The moonshot entrepreneur may ask the big "what if" questions—dreaming dreams that are so big that people think he's crazy—but there is not a more clear-sighted, perceptive, or discerning thinker on the planet. What's crazy is the short-sighted incrementalism of linear approaches to problems of exponential proportions—and believing they'll make any difference at all.**

The moonshot entrepreneur may ask the big "what if" questions—dreaming dreams that are so big that people think he's crazy—but there is not a more clear-sighted, perceptive, or discerning thinker on the planet. What's crazy is the short-sighted incrementalism of linear approaches to problems of exponential proportions—and believing they'll make any difference at all. Yet this is the best that the pessimist will ever hope for. And in doing so, he radically foreshortens the untapped power of human imagination, curiosity, imagination, creativity, ingenuity, innovation—and optimism. In times of great change, these are the greatest resources for taming the risks of an uncertain future.

Indeed, the alternative is no less than the end of history. "Everything beyond a certain distance is dark," writes Francis Fukuyama. "The end of history will be a very sad event. The struggle for recognition, the willingness to risk one's life for a purely abstract goal, the worldwide ideological struggle that called forth daring, courage, imagination, and idealism will be replaced by economic calculation, the endless solving of technical problems, environmental concerns, and the satisfaction of sophisticated consumer demands. In the post-historical period there will be neither art nor philosophy, just the perpetual taking of the museum of human history."

The light versus the darkness, optimism versus pessimism. Is this not the continuing story of human history? The optimistic entrepreneur wants only to shine light into that darkness, to illuminate a vision beyond a certain distance, to inspire a dream of a better future for everyone. Could it be that all really is light and we just need to remove the blindfolds? Is that not the true objective of the moonshot?

> " The optimistic entrepreneur wants only to shine light into that darkness, to illuminate a vision beyond a certain distance, to inspire a dream of a better future for everyone. Could it be that all really is light and we just need to remove the blindfolds? Is that not the true objective of the moonshot? "

When you wake up each morning, you get a fresh opportunity to make a choice. Will you choose to be happy or unhappy? If you bring an optimistic outlook to your day, I guarantee that you'll discover 10 reasons why your life is wonderful already and is only about to get better. On the other hand, if you default to pessimism, you'll be sure to find 10 reasons why your life, however wonderful, sucks compared to those you might envy or aspire to. How sad it is that the world's beauty is a stranger to so many people, and yet how close at hand it is—if only they had eyes to see it. The closing scene in the first season of HBO's *True Detective* brings this sentiment into most poignant relief in a conversation between the show's tarnished heroes:

Marty: "Didn't you tell me one time, dinner once, maybe, about how you used to ... you used to make up stories about the stars?"

Rust: "Yeah, that was in Alaska, under the night skies."

Marty: "Yeah, you used to lay there and look up, at the stars?"

Rust: "Yeah, I think you remember how I never watched the TV until I was 17, so there wasn't much to do up there but walk around, explore, and ..."

Marty: "And look up at the stars and make up stories. Like what?"

Rust: "I tell you Marty, I been up in that room looking out those windows every night here just thinking, it's just one story. The oldest."

Marty: "What's that?"

Rust: "Light versus dark."

Marty: "Well, I know we ain't in Alaska, but it appears to me that the dark has a lot more territory."

Rust: "Yeah, you're right about that."

Rust pauses, considering the point further.

Rust: "You're looking at it wrong, the sky thing."

Marty: "How's that?"

Rust: "Well, once there was only dark. You ask me, the light's winning."

CHAPTER 11

Ripples in the Pond of Possibility

Running a startup is like chewing glass and staring into the abyss.
After a while, you stop staring, but the glass chewing never ends.

—Elon Musk

S O WHY DOES THE ENTREPRENEUR DO IT? Why would anyone want to stare into the abyss while chewing glass? In short, it is because entrepreneurship is, more than anything else, a *calling*. Some might simply call it a passion. A calling, though, has an extrinsic aspect: while you might experience a calling or a passion as a strong inner impulse, it is also invariably accompanied by what seems like a divine influence, manifested as an inspired vision that takes hold of you and will not let you go. A calling calls you out. And when you answer that call, it blossoms as a motive life force, and so decisively so that you come to organize your whole world around it.

The entrepreneurial calling is important because it is that knock on the door that asks you to dedicate and bring to bear your unique qualities to solving the world's grand challenges. Everything you are and do is then lived out as a response to this strange and singular summons. And yet it is not deterministic. A calling, compelling though it may be, can always be denied. And sadly, it is denied far more often than it is affirmed.

As we saw earlier, people tend to live far within their limits—as if they have any idea what those limits actually might be. Their life habit is too often a retreat to comfort. Consequently, they energize far below their potential, completely unaware—or simply afraid—of their actual potentialities. There is no question that entrepreneurship is not exactly the path of least resistance. But entrepreneurs are more fully alive because as they engage radical possibility, they also align themselves to hope. Those who won't venture because of the possibility of failure align themselves to fear.

Fear is one of life's greatest illusions. It does indeed require courage to allow oneself to be disillusioned of false but closely held beliefs, but it is the only way they can be dispelled. Of course many desire the visible aspects of successful entrepreneurship, but few are willing to commit themselves to the entrepreneur's path. They want the benefits without the costs, and yet they are oblivious to the costs—to themselves and the world—that they're actually paying to play it safe.

The truth is that there can be no passion without struggle. While the entrepreneur's optimistic vision is impelled by infinite possibility, his passion nonetheless can also be marked by dread—the dread experienced as "the dizziness of freedom." Hard decisions are made in fear and trembling, and always accompanied by the sounds of gnashing glass.

○ ◑ ● ◖

The entrepreneur knows it is his responsibility to determine what he ought to do. As an entrepreneur with existentialist sensibilities, he knows that "existence precedes essence," meaning it is up to him to determine his purpose in life. Once he decides, he moves and acts accordingly. Only when he answers his "call to be" does his essence emerge as a true self-realization. Otherwise, he lives in bad faith. The other ready alternative is to live by the expectations of others. Most people do, in fact, live by concepts developed by other people and handed down to them. And consequently, they become exhausted by an ambition that always hangs upon the decisions of others.

> **Most people live far within their limits—as if they have any idea what those limits actually might be. Their life habit is too often a retreat to comfort. Consequently, they energize far below their potential, completely unaware—or simply afraid—of their actual potentialities.**

It is tragic how few people truly possess themselves in life. Most people seem to live vicariously, think the thoughts of others, and live lives that are essentially a mimicry, a quotation.

This sentiment was punctuated by Steve Jobs in his 2005 Stanford commencement address. "Your time is limited," he said, "so don't waste it living someone else's life. Don't be trapped by dogma—which is living with the results of other people's thinking. Don't let the noise of others' opinions drown out your own inner voice. And most important, have the courage to follow your heart and intuition. They somehow already know what you truly want to become."

These thoughts not only embody the first principles of existentialism, they are the first principles of entrepreneurship. Each and every one of us has the opportunity to construct our lives and significance in ways that are utterly unique and special. And we are absolutely free to choose to *will* our existence, which, even while finite, is ever open to the infinite. To choose *not* to choose is still a choice for which you are solely responsible.

> **These thoughts not only embody the first principles of existentialism, they are the first principles of entrepreneurship. Each and every one of us has the opportunity to construct our lives and significance in ways that are utterly unique and special.**

But again, as we have seen, it's not just about us. While man is certainly responsible for what he is, he is, by virtue of his decisions and actions, responsible to all men. In actualizing the fullness of possibility, he fashions a new image of man—one that is empowered to do likewise, giving rise to new meaning in the world. It's a mystery as to how life works, but whenever you commit yourself to something, you are not only choosing for yourself, but at the same time deciding for the whole of mankind. Herein lies a man's profound responsibility. Yet this awesome realization turns hubris into equally profound humility. Man's choice truly does involve mankind in its entirety.

I'm as big a fan of Ayn Rand's *The Fountainhead* as anyone, but the sensibility we're discussing here lies in stark contrast to the corrupted existentialism of Rand's characters—protagonists portrayed as heroic figures who stand by their principles and live on their own terms, and to hell with everyone else. Rand calls this the "virtue of selfishness." Such a person may certainly change the world, but it won't necessarily be for the better.

○ ◐ ● ◑

Is it true that man is essentially only concerned with "gratifying needs and satisfying drives?" Are we "self-actualized" when we do? Is that it? Or is human existence more fundamentally directed to something, or someone, *other* than itself? If so—and I prefer to believe that this is the case—then does it also follow that self-actualization can also be a byproduct of self-transcendence? If this is true, then one's "search for meaning" would displace his "search for himself"—and to world-changing effect. I believe it does, in fact, work this way. It's true that the more one forgets himself, allowing himself to be absorbed in causes other than himself, the more he actually *becomes* himself. In this way, doing good and doing well are by no means mutually exclusive. In fact, they are absolutely *mutually dependent* if we are to bring about a different vision for the future. It seems to me that this is existential in the highest degree!

> ❝ **The point is that each person's pride is in competition with everyone else's pride, and the end result is that the prideful suffer without benefit. Complete self-confidence is, therefore, a weakness.** ❞

The opposite is a corrosive Randian pride that consists in drawing one's strength entirely from oneself. The prideful cut themselves off from their fellow men, making for inevitable breakdowns. Their destructiveness, as history shows time and time again, comes back on themselves. The point is that each person's pride is in competition with everyone else's pride, and the end result is that the prideful suffer without benefit. Complete self-confidence is, therefore, a weakness.

Only the humble can count themselves among the truly successful. The entrepreneur who has tasted the bittersweet quality of humility has learned that he must purge every shred of arrogance if he is to truly actualize his potential and realize his great purpose. Faults and failures will then turn to good, and discouragement will be a stranger. Discouragement, after all, is simply the despair of wounded pride. The best way of profiting by the humiliation of one's own faults is to face them in all their glory.

The true rite of passage in life occurs with the death of egotism; maturity begins when one begins to live for others. This is no less true for the entrepreneur—and especially so for the moonshot entrepreneur. Humility in no way means hiding our talents and virtues or in thinking little of ourselves, but in possessing a clear knowledge of our shortcomings (of which there is no shortage. If you are to boast, then boast that you have more of them than anyone else!). In fact, true audacity of vision requires humility. The fact is, the entrepreneur cannot endure his own littleness without translating it into meaningfulness at the greatest possible scale!

This is the paradox. There is indeed unimaginable power in humility. Humility releases a very different and attractive kind of energy. And it's a hell of a lot harder to acquire than pride, which requires no effort at all. Unfortunately, though, for the same reason that most people energize far below their capacity, nothing in the world is more repulsive to a man than to take the path that leads to humility.

Of all the things the entrepreneur must manage, none is harder than the management of himself. The challenges of daily living meet their matches in temperament, expectations, weaknesses, and temptations. It is appropriate then, not only for the entrepreneur—but certainly for the entrepreneur—to shift focus from time to time from the externally oriented activism of his mission to a bit of private, self-addressed activism.

Indeed, one can change the world through one's discoveries and cleverness; one can even explain the whole of nature and yet not understand himself. Everyone dreams of changing the world, but few realize that the process begins with changing oneself. Instead, we live by the many unexamined assumptions that form our defaults, never considering that, even in the shadow of massive human potential, the unexamined life really is not worth living.

> " The entrepreneur who has tasted the bittersweet quality of humility has learned that he must purge every shred of arrogance if he is to truly actualize his potential and realize his great purpose. Faults and failures will then turn to good, and discouragement will be a stranger. "

Yet think of the benefits when we do. These existential orientations are vital to the entrepreneur because they help him define not only himself, but the company he creates—a company that is distinguished from all other companies by virtue of its deeply examined mission and purpose. When entrepreneurs are able to convey their essence *and existence* in this way, they naturally connect more deeply with their constituencies.

Disruption can only be countered by a radical self-awareness. "Why are we here and why should anyone care that we exist?" are the questions organizations should unceasingly ask. Most don't take this path because the answers are often uncomfortable. But failure to do so may ensure their irrelevance and ultimate vulnerability to disruption.

The dearth of such active and intentional mission-driven visionaries leaves us—and the world—with a big problem: there are not enough conscientious entrepreneurs to meet the growing scope of problems that need solving. We've got an abundance of everything else, but we've got a critical shortage of the special breed of entrepreneurs who are willing to join that "worldwide ideological struggle that calls forth daring, courage, imagination, and idealism." The harvest is great, but the workers are few. And while many are called, since so few *choose* to be chosen, few *are* chosen. "But never doubt," as Margaret Mead once said, "that a small group of thoughtful, committed citizens can change the world; indeed, it's the only thing that ever has." And the opportunity has never been greater.

> This is the paradox. There is indeed unimaginable power in humility. Humility releases a very different and attractive kind of energy. And it's a hell of a lot harder to acquire than pride, which requires no effort at all.

Whether that opportunity exists in the world and is simply waiting to be discovered or does not exist until an entrepreneur creates it, hardly matters. What matters is the entrepreneur's response to the opportunity, when and however it is encountered. But opportunities are encountered only by those who are able to perceive them; they resonate only when they are in tune with the purpose one has chosen for his life.

The fact that you're reading this book tells me that you are or aspire to be one of this small, thoughtful, and committed group of entrepreneurs. If I may, let me venture to tell you who you are. For starters, unlike those who seek instant gratification, you know the power of the long view. You love ideas. Big ideas. You're not one to shrink from change. In fact, you embrace change, because, in spite of any anxiety you might feel about it, you recognize that opportunity is inherent in change. You are also innately curious; therefore, you are continually learning, constantly exposing yourself to ever more ideas and opportunities. What's more, you're not content to merely work for wages; you seek a much bigger prize. And finally, you relentlessly challenge the status quo—and yourself—by daring to ask, "*What if?*"

And if you find yourself lacking in any of these qualities, you can learn them.

If you're willing to search, you will discover the passions for your life that drive you to develop and deepen them. There is, after all, a certain discipline to hope.

At the end of every day, I ask myself, did I get just a little bit better intellectually, emotionally, or spiritually? If not, then I resolve to try harder tomorrow. And to prepare myself for such daily improvement, I start each day in meditation. When you set out to improve a little each day, eventually big things happen. But this, too, is a discipline. If you're only out for the quick, big improvement, you'll never develop the muscle to sustain it. There are no shortcuts to meaningful personal change that lasts.

Likewise, just as our cells change day by day, so ought our minds—one day at a time. We actually have very few cells that we had just five years ago. By the same token, as we constantly push the limits of our intellectual curiosity, we should find that we don't have as many *answers* as we did a few years ago either. Our bodies change, the world changes, our questions change. And through it all we are continuously renewed—body, mind, and soul. But while we work to solve the mysteries of the world—and the universe, for that matter—what a mystery *we* remain! We are, indeed, the most enigmatic of unexplored territories. What I can promise you is, if you will venture into this territory, you will discover when you arrive a heretofore unrealized capacity for possibility. Radical possibility. On the other hand, if you don't know or care where you're going, then any road will get you there.

○ ◑ ◉ ◐

What is it to believe in something that does not yet exist, has no proofs, cannot be examined, measured, or even seen? It means that if we believe in it because we can conceive it, then we must create it! In the act of creating we pass from imagination to faith to knowledge. More important, in the end, we learn that the nonexistent is whatever we have not yet sufficiently desired or imagined. To imagine is to be born anew every day.

We live in a finite world, but imagination makes it seem infinite. Even a small amount of imagination—or faith the size of a mustard seed—can move mountains. Radical possibility feeds on this type of faith.

> **The harvest is great, but the workers are few. And while many are called, since so few *choose* to be chosen, few *are* chosen.**

Faith, like curiosity and imagination, is not an opinion but a *state*—a way of being and doing. Faith transcends the limits of the present reality. It enables us to imagine a different, better future, and then believe that it is actually possible. Through this faith, one is able to affirm himself, because he is affirmed by the power of being itself. This is the wellspring of the entrepreneur's courage.

Again, that's not to say that faith does not admit doubt. It does—and indeed, it must. Doubt merely tells us that we've found an edge to faith. And discovering that edge means to define it so that it, too, shall be traversed and extended. Doubt is a staple of the human story. It's also what drives us to continue to grow—to imagine ever greater heights, to keep pushing beyond. And we know we've gone just far enough when people again begin to tell us we're crazy.

> **If you will venture into this territory, you will discover when you arrive a heretofore unrealized capacity for possibility. Radical possibility. On the other hand, if you don't know or care where you're going, then any road will get you there.**

It is true that faith has a certain nonrational dimension to it, but that does not mean it takes flight from rationality. Reason is not the basis of faith, nor is faith a substitute for reason; instead, reason is the *servant* of faith. It is the mechanism by which we "figure out" how we will get from the impossible today to the possible tomorrow. As such, there can never be a conflict between faith and reason. To the extent that anyone suggests that there is, or insists on reason colonizing the domain of faith, then either his faith, reason, curiosity, imagination—or any combination thereof—is woefully deficient. As is his understanding of the nature of these two very different but amazingly complementary domains. But just as the entrepreneur seeks to mitigate risk, he is also determined to convert faith, through discovery, to knowledge, establishing as he does so new, further-flung outposts for a renewed exercise of faith. It's a faith that never stops questioning. Once you stop questioning, then that ever-reaching faith becomes static—a mere dogma. Science itself suffers this fate when it stops imagining. Whenever it declares "settled science," it moves itself into the dogmatic realm of scientism. The curse of the expert revisited.

The moonshot entrepreneur believes that by virtue of potential alone, anything can come to exist. Anything. We don't know what or how; we can't see the unseen. But we can always ask, what if? When the entrepreneur focuses his energies on that question, he frees imagination to do its creative work. And when he puts his hand to it, it starts a ripple. Amazing things happen from that little drop into the pond of possibility. That is the beauty of the audacious goal: it takes just one person to get it started, to suggest to the rest of the world what is possible.

No doubt, that fledgling ripple will encounter the interference patterns caused by other pebbles tossed into the pond— competing or limiting views of the future that seek to cancel out that hopeful start. Sometimes, though, the new ripples are actually in phase, and the combined energies increase the amplitude of the little ripple we initiated, creating a wave. If only it were always so!

There is a cult of optimism promulgated by Norman Vincent Peale's *The Power of Positive Thinking*. But let's be clear: the moonshot entrepreneur—even the most optimistic of them—is not given to the power of positive thinking. He is given to the power of positive *doing*. He knows that the moonshot is going to be difficult. In fact, the conventional wisdom is that what he seeks to accomplish is not merely difficult, but "impossible," and that he is "crazy" to even contemplate it. This is his starting point. And mere positive thinking is no match for this reality. Moonshots are not for mere dreamers.

Dreamers are seldom doers. Merely thinking and dreaming about the future actually makes people less likely to achieve their goals. Somehow our minds become satisfied that a goal is actually attained when it is still only a vapor. I'm sure you know a few dreamers. They talk a good game, but can they point to any results? Few can. For all practical purposes, they have already forgone the realization of their dreams. The most surprising counterintuitive idea is that when we take a realistic inventory of the obstacles that we believe impede the realization of our goals, we can actually hasten their fulfillment.

> **Reason is not the basis of faith, nor is faith a substitute for reason; instead, reason is the *servant* of faith. It is the mechanism by which we "figure out" how we will get from the impossible today to the possible tomorrow.**

Acknowledging obstacles forces us to engage directly with the reality of the current paradigm or state of affairs that might stand in opposition to our vision. Going into the headwind—and sustaining one's resolve—requires yet another vital character element: *grit.*

Psychologist Angela Duckworth has identified this characteristic as standing out above all others as a predictor of success, rating higher than social intelligence, higher than good looks, higher than IQ. "Grit," she explains, "is passion and perseverance for very long-term goals. Grit is having stamina. Grit is sticking with your future, day-in, day-out. Not just for the week, not just for the month, but for *years*. And working really hard to make that future a reality."

Earlier, we described the attributes of the moonshot entrepreneur that mark him as "one of the few." Now let us list the attributes that you *won't* necessarily find in the profile that marks the successful entrepreneur: talent, education level, experience, high IQ, age, gender, race, religion, parentage, expertise, wealth, zip code. For the entrepreneur, none of these things matters.

I've now described the entrepreneurial mindset to paint a picture of the moonshot entrepreneur as a curious futurist who imagines unexplored possibilities, and whose inspirational vision, faith, and humility attract others to join him. His grit then fuels his ability to make the impossible possible. All these characteristics can be learned through intentional practice. And, now for the best part: these characteristics age well. So well, they overcome innate talent.

To make it even clearer, we can reduce it all to a simple formula:

Skill X Perseverance X Purpose = Achievement

Put another way, the harder you work, the more talented you will appear.[1]

We want to pick off one more attribute here, and that is age. Whether it is creativity, optimism, imagination, or curiosity, the conventional wisdom says these qualities are found in abundance only in the young. There is a lot to support this view. Earlier, we noted that even Albert Einstein, who made his great discoveries while still in his twenties, told the world, "A person who has not made his great contribution to science before the age of 30 will never do so." Not only is this a

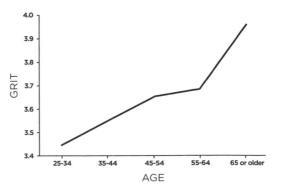

claim that no longer holds water, but youth actually has a serious downside. Comparatively speaking, younger people tend to have less grit. Older entrepreneurs, however, have it in spades. In fact, technology entrepreneur Vivek Wadhwa has researched old and young entrepreneurs and has found that older entrepreneurs tend to be more successful. People simply become grittier with age. Life has a way of doing that.

So there you have it: the two most overrated qualities in an entrepreneur—youth and talent. But that's not to say that we don't have an entrepreneurial generation gap. We most certainly do. And if we don't do anything to address this problem, it's beginning to look like moonshots just might skip a generation. And that would be tragic.

○ ◐ ● ◖

We all begin life as a *tabula rasa*, wide-eyed, taking in the world and making sense of it. Curiosity unimpeded, imagination unconstrained, creativity unhindered. Then the socialization processes begin. We learn the limits of the world—and our place in it, what we can and cannot do, what we're entitled to, what we have to fight for. But in the age-old arguments between nature and nurture, it's clearly not one or the other. The two go hand in hand for good and for ill. We also know that our natural curiosity is nurtured out of existence; our familial and community narratives chart narrow paths of possibility, socioeconomic conditions predetermine and reinforce continuing cycles of outcomes. Mindsets and world-views are formed and fixed. And just as one can never step into the same river twice, the age into which we are born determines the rest. And here we find massive differences in outcomes, as respective generations interact with the world as each of them finds and fashions it.

> **The two most overrated qualities in an entrepreneur: youth and talent. But that's not to say that we don't have an entrepreneurial generation gap. We most certainly do. And if we don't do anything to address this problem, it's beginning to look like moonshots just might skip a generation.**

For example, Baby Boomers, born between 1945 and 1965, came of age with rotary telephones and tube televisions—and only three local network affiliates. Our version of the tablet was the Etch A Sketch. Cars had big V8s and no seatbelts. The closest thing we had to the microwave oven experience was Jiffy Pop. We are the children of the so-called "Greatest Generation" that won the war, invented the suburbs, and put man on the moon.

> We all begin life as a *tabula rasa*, wide-eyed, taking in the world and making sense of it. Curiosity unimpeded, imagination unconstrained, creativity unhindered. Then the socialization processes begin.

Millennials, born between 1980 (their vanguard would come of age in the new millennium) and 1998, are the children of Baby Boomers. They entered a world that was vastly different from the one their parents inherited—a world that saw rapid technological development, a massive economic expansion, and the mainstream liberalization of society.

Generation Z (Gen Z) were born after 1998, making them the first true digital natives. Consequently, they see the world through the lens of technology, which, combined with their experience of the economic crash, has yielded a very different worldview than that of their immediate predecessors. Indeed, it is their approach to the world that will do the most to reshape the future. Gen Z will be wholly responsible for shaping the future of technology.

If you really want to follow the trajectories of technologies and trends that are now in accelerated motion, if you really want to know where the puck *will be*, you'd do well to factor in the impacts that these three overlapping generations will have as the future plays out. We'll start this assessment with the Millennials, as their contribution to our current state of affairs is of the greatest consequence.

Millennials get a bad rap these days. A really bad rap. Is it deserved? It is true that Millennials are gaining a reputation as being tough to manage or even motivate. Simon Sinek, who spends a great deal of time speaking to Millennial audiences, says, "They are accused of being entitled and narcissistic, self-interested, unfocused, and lazy—but entitled is the big one. Because they confound the leadership so much, leaders will say, 'What do you want?' And Millennials will say, 'We want to work in a place with purpose, we want to make an impact, we want free food and bean bag chairs.' ... And so Millennials are wonderful, idealistic, hardworking smart kids who've just graduated school and are in their entry-level jobs, and when asked, 'How's it going?' they say, 'I think I'm going to quit.' And we're like, 'Why?' and they say, 'I'm not making an impact.' To which we say, 'You've only been there eight months!' ... It's as if they're standing at the foot of a mountain, and they have this abstract concept called *impact* that they want to have on the world, which is the summit. What they don't see is the mountain. I don't care if you go up the mountain quickly or slowly, but there's still a mountain. So there is this institutionalized sense of impatience, no patience for the journey."

Duckworth, in a blog post, asks rhetorically, "What's wrong with Millennials? ... Why do they keep changing their minds about what they want to do with their lives? Why does even a hint of critical feedback send them into a tailspin of self-doubt? In a word, why don't they have more *grit*?"

Surprisingly, Duckworth, noting the correlation of grit to age, concludes with a big pass for Millennials. "So what's wrong with Millennials?" she asks. "Nothing. They just haven't grown up." I don't think this is correct. Moreover, this conclusion seems to lack a certain internal consistency with her greater body of work. Undoubtedly some will "grow up," but if they do, it will mean consciously, deliberately—and grittily—going against the very grain of their formation—a formation steeped in a sense of entitlement and easy answers. They'll have to summon tremendous courage, willpower, and perseverance over the long haul to pull off this "growing up." But these resources are notably in short supply within the greater Millennial mindset. Consequently, it's a conundrum that presents the greatest existential challenge for the Millennial generation. And they're going to need help. If Millennials fail to meet this challenge, they bear the risk of becoming increasingly marginalized as the inherently grittier, far more competitive Gen Z take their jobs and, in short, kick their collective asses.[2]

> **If you really want to follow the trajectories of technologies and trends that are now in accelerated motion, if you really want to know where the puck *will be*, you'd do well to factor in the impacts that these three overlapping generations will have as the future plays out.**

While age plays a role in one's grit aspect, observe that Gen Z are the youngest of the generational lots, and they are already displaying more grit than the others combined. Then again, perhaps they're just growing up a lot faster.

Gen Z is a fascinating demographic. While Millennials came of age in a time of great economic prosperity—and learning that getting whatever they wanted was easy—Gen Z came up through the Great Recession. They likewise learned from their parents' experience—an experience that saw incomes and net worth decline precipitously. No sense of entitlement here. Consequently, they're more pragmatic than idealistic. Millennials want to change the world, but so do Gen Zers. They just want to be paid first! And as for the Millennials' penchants for collaboration and open workspaces? "Screw that," says Gen Z. As one observer noted, "They'd rather share socks than office space." Clearly, Gen Z is a different breed of cat. (What might this portend for the overinflated office-sharing company WeWork?)[3]

> **If Millennials fail to meet this challenge, they bear the risk of becoming increasingly marginalized as the inherently grittier, far more competitive Gen Z take their jobs and, in short, kick their collective asses.**

The differences are even starker when considering entrepreneurship. Given what we've seen thus far, is it any surprise that Millennials are not terribly entrepreneurial? In the US, just 2 percent of Millennials are self-employed. (Indeed, a generation given to groupthink and "bred-in-the-bone collectivism," by definition, will yield the opposite of individualism and entrepreneurship.) Between 1996 and the present, the number of 20- to 30-year-olds (Millennials) launching startups *halved*. Gen Zers, on the other hand, are starting businesses in high school. Research conducted by Monster shows that Gen Zers will do whatever it takes to reach their goals—and entrepreneurship is a major priority. Seventy-six percent of Gen Zers see themselves as the owners of their careers, with nearly half expecting to have their own business. Moreover, two-thirds of them are willing to relocate for a good job, and are more than willing to work nights and weekends for a better salary. In addition, they embrace the concept of the "always on" work world.

The Gen Zer's work ethic also translates to a very different worldview than that of the Millennials. Research by The Center for Generational Kinetics, for example, shows that 78 percent of Gen Zers believe the American Dream is attainable, which is higher than any other generation. In fact, they believe they've got the wind at their backs, with two-thirds of them saying that the American economic system works *for* them. And they're more than willing to work hard to reciprocate. On the other hand, more than half of Millennials believe that America's economic system works *against* them. So, then, combined with everything else we've learned, is it any surprise that half of Millennials also say they would rather live in a socialist or communist country than a capitalist democracy? These are deeply worrisome trends, to say the least.

As a transitional generation between the Boomers and Gen Z, the Millennials are a hinge—and a squeaky one at that. Some would even say they are unhinged. Ultimately, though—and unfairly—the weight of the Millennial generation will be borne by Gen Z, particularly as the narratives of the Millennial ideologies radically constrain their future options. A little existential introspection might help to break this particular self-fulfilling prophecy.

○◐●◑

In the end, we all exist in time—and not for very long. This should lend some urgency to the whole idea of our existence. We can choose to stroll through life, going around problems, and do just fine copying what everyone else does. After all, this is exactly what most people do. But to live this way is to sacrifice one's individuality—and the possibilities that it could present to the world. The rigors of being faithful to one's unique potential involves faithfulness to that very individual uniqueness, and to the larger world we impact when we exercise it to the full.

Seneca challenged his 1st-century followers when he told them that it's not that we have a short time to live, but that we waste so much of it. "Life is long enough," he asserted, "and a sufficiently generous amount has been given to us for the highest achievements if it were all well invested. But when it is wasted in heedless luxury and spent on no good activity, we are forced at last by death's final constraint to realize that it has passed away before we knew it was passing. So it is: we are not given a short life but we make it short, and we are not ill-supplied but wasteful of it ... Life is long if you know how to use it."

> **If our years were in greater abundance would we squander them? I'm not sure. The fact is, people squander short lives. I'm reminded of David Cassidy's last words, "So much wasted time." Indeed, it is vanity to wish for long life and to care little that the life is well-spent.**

If our years were in greater abundance would we squander them? I'm not sure. The fact is, people squander short lives. So much precious time is wasted. Indeed, it is vanity to wish for long life and to care little that the life is well-spent. Millions may dream of immortality but do they know what to do with themselves on a rainy Sunday afternoon?

....

Entrepreneurship for the Curious

As curious and imaginative people, we are always pursuing the questions, what can be known, and how can we know it? But the entrepreneur is concerned with another question—an ultimately more important question: what is to be *done*? Indeed, for anything to change, *someone* has to start acting differently.

It's easy to think of an entrepreneur as someone who starts a business. But entrepreneurship isn't about starting a business; it's about solving a problem. Most people, however, spend more time and energy going around problems than in trying to solve them. And consequently, many problems go unsolved. Regina Dugan, the former director of DARPA and Facebook's Building 8, has observed of problems in general, "We think someone else—someone smarter than us, someone more capable, with much more resources—will solve that problem. *But there isn't anyone else.*"

In the end, it's the entrepreneur who steps in to fill the gaps. To the entrepreneur, problems are opportunities in sheep's—or is it wolves'?—clothing. The entrepreneur is the person who wakes up in the morning and resolves to be the solution. So many of the world's problems require only a catalyst to set even bigger solutions into motion—like accelerating a chemical chain reaction. Acting as the stimulus, the spark, the impetus—the pebble tossed into the pond—the entrepreneur enables a new creation, *de novo* and full of surprise. It's the surprise that counts, because surprise means the world has rid itself of another impossibility. As such, it is a profound experience, and one that transcends mere materialistic concerns. This is how humanity is lifted up and dignified. This is the real fruit of the entrepreneur's work and calling. And what could possibly be more fulfilling, rewarding, or thrilling?

The very word *entrepreneur* is translated as "adventurer." For the entrepreneur, the opportunities to slay impossibilities provide endless adventure. And we'll never be without them. While we may only be able to see a short distance ahead, we can clearly see that there is much to be done.

Thomas Edison said that if we all did the things we are really capable of doing, we would literally astound ourselves. There's no question about it. But make no mistake—the journey of entrepreneurship will test every fiber of your being. And yet that's just another twist: when the going is *not* difficult, it could mean trouble. To the entrepreneur, stagnation masquerades as smooth sailing, and stagnation invites certain disruption.

Of course there will be moments when you catch the wind in your sails, the views from the summit, the lightning in a bottle. But the fact is, entrepreneurship is the path of *most* resistance, where the effortlessness of *wu wei* is an utterly foreign concept. Yet entrepreneurs experience *wu wei* in their own way: their path is as sure as that of water flowing in a downhill stream. The resistance comes in the form of the myriad minds it encounters along the way—the stones and boulders in the stream. And yet, somehow, in the face of all that resistance, entrepreneurs are still supposed to be able to "go down deeper, stay down longer, and come up drier than anybody else." And somehow, many of them actually do!

Machiavelli, a shrewd shaper of his own world, said, "Entrepreneurs are simply those who understand that there is little difference between obstacle and opportunity, *and are able to turn both to their advantage.*" To the entrepreneur, it really is all the same.

---

1. To this point, Garry Kasparov adds, "The ability to push yourself, to keep working, practicing, studying more than others is itself a talent. If anyone could do it, everyone would. As with any talent, it must be cultivated to blossom."

2. The Millennial mindset is in no way unique to America. The so-called "Buddhist Youth," China's nickname for their millennial generation, are in their own way embracing a laissez-faire and low expectations approach to life.

3. Rhett Jones, writing for Gizmodo, says, "Of all of the mega-funded startups out there, WeWork probably baffles me the most." With valuation on par with that of SpaceX, it is baffling, indeed. "But unlike Elon Musk's rocket startup," Jones continues, "WeWork has no moonshot ideas. It just rents real estate and brands properties. WeLive is its communal housing offshoot. A bunch of people live in a place and share common areas. This is called 'co-living' in the world of WeWork. In the real world, it's called having roommates. If you elect to have a roommate rather than 'co-living' with someone, it tends to be cheaper, and you get to choose your own decor."

CHAPTER 12

In the Light of Mind

Everything has changed except our way of thinking.

—*Albert Einstein*

GROUP OF PRISONERS HAS BEEN CONFINED in a cave their entire lives. They have no knowledge of the outside world. They are chained and shackled, facing a wall, unable to turn their heads in any other direction. Behind them, a fire burns, its glow casting a flickering light. Sometimes people pass in front of the fire carrying various objects, casting shadows on the wall as they go. And when they speak, the sound of their voices echoes off the wall, giving the prisoners the impression that the voices are emanating from the shadows themselves. Over the long term of their imprisonment, they come to name and classify these manifestations, which, to their senses, are real entities. Suddenly, one of the prisoners is freed from his confinement and forcibly brought outside the cave for the first time. The sunlight momentarily blinds him, and he struggles to find his balance. He is disoriented. He is then told that what he sees all around him is real and substantive, and that the shadows are mere images, immaterial. In time, his eyes adjust and he is able to take in this new and phenomenal world. But then the prisoner is returned to the cave, where he shares the news of his startling epiphany. The other prisoners think he's gone mad. And because his eyes are now having trouble adjusting to the darkness of the cave, they also believe he's gone blind. But when he attempts to set the other prisoners free so that they can experience this wonder for themselves, they resist violently. They would, in fact, kill him if they could.

Before you're tempted to condemn our captive cave dwellers, ask yourself, are there any illusions to which you hold yourself captive? Are there any areas of your life and thinking that, hidden from the light of day, remain unexamined? Are there certain personal and professional challenges that are more comfortably and conveniently left in the dark? If so, then you are in good company: 98 percent of the population proceeds in life upon one false basis or another—and actually believe they are served by them.

Plato's classic allegory not only exposes this state of affairs, but also tells us what happens when we dare to step outside the confines of our programming. Humans are remarkably adaptable when it comes to accommodating and enforcing illusions and limitations of every kind—especially when they are threatened. This book is written to the outliers, the 2 percent who will actually dare to unlock the chained doors of imagination and possibility—the few who realize that no one keeps us from the light of common day but ourselves.

The sum of your knowledge, beliefs, dispositions, openness, experience, and attitudes about the world and your place in it comprises this most powerful entity called the mindset. It can enable you to reach for the stars or condemn you to a cycle of poverty and despair. Mindset is the stuff of your being and becoming, the measure of your grit, the limit of your aspirations. As a mental construct, it is both as abstract and as real as possibility. And the freedom it presents is either a liberating or a terrifying prospect. Either way, mindset—the entrepreneurial mindset—is central to everything we've discussed thus far.

Nothing comes to your mind but by the filter of your mindset. By virtue of what it admits or denies, it is the engine of the self-fulfilling prophecy, for good or for ill. But it, like the future, is also malleable. While many external factors work to mold and shape your mindset, you do get a vote in the matter. You can question the underlying assumptions. You can test the theses. You are not required to accept any of the default settings. You are always free to reject one belief and replace it with another. And when you reinforce that new belief, your outlook and your behavior will change. Your perception really is your reality, and

> **While many external factors work to mold and shape your mindset, you do get a vote in the matter. You can question the underlying assumptions. You can test the theses. You are not required to accept any of the default settings.**

if you don't like what you see, you can change the underlying reality and your perception with it. To this end, the mindset can be thought of as one's "disposition to possibility." And its effect, like the self-fulfilling prophecy, is circular.

One of your greatest freedoms is the freedom of opinion. If you can resist the indoctrination of the established order of expectations, then you'll be sufficiently independent of the existing paradigm that you can smash it. That's what a moonshot does—it openly defies the majority opinion. "Whenever you find yourself on the side of the majority," Mark Twain warned, "it is time to pause and reflect." Indeed, as an entrepreneur, you cannot afford to allow other people to tell you who you are. Rather, you must always resolve to consider everything in its true light.

> **If you can resist the indoctrination of the established order of expectations, then you'll be sufficiently independent of the existing paradigm that you can smash it. That's what a moonshot does—it openly defies the majority opinion.**

This bears saying only because, as an entrepreneur, you are sure to encounter a wave of opinion—largely that your dream is an impossible dream. And here again is mindset at work. When someone tells you that something is impossible, they're absolutely correct: it *is* impossible—*for them*. You, on the other hand, are under no obligation to accept the oppressive restrictions of third-party mindsets.

As an entrepreneur your context is far broader. Your vision is radically different and therefore strange to other minds that are not in sync with your own. Consequently, these others can contribute nothing to your enterprise. Rather, you need to guard and protect your mindset from such cross-contamination. This is also why you must never evaluate or compare your ambitions and expectations with those of others in relative terms, but always in absolute terms. Anything less is deadly compromise.

Imitation is the default expectation. Conformity maintains the established order of things. Therefore, you must fight for your mindset as hard as others fight to protect their own. Indeed, every battle in the history of the world was fought over differences in mindsets.

Many people, though, manage to avoid the conflict that can arise from the independent development of mindset by simply copying others. Many would-be entrepreneurs are no exception. Blockbuster books notwithstanding, following the practices, behaviors, and rituals of other successful people will *not* make you successful. If you are to imitate anything, make it their thought processes, not, with all due respect to Mr. Covey, their "seven habits." For example, Tony Robbins takes an ice bath every morning. I guarantee you, if you take three ice baths every morning, you are not going to become Tony Robbins. You'll get to be like Tony Robbins by *thinking* like Tony Robbins. The only shortcuts to the formation of mindset are the ones that strip you of all possibility of ever achieving a dream.

Think about this: thinking for yourself really means learning how to exercise control over how and what you think. Indeed, the world as we have created it is a product of our thinking. The world "as it is" is a function of our collective mindsets. That world cannot be changed without changing the thinking behind it. And if we venture to bring meaningful change at the scale we imagine, it will require a radical *metanoia*—a massive U-turn of the mind, a digging up and a plowing under.

There's no use in trying to cultivate a garden on barren soil where only weeds can grow. That soil needs to be turned over, amended, and replanted with good seeds. You have to make room for a new mindset—it cannot share the same space with the old. And that means there first has to be a good deal of unlearning—a pulling up of the weeds. When you do that, you'll be disposed in a completely new way. To do something different, you must first *become* something different. A new life of inspired possibility then lies within your grasp. And then, as Marcus Aurelius wrote, "You have only to see things once more in the light of your first and earlier vision, and life begins anew."

There are great challenges, of course. Many of us have decades of accumulated mind-making work behind us. And many of us were trained from childhood to modulate our expectations in life— even by those who love us. Indeed, we get a lot of mental programming—programming that sets up automatic and conventional responses to our experiences in the world—and not all of it enhances

> **What really matters to cognitive performance is not so much the brain's hardware as its onboard *software*. Software can be buggy, but it can also be patched, updated, and upgraded. But mostly, it's just copied.**

our performance. It's true that what really matters to cognitive performance is not so much the brain's hardware as its onboard *software*. Software can be buggy, but it can also be patched, updated, and upgraded. But mostly, it's just copied.

Someone once observed that children have never been very good at listening to their parents, but they never fail to imitate them. I guess I was lucky. As I mentioned earlier, one could argue that there was no chance for me to escape the cycle of poverty in India as I was growing up. And I certainly would have had no chance had I continued to think the way I was expected to. Had I followed the rules, I would have never left home. I would have remained stuck within the bell curve of the societal norms and expectations for someone of my "social standing."

Expectations matter a great deal to our life outcomes. If expectations are low, we will not be surprised when we don't advance. We won't even notice that we're not advancing. That's the way the brain works, and the brain is quite willing to accommodate whatever mindset we choose to feed it. High expectations can certainly lead to better outcomes, but what happens when we fail to achieve them? If, on the other hand, we have no great expectations, we can never be disappointed.

As we saw earlier, holding low expectations in order to protect us from disappointment is mitigated by that tricky state called defensive pessimism. But low expectations do not diminish the pain of failure. In the end, low expectations serve no one.

Expectations are absolutely essential to achieving goals. They go hand in hand with the grit that reflects our belief that we can, and will, accomplish our goals. But expectation is different from hope in that it gives you the inner conviction that your goal is attainable, even if it seems irrational. And it has a physiological effect. When you strongly believe in something, you actually stimulate those parts of the brain

> **In any discipline, students need mentoring, as well as peer support, and a good deal of personal reflection in order to succeed. Entrepreneurship is no different.**

that involve motivational activity. You set up a virtuous cycle, a self-reinforcing feedback loop that spurs you on.

In this respect, mindset is no different than a muscle or a habit. In order for it to become strong and effective, it must be developed and exercised. Like everything, change begins with desire—even a negative desire, like the refusal to accept the existing reality. Once a conscious decision to change is made, you must train yourself to remain focused on your goal. This business of reinvention is never finished, though, because we are in a constant state of becoming. In any event, if there is just one defining difference that marks the successful entrepreneur, it is his mindset. Every other factor—socioeconomic status, intelligence, talent, etc., melts away in the face of a muscular and determined mindset—a mindset that is prepared to do "whatever it takes."

○◑●◐

Remember that entrepreneurship really isn't about starting a business. Rather, it's a state of mind, a way of looking at the world, and seeing opportunity where others see only obstacles. This is the entrepreneur's special "talent." His expertise lies in the shape of his mindset—that conductor of a symphony of intellectual curiosity, active imagination, free-range possibility, forward-looking optimism, prescient perception, and, of course, grit. You've seen these people in action. They are as amazing to watch as any professional athlete or virtuoso musician. They are at the top of their game. They are *different*. None of the attributes that comprise this mindset, though, are static; they are not driven or constrained by knowledge. There are no certifications. There is no equivalent of the Mensa Society admission test for this kind of cognitive prowess. But neither do they operate alone.

Entrepreneurial circles function more like *salons*—like those of Gertrude Stein, who hosted the likes of Ernest Hemingway, Pablo Picasso, James Joyce, and other voices of their generation. Or the Algonquin Round Table, where birds of a literary feather would gather to compare notes and match wits. Or the Vagabonds—Henry Ford, Thomas Edison, and Harvey Firestone—industrialists who embarked on "camping trips" together. Each of these gatherings of minds created and fostered environments that allowed their members to feed off each other's energies and intellects. In other words, they surrounded themselves with the right people in order to up their respective games. Today's great entrepreneurs do the same. We now have hundreds, if not thousands, of "startup communities" around the world where like minds come together for inspiration, encouragement, and strategic networking. Other leading entrepreneurs generously make themselves available to advise entrepreneurs in the making.

I'm thinking of entrepreneurship mentoring programs that bring tremendous community resources together to nurture the development of entrepreneurial mindsets. In many ways, they're not unlike the peripatetic schools where eager students gathered and sat at the feet of the likes of Aristotle in the Lyceum. It's true that when the student is ready, the mentor will appear.

The point is that a community of like minds is essential for developing entrepreneurial competence—but always with the perpetual spirit of a novice. Indeed, conventional domain experts structure their domain knowledge very differently. The entrepreneur's brand of expertise is a very different breed of cat.

The people you spend time with play a huge role in your life, so you need to choose them carefully. You're the average of the five people you spend the most time with. It's very true. This is one reason why I'm involved with Singularity University. Here is an amazingly fertile and creative environment where I can surround myself with people who believe, for example, that the singularity is possible, that an abundance of resources is possible, that meeting all the world's grand challenges is possible. When you immerse yourself in the company of such people, it changes your mindset. You will always encounter two types of people in this world—those who build and those who tear down. Surround yourself with the builders. The others will only be parasites on your energy. They will suck you dry with their negative energy. When you encounter them, do yourself a great favor and just walk them out of your life.

○◐●◑

There is also a cultural aspect to mindsets. Growing up in India, I am well acquainted with the concept of poverty and the mindset that attends it. There were times when we had no food to eat or even a place to call home. Of course, there is also poverty in America, but the stats really don't define the true state of the American experience of poverty. Real poverty is more a state of being rather than a matter of financial condition. The problem is that we define poverty too narrowly.

Consequently, poverty is a condition that is rife with partial truths—and partial truths can be far more insidious than total falsehoods. Where mindsets meet reality, valid partial truths can grow up to be false total truths. And when that happens, the defective mindsets that result yield the acids of failure—a virus of the mind that will be with us for generations.

Mental crimes occur when error and false theories taint the soul. In these cases, the good fortune allowing for a state of grace must happen for affected people to be in a condition to make the choice of possibility. If people believe they are locked out of opportunity, they need to understand that it's just a four-digit combination lock. If you have only three digits, it won't open. It's not rocket science. But let's say that it is rocket science. It's rocket science that is well understood. And there are plenty of rocket scientists who will help you get to where you want to be in life. You just have to ask them.

The biggest problem is that people living in poverty are not inspired, and so they default to choices that are counterproductive. (It's always the people who have the least amount of money who buy lottery tickets.) People in their own communities tell them they are worth nothing, and so they become convinced that society is against them. They then create a belief system—a mindset—that makes them feel better about their condition; they believe that the reason they can't succeed is because everyone is against them. They become victims of their mindsets.

> **Valid partial truths can grow up to be false total truths. And when that happens, the defective mindsets that result yield the acids of failure—a virus of the mind that will be with us for generations.**

According to research at Stanford, the people who suffer the most from a given state of affairs (the disadvantaged, those living in poverty) are paradoxically the *least likely* to question, challenge, reject, or attempt to change it. They accept their lot in life and actually work hard to justify it when they could just as easily ask, "What if I try? Who is stopping me?" And when they do try, they discover that no one is stopping them, that people are actually supporting them, that the wind is at their backs. The headwind they assumed is nonexistent.

When people try, they tend to succeed. Anyone can set for themselves a series of small intermediate goals and achieve them. There are very few people who can honestly say, "I tried, and I failed." Rather, people tend to conform to their own specifications. As Napoleon Hill said, "Remember, no more effort is required to aim high in life, to demand abundance and prosperity, than is required to accept misery and poverty."

The fixed mindset is the enemy of possibility. It's also the brain's default condition, which means it requires some effort to adjust. The brain is a remarkable self-organizing mechanism that is tuned specifically to form patterns. Once those patterns are formed, all the brain needs to do is to recognize the appropriate pattern and then follow along. It's a useful feature, because it's through the use of established, routine patterns that we are able to cope so well with an otherwise overwhelmingly complex world. The downside of patterns is that once we have set them up, we become trapped by them. So we need the ability to challenge these patterns from time to time to set up better patterns—patterns that rise to the level of possibility. And that's tough, because for an entrepreneurial mindset, those can be crazy patterns.

Here's the rub: the people who are crazy enough to believe they can change the world are the ones who actually do. Steve Jobs famously said that it's the crazies who change the world. So I've always said, *think so big that people will think you're crazy*. And there's a simple test for crazy. If people believed the "crazy" thing could be done, it would have already been done. That it hasn't been done means that people believe it to be impossible and have simply taken themselves out of the arena, which in turn means that you have no competition. If people think it's a crazy idea, they'll never attempt it, and you'll have the road to yourself.

> ❝ Steve Jobs famously said that it's the crazies who change the world. So I've always said, *think so big that people will think you're crazy*. And there's a simple test for crazy. ❞

"Those who dream by night in the dusty recesses of their minds," wrote T.E. Lawrence (of Arabia), "wake in the day to find that it was vanity: but the dreamers of the day are dangerous men, for they may act their dream with open eyes, *to make it possible*."

And that really is the essence of the entrepreneurial mindset—out of the dusty recesses of the cave and into broad daylight.

Special Ops Entrepreneurship

"It's just sad," said one of the officers. "It's disappointing because these men have proven to be physically tough. They just have to overcome the fear of drowning." The officer was speaking of aspiring Navy SEALs who didn't make the cut. All because of a trifling thing like being afraid of drowning.

Wait. What?

It's true, physical strength alone does not a Navy SEAL make. Unless, that is, you consider the brain to be the strongest muscle of all. Mental toughness is what really counts in the special forces. This drowning business is a case in point: trainees have to stay underwater for 20 minutes while their instructor assaults them, ripping off their face masks, shutting off their oxygen tanks. In another underwater exercise, they must remain submerged for a duration with their wrists and ankles tied, simulating pretty convincing drowning conditions. Could you pass these tests?

The point of the training, of course, is to develop the SEALs' ability to control their mental states so thoroughly that they can turn off the brain's automatic fear responses in order to carry out their difficult missions. And not all of them can do it. So the Navy enlisted the help of neuroscientists and psychologists to devise techniques that might help increase the graduation rate. What they discovered is that special forces training creates stress levels in the body higher than those experienced by people who are landing on an aircraft carrier at night for the first time, higher than those who are skydiving for the first time. The effect of neuropeptide Y—a neurotransmitter associated with reducing anxiety and stress—is so pronounced, they observed, that they can identify a member of the special forces by a blood test alone.

Interestingly, the techniques the researchers developed were a set of interventions designed to buffer the negative impact of stress on the trainees' cognition, memory, and operational performance levels. In other words, a recipe for a mindset that could actually override the brain's response to life's threatening situations. A big part of accomplishing this is effectively raising the threshold of the brain's "smoke detector," the amygdala.

The amygdala, part of the limbic system, is responsible for detecting fear and preparing the body for a fight or flight or freeze response. Known also as the "lizard brain" because the limbic system is about all a lizard has for brain function, it is in charge of our responses to threatening stimuli. When the amygdala's alarm is tripped by perceived danger, the brain releases a flood of chemicals and hormones such as adrenaline and cortisol. The amygdala serves us well in these situations because it processes visual and sound information without having to wait on other cognitive functions to make judgments about the threat. That means it can react very quickly. Your heart starts pounding, your breathing becomes quick and shallow, and your muscles tense, readying the body for its defensive action. But something else happens. When the amygdala kicks into gear, it immediately shuts down the neural pathway to the prefrontal cortex, giving the brain a kind of cognitive tunnel vision. Consequently the capacity for complex decision-making disappears.

And suddenly it becomes clear why special forces need to maintain robust conscious awareness even—and especially—under such conditions. Control these hormones, and you control your performance. It's not natural, but the brain can be trained to pull this off. Not that the entrepreneur in training has to endure such extremes as simulated drowning, but there is much he can draw from these kinds of practices. For that matter, there is much that we all can take from such practices to simply endure watching the daily news!

Because the amygdala is essential to survival, it constantly scans the horizons of its inputs for anything that might constitute a threat. The media knows this. If you've watched *Crisis News Network* recently, then you know they've made an art form of serving up a continuous stream of negative stories. They shamelessly pander to the brain's "negativity bias"—the right brain's yang to the left brain's optimistically biased yin. On the whole, though, because of the amygdala's defensive function, we are asymmetrically wired to favor the negative. As psychologist Rick Hanson says, "The brain is like Velcro for negative experiences but Teflon for positive ones." While negative stimuli hold sway over our psychological state, being mindful of this propensity will help us overcome it.

We'll also have to become more mindful of the nature of our so-called self-talk. Research has discovered that as much as 77 percent of self-talk is negative and counterproductive. Indeed, thoughts influence our emotional and physiological responses. Because of self-talk's power to shape and reinforce one's mindset, it is vital to recognize that most negative thinking is flawed, if not self-delusional, and to replace harmful thoughts with ones that are actually rational.

Getting a grip on one's amygdala, then, is crucial in the development of an effective entrepreneurial mindset. When you do, you will feel less anxious and actually be more productive; you'll have greater control of your circumstances, enjoy increased clarity and resolve, and develop an increased capacity for concentration. Before we know it, our old habit of fight or flight is changing, and the world is a safer place.

So how, exactly, do the SEALs do it? Let's take a closer look at those interventions known as the "Big Four" that the Navy developed. When put into practice, these techniques actually boosted performance by 80 percent or more. Here they are in a nutshell:

- Set challenging but achievable long- and short-term goals.
- Connect these goals to your life vision.
- Practice deep breathing techniques to control the stress response and center the mind.
- Visualize anticipated experiences and outcomes to improve concentration, reduce anxiety, and build confidence.

Sound simple enough? Whole books, of course, are written about these techniques, but it is interesting how consistent these few insights really are across nearly all forms of mental coaching in nearly every field. When applied to developing the entrepreneurial mindset—and combined with all the other elements discussed thus far—they can truly help to produce the grit needed to persevere when the going gets tough.

Mark Divine, former SEAL commander and author of *The Way of the SEAL*, elevates and expands the Big Four as he applies it to approaches to leadership. Wary of the myriad management styles *du jour*, Divine finds that their formulaic approaches tend to treat leadership simply as a skill. "But what if leadership is not a skill?" he asks. "What if it's a *character*? We wonder why things don't work or continue to feel wrong when we spend so much time seeking the holy grail of leadership models instead of looking within, instead of building that character." His big takeaway is that if you lack the underlying commitment to self-mastery and growth, then even the best management theory won't help you lead yourself or your team to success.

It turns out that the core tenets of *The Way of the SEAL* exactly parallel the way to develop an entrepreneurial mindset. Adopting it will not only create a better you, but you'll also help create a better world. Here, then, are Divine's eight steps to accomplishing any goal in any area of your life that you may set for yourself:

- Live an examined life. What I mean by this is that the most important aspect of mental toughness is to know yourself, what drives you and motivates you deeply.
- Master your body, mind, and emotions to excel at an elite level. To do this requires the knowledge, skills, and commitment to a life of training and daily improvement.
- Take your eyes off yourself and put them on others, in service.
- Learn to win in your mind before you set foot in the arena.
- Learn to select the right targets, connected to your main purpose in life.
- Employ KISS (keep it simple, stupid) planning and be willing to execute with an imperfect plan.
- Take massive action using micro-goals, then fail forward fast.
- Never quit, period.

PART TWO

Moonshots Masterclass

CHAPTER 13

To the Moon—And Beyond

Earth is the cradle of mankind, but one cannot live in the cradle forever.

—Soviet Rocket Scientist Konstantin Tsiolkovsky

SINCE TAKING OUR FIRST STEPS BEYOND THAT CRADLE with Yuri Gagarin's historic 1961 Earth orbit, mankind began its journey as a spacefaring species. In the nearly 60 years since, however, fewer than 600 people have been to space, and only a dozen have ever set foot upon another celestial body. It would appear that in the face of such promise, we've once again been energizing far below our potential.

Mankind, having left the cradle, was really just beginning to crawl when the remaining three Apollo missions were unceremoniously canceled, bringing an end to the era of manned moon ventures. More terrestrially related concerns of the time shifted the nation's priorities as the public yawned with each subsequent launch. Consequently, with no strategic or economic drivers to continue the journey, NASA stalled out in low Earth orbit.

On December 14, 1972, Gene Cernan became the last human to step off the moon's surface, radioing as he climbed back into Challenger, the mission's lunar module, "... I take man's last steps from the surface ... for some time to come, but we believe not too long into the future. I'd like to just list what I believe history will record that America's challenge of today has forged man's destiny of tomorrow. And, as we leave the moon at Taurus Littrow, we leave as we come and, God willing, as we shall return, with peace and hope for all mankind. Godspeed the crew of Apollo 17."

Little did anyone know, though, that the Apollo program's ultimate—but as yet unknown—legacy would be established when NASA caved to the pressure mounted by the scientific community, which demanded that one of their own crew an Apollo mission. They got their man in geologist Harrison "Jack" Schmitt, who, along with Cernan, returned with a motherlode of moon rocks that concealed a powerful but hidden element—helium-3.

What's so special about helium-3? It turns out that helium-3—a light, non-radioactive isotope of helium—is an ideal fuel for fusion power production. At the time, however, NASA had no idea. Today, nuclear power plants rely upon nuclear *fission* to produce heat (releasing energy when very large atoms like uranium or plutonium are split), turning water into steam, which in turn drives a turbine to produce electricity. In nuclear *fusion*, energy is released when two lighter atoms are smashed together and fused into a larger one.

Conventionally, hydrogen isotopes are used as the fuel in a fusion process, which is how the sun—a giant fusion reactor itself—generates its energy. The downside to both of these types of nuclear reactions, of course, is radioactive waste. But if helium-3 is used as the fuel, no neutrons are generated as a reaction product, and consequently, no nuclear waste is produced.

Not only is it clean, it is astoundingly efficient. Imagine replacing a coal train more than a kilometer long, loaded with 5,000 tonnes of coal, with just 40 grams of helium-3. Just 25 tonnes of helium-3 could power the United States and Europe combined for a year! And with more than a million tonnes of the stuff on the moon, we could potentially keep up this pace for thousands of years. Energy problem solved.

Helium-3 is emitted by the sun and scattered throughout our solar system, driven at high velocity by the solar winds. That wind, however, is repelled by the Earth's magnetic field; only a tiny amount of He-3 makes it through our atmosphere in the form of cosmic dust, making its occurrence very rare. (The United States' helium-3 reserves are just shy of 30 kilograms.) Consequently, people pay upwards of $20,000 an ounce for it. Gold, in comparison, goes for a mere $1,200 per ounce. But there's no shortage of the stuff on the moon, which has a weak magnetic field and no atmosphere. That makes the moon a fertile receptor of everything the solar wind blows its way, hence the massive deposits of helium-3 and other elements that have accumulated on its surface over billions of years.

In retrospect—and now looking forward—Schmitt believes the discovery of helium-3 is one of the most significant contributions of the Apollo missions. But it wasn't until Schmitt met Gerald Kulcinski, director of the Fusion Technology Institute at the University of Wisconsin at Madison, that a larger vision emerged. "The NASA folks knew that there was helium-3 on the moon," Kulcinski says, "but they didn't know what it was good for. We knew what it was good for, but we didn't know where it was." Kulcinski and Schmitt then teamed up to define more specifically how they might access the lunar resource "and," Schmitt said, "make it available to people on Earth." Kulcinski adds, "There's actually more energy in the helium-3 on the moon then there ever was in all of the coal, oil, or natural gas on Earth."

With that, the moon graduated from a desolate wasteland to an unimaginably resource-rich "eighth continent." Suddenly there is great interest in returning to the moon—the gateway not only to the solar system, but to a future of unlimited abundance. What's more, when we are able to make space and its resources truly accessible, we will have moved humanity forward by simply making us a multi-planetary society.

....

Helium-3 Fusion—How Far Away? A Conversation with Professor Gerald Kulcinski

No question, a demonstration of commercially feasible helium-3 (He-3) fusion power would be a moonshot in its own right. But it is within sight. Apollo 17 astronaut and geologist Harrison "Jack" Schmitt notes that historic progress has been made in the use of helium-3 fuels to produce controlled fusion reactions, as he has witnessed working with his colleague Gerald Kulcinski at the University of Wisconsin-Madison. Schmitt and Kulcinski believe that the energy contained in the raw lunar soil could be unleashed at a scale that could transform the moon into the "Persian Gulf" of the solar system.

The big idea is built upon a trio of contingencies: a commercial fusion reactor, an efficient lunar mining operation, and, of course, a means of transporting the material to Earth. We talked with Professor Kulcinski to learn more about the state of the technology.

How viable do you consider helium-3 fusion to be at this stage?

Perfecting the He-3/He-3 fusion fuel cycle could be the answer to the world's need for abundant, clean, and safe energy for generations to come. To be able to provide nuclear energy without any nuclear waste is a goal that would be truly game-changing. And I believe it will eventually be achieved, if not in my lifetime then perhaps in my students' lifetimes. I know of no other energy resource that can provide base load electricity for 1,000 years or more at the level needed to provide electricity for the entire Earth.

Are you able to forecast when such technology might become practical?

Large-scale (100s of megawatts) nuclear fusion with the deuterium-tritium (DT) fuel cycle will be first demonstrated by the ITER device, currently being built in France, in the 2030 timeframe. Other private companies such as TAE Technologies are already constructing smaller devices that will be able to "burn" advanced fusion fuels (p11B) in the next 10 to 20 years. If they can demonstrate *net* energy production (energy out> energy in) with p11B (proton-boron fusion), then they certainly can use D-He-3. It would then be up to scientists to build on that fuel cycle to get to the He-3/He-3 cycle, the ultimate fusion fuel. The issue of procuring He-3 fuel from the moon (≈ 1 million tonnes resource base) then becomes the only barrier to that future of abundant, clean, and safe nuclear energy.

What are your thoughts about the mining and transport of helium-3 from the moon? What do you believe are the greatest logistical challenges?

I believe that the mining of helium-3 from the moon is only an engineering issue, not a physics issue. We are on our third lunar He-3 miner design, and when industry gets involved, we feel that providing He-3 for terrestrial use will be much easier than solving the burning of He-3 fuels. The current issues to be faced in mining are about how small we can make the lunar miners to reduce the cost of the He-3 fuel. Currently our designs are in the 10 tonne range for production of ≈50 kg of He-3 per year. That amount of He-3 would power one 500 MWe power plant full time for a year.

How will you determine the most advantageous areas to mine?

The amount of He-3 we have comes from the samples brought back to the Earth by the Apollo 11, 12, 14, 15, 16, and 17 missions, as well as the Russian Lunokhod samples sent back to the Earth. In addition, there seems to be an association of the He-3 retained in the lunar regolith and the titanium content of the minerals. So mapping the Ti concentration could lead us to the highest concentrations on the moon.

How would you estimate the years of power consumption in the US (and/or world-wide) that helium-3-based fusion could satisfy?

The energy in a tonne of He-3 burned in a fusion reactor is ≈10,000 MWe-y. Since the US produced ≈470,000 MWe-y of electricity in 2016, that would mean that we would need ≈50 tonnes of Helium-3 to replace all of the electrical power plants in the US. Since there are an estimated 1,000,000 tonnes of He-3 on the moon, this would indicate that if only the US used He-3 for all of its electrical needs at the 2016 level, the helium-3 reserves would last for thousands of years. Even if we could only extract 10 percent of the helium-3 on the moon, the He-3 reserves would last ≈2,000 years.

But it won't be NASA that will do it.

Schmitt believes that NASA would have to be totally restructured in order to carry out such a mission—a tall order in the current political environment. "The option of rebuilding NASA," he explains, "is highly unpredictable and its sustainability may depend on the appearance of a set of world circumstances comparable to those that faced the Congress and Presidents Eisenhower, Kennedy, and Johnson in the late 1950s and throughout the 1960s. Some, including myself, would argue that those circumstances exist today, but no clear bipartisan consensus prevails on this point as it did in 1961 ... If the government of the United States wishes to lead the return of humans to deep space, its space agency of today is probably not yet the agency to undertake this new program ... NASA lacks the critical mass of youthful energy and imagination required for work in deep space. NASA also has become too bureaucratic and too risk-averse ..." [2]

> Thanks to a cascading series of exponentially enabling technologies, we are witnessing the dawn of the entrepreneurial space age, with more than 250 space ventures receiving non-government equity funding to date. Billions of dollars are flowing into this nascent and inspiring industry.

That last point was actually confirmed by NASA itself. The agency commissioned a review of its operations, which concluded that, because of its bureaucracy and practices, its current plans for returning astronauts to the moon are not affordable and likely won't produce sustainable, long-term economic benefits.

As it is, while we remain essentially stalled in low Earth orbit, the US relies on Russia for transport to and from the International Space Station, thanks to the retirement of the shuttle fleet. Moreover, over the past decade, with very few new projects having been approved—and a generation of missions coming to an end—there is very little in NASA's development pipeline.

Under the Obama administration NASA's charter was redirected to Earth science and long-term planning for a manned mission to Mars, with an asteroid encounter as an intermediate goal. The moon, meanwhile, was cut completely out of the loop. "Been there, done that," they said. The Trump administration, however, has signaled a reversal of this policy, signing Space Policy Directive 1, which puts a manned mission to the moon back in the mix—with the signing, attended by Schmitt, coinciding with the 45th anniversary of the Apollo 17 mission. But clearly, there is a lot of rebuilding to do, and a return to the moon by NASA won't be happening anytime soon.

> " As a species, we were made to explore, to settle, to cultivate, to push every limit to discover whether there really are any limits at all. "

If not NASA, then who? Schmitt is putting his money on the private sector—entrepreneurs—whose innovative, audacious, profit-driven initiatives he expects will pick up the dropped baton and even exceed the technological and financial pace of publicly funded space efforts.

And why not? To paraphrase Kennedy, today's spacefarers choose to go to the moon not because it is hard, but because it is good business! And they are in increasingly good company: Moon Express, Richard Branson's Virgin Galactic, Peter Diamandis' Planetary Resources, Paul Allen's Stratolaunch, Jeff Bezos' Blue Origin, Elon Musk's SpaceX, Peter Beck's Rocket Lab—all dedicated to bringing down the barriers to space, and already creating massive opportunities by and for entrepreneurs. If we waited on NASA, none of this would be happening.

Another case in point is that while NASA has been building rockets for 60 years, they've never bothered to build a reusable or otherwise economical rocket—they've had no financial incentive to do so. Indeed, you can be sure that the management styles practiced at NASA and those of the likes of SpaceX or Moon Express bear very little resemblance to one another—they're very different animals with very different objectives.

But now, thanks to a cascading series of exponentially enabling technologies, we are witnessing the dawn of the entrepreneurial space age, with more than 250 space ventures receiving non-government equity funding to date. Billions of dollars are flowing into this nascent and inspiring industry. "It's not a mad man's dream," Schmitt says, "to go to the moon and access its resources. We've been there, we know how to do it; we can estimate the costs." And entrepreneurs have most definitely answered the call.

What's more, the technologies and know-how already exist for mining the moon's resources. Robotic machines would perform much of the work. The processes involved in separating helium-3 from its ore are equally straightforward, and easily and economically accomplished. In fact, Schmitt suggests that the total investment required would be comparable to building a major transcontinental pipeline—but one with a vastly more productive payback. And we'd get a permanent lunar base in the bargain—a base that could serve every need from resupply to training to supporting Mars missions to unimagined potentials for scientific discovery.

Contrast this very realizable and world-changing dream with, for example, the budgets of Formula 1 teams like Ferrari, McLaren, and Red Bull. They each spend an average of $320 million *per year*—and they don't even get off the ground! It is astounding that for comparable costs, we can unlock the vast hidden resources of the moon—which also include magnesium, platinum, and titanium—and pave the way for ultimately developing a space colony to support mining operations, which will be necessary if we are to meet what could be a 10-fold increase in energy demand by 2050.

Think of it: in our lifetime, people will be living on the moon, Mars, Europa, Titan, and possibly beyond. Humanity will become a truly multi-planetary society. This may, in fact, be key to our survival as a species. Preservation of the Earth and our civilization is precisely the reason we need to expand our economic and societal sphere into space. And again, why not? Our citizenship extends to the ends of our solar system. But really, who or what establishes our boundaries? As a species, we were made to explore, to settle, to cultivate, to push every limit to discover whether there really are any limits at all. And to achieving all these ends, our moon is an ideal base camp—a fabulous point of departure to the entirety of the solar system—a celestial waystation seemingly made to order.

Water, it is said, is the oil of the solar system and the key to developing a colonizing presence on the moon. It was only in 2009 that NASA discovered vast quantities of water on the moon, locked up in ice (and perhaps in a recently discovered network of lava tubes beneath the lunar surface) that can be used not only in the production of rocket fuel (water being composed of hydrogen and oxygen—rocket fuel's essential ingredients), but provide crucial life support. This is a real game-changer, not only for the viability of a lunar base station, but for supporting the logistics of reaching Mars and other deep space destinations.

> " Our ongoing expeditions to the moon will continue to collapse the cost of lunar access and enable new markets and opportunities to arise, bringing the moon within reach by creating frequent opportunities for democratized lunar exploration by scientists, researchers, students, and, of course, entrepreneurs. "

At Moon Express we've laid out an ideal vision for our mission to moon and beyond. It's not just about boldly going; it's about boldly *staying*. It's about moving the economic sphere of Earth outward in a way that uses the material wealth of space to solve the urgent problems we now face on Earth: to bring the poverty-stricken segments of the world up to a decent living standard, without recourse to war or punitive action against those already in material comfort; to provide for a maturing civilization the basic energy vital to its survival.

Likewise, Jeff Bezos envisions the creation of an "infrastructure" to enable the next generation of people to realize a dynamic, entrepreneurial explosion into space. "I want thousands of entrepreneurs," he says, "doing amazing things in space, and to do that we need to dramatically lower the cost of access to space. We shouldn't be doing heavy industry on Earth. Resources are more plentiful in space. We were able to start Amazon with just four people because all the infrastructure was in place—we didn't have to build the internet, payment system, or the delivery system—we got to rest on top of them. That's why we don't see much entrepreneurial activity in space. It's completely unlike the internet. Two kids in a dorm room can change the industry completely. You can't do that in space yet—the price of admission is too high."

But not for long. Here's why: Elon Musk brought the cost of the rocket from around $300 million down to $60 million to $70 million through reusable components and vertically integrated technologies. The rockets are not only becoming less and less expensive, they're becoming more and more versatile. But Rocket Lab's low-cost Electron rocket will launch our robotic MX-1E lunar lander for under $5 million! Entrepreneurs are already building them for $1 million, and before long, tens of thousands of dollars. As a result of the myriad innovations and exponential technologies that are making these cost reductions possible, our mission to the moon, which is currently projected to cost (on a marginal basis) well under $10 million, is likely to fall to less than $1 million, making everything even cheaper.

Another reason we are able to accomplish this is because we are thinking like software engineers, not rocket scientists. Let me explain. Everyone who contemplates going to the moon always assumes you need a massive rocket to get you there. But it's not true. Likewise, good software is never written as a monolithic whole. It's built with modules, each of which performs a specific and compact function. These modules can then be assembled like Legos into larger programs. They can be swapped out, upgraded, replaced. It doesn't matter how big the challenge or dream may be if you can slice it into smaller, manageable tasks that you can execute with relative ease.

Likewise, we've broken our lunar mission into smaller pieces that actually enable us to do more with less. For example, our initial thought was to use a rocket that can take us into a geosynchronous orbit, and then deploy a smaller propulsion system that would take our lander out of that orbit, using the fuel savings to complete the journey to the moon. But then we realized that we could break it down even further. What if we only needed the rocket to get us to low Earth orbit, which costs less than $5 million, versus the $70 million we'd have to spend with SpaceX to get us into geosynchronous orbit? In that case, our lander itself could have a booster built into it, and that booster could take us to geosynchronous orbit and ultimately all the way to the moon. That's exactly what we're doing. The craft will make several elliptical orbits around the Earth, moving into a higher orbit on each pass. Once its orbit is high enough, the moon's gravity will take over, and our lander will do a burn to transfer to lunar orbit before navigating the soft landing. And we will accomplish all this for less than $10 million.

The cost of going to space really becomes then, on a marginal basis, the cost of the fuel. And we know that 93 percent of the weight of the rocket is contributed by the fuel. That means quite literally for every drop of fuel you have to carry, you have to carry another drop of fuel to move it. Imagine if you didn't have to carry all the fuel from planet Earth and could instead refuel in low Earth orbit, or geosynchronous orbit, or the lunar orbit for deep space missions. Now it's just a matter of docking with fuel depots along the way. At that point, the cost of accessing space becomes really cheap.

Our ongoing expeditions to the moon will continue to collapse the cost of lunar access and enable new markets and opportunities to arise, bringing the moon within reach by creating frequent opportunities for democratized lunar exploration by scientists, researchers, students, and, of course, entrepreneurs.

> **Capital is not patriotic. Capital goes where the opportunities are. Boundaries are created by politicians for their own purposes. Entrepreneurs don't create boundaries; they expand them far beyond any visible horizon on Earth or beyond.**

The astounding opportunities notwithstanding, industrial-scale mining operations aren't the only reason for a return to the moon. Even with all the satellites currently deployed, for example, we can't get a full view of the Earth to enable continual full Earth monitoring. A vantage from the moon, however, would certainly provide that. Astronomers would also like to see a radio telescope deployed on the far side of the moon, where it would receive no radio interference from Earth, and for 13 days a month, none from the sun.[1]

All that said, NASA will still tell you that it costs a billion dollars to go to the moon. The reason we're able to do it for less, aside from our engineering approach, is that we don't have to worry about achieving "Five 9s"—that is, Six Sigma performance. It's the last three nines that contribute 90 percent of the cost. If the rocket blows up, we're actually okay with that; we can easily recover. We can afford to blow up 10 rockets! But if NASA blows up a rocket, they lose their funding. Consequently, they'd rather spend a billion dollars to avoid failure. So we go with 99 percent confidence versus 99.999 percent confidence; we go with 1/10th the cost and just insure the damn thing.

To date, only three nation-states have ever landed on the moon. Moon Express is working to become the first private enterprise to do so, reopening the lunar frontier in the process. Let me tell you what we have in mind.

Our three-fold mission involves a set of staged objectives: arrive, prospect, and return. The Lunar Scout MX-1 mission will be the historic event that demonstrates the cost-effectiveness of entrepreneurial approaches to space exploration, carrying a diverse manifest of payloads. This includes the International Lunar Observatory, which will deploy a "mooncam"—a small astronomical observatory—accessible on the internet. (Google plans to provide access to its images through YouTube.) Also included is MoonLIGHT by the INFN National Laboratories of Frascati and the University of Maryland, which will deliver a new generation of lunar laser ranging arrays to test principles of Einstein's general relativity theory, add to international scientific knowledge about the moon, and increase lunar mapping precision that will support Moon Express' future lander missions. A Celestis memorial flight will also be included.

> **Because the nation-states have backed off investing in space exploration and other crucial sciences, they are going to increasingly lose power to influence where the world is headed. And because entrepreneurs have stepped up to close the gap, entrepreneurs are going to take the lead.**

The second leg, *Lunar Outpost*, will enable the first commercial presence and exploration of the lunar south pole. The poles of the moon have high concentrations of water and other valuable resources, as well as "peaks of eternal light" where nearly continuous sunshine and direct communication with Earth are possible. The primary goals of this mission are to set up the first lunar research outpost, prospect for water and useful minerals, and deploy a variety of research instruments for our expedition partners.

The third leg is the most exciting. The *Harvest Moon* expedition will be the first commercial endeavor to return samples to Earth, launching the business phase of lunar resource prospecting.

Now, you might ask, how is it that we have permission to do all this? It's a good question, because it turns out that there is no "Federal Department of Moon Permits." Still, the question remained: would the US government actually give us permission to fly? In early 2016, after visiting a number of federal agencies involved in the interagency review of launch licenses—the NSA, CIA, the State Department, NASA—it became clear that although any of the agencies could potentially say "no," no one agency actually had the independent authority to say "yes."

Until recently, the business of space was the sole province of state governments. And those governments certainly did not anticipate non-governmental actors getting involved in space, let alone those with private commercial aspirations. The "Treaty on Principles Governing the Activities of States in the Exploration and Use of Outer Space, Including the Moon and Other Celestial Bodies," known more briefly as the Outer Space Treaty of 1967, sheds some fascinating historical light on this subject. Inspired by the Antarctic Treaty, it sought to prevent "a new form of colonial competition." More than 100 countries signed on to the idea that the exploration and use of outer space, including the moon and other celestial bodies, should be carried out for the benefit and in the interests of all countries, "irrespective of their degree of economic or scientific development, and shall be the province of all mankind." Moreover, space would not be subject to national appropriation by claim of sovereignty, by means of use or occupation, or by any other means. And it banned the deployment of weapons in space.

The treaty, however, did not explicitly define any rules regarding ownership of natural resources that might be mined in space or on the moon—a question that was ultimately cleared up with the "Spurring Private Aerospace Competitiveness and Entrepreneurship Act of 2015," or the SPACE Act, signed by President Obama. It does explicitly entitle US citizens to "possess, own, transport, use, and sell" extracted materials, subject to the obligations of the United States under the various treaties it has previously signed. Hailed as a "giant leap" for private space exploration, it eliminated the ambiguity that was hampering entrepreneurial investment in space.

> " The next set of superpowers is most likely to be entrepreneurs—entrepreneurs who are not waiting on governments to solve problems or address the things that they care about. "

But still lacking was any prescribed process or clarity of regulatory authority for actually launching an expedition. So in this absence, we proposed a "Mission Approval" framework, intended as an interim "patch." It built on the existing payload review process of the Federal Aviation Administration Office of Commercial Space Transportation (FAA/AST) with a series of additional "voluntary disclosures" intended to help satisfy US obligations under the original Outer Space Treaty. We worked independently with all the stakeholder federal agencies, who in turn worked collaboratively and creatively to find a way to approve our *ad hoc* approach, even as Congress and the Administration determine a more formal framework.

As a result of these efforts, on July 20, 2016, Moon Express became the first commercial entity to receive formal US government approval to send a robotic spacecraft beyond traditional Earth orbit and to the moon. This was in fact the first time in history that any government signatory to the Outer Space Treaty exercised its rights and obligations to formally authorize and supervise a commercial entity to fly a mission beyond Earth orbit. As a further result, Ben Roberts of the White House Office of Science and Technology Policy, a tremendous ally throughout this process, ultimately joined Moon Express as its vice president of government affairs. And, at the time of this writing, Moon Express remains the only company with per-

> " A government mired in gridlock wrapped in bureaucracy is the entrepreneur's opportunity. Governments are not wired for responsive agility. Entrepreneurs are. "

mission to leave Earth orbit. Best of all, thanks to the SPACE Act, we'll own anything we bring back from the moon.

The moon will ultimately be treated no differently than international waters. No one owns the oceans, but those who invest their money and effort to find fish are entitled to profit. Likewise, there is strong legal precedent and consensus around the concept of "finders, keepers" for resources that are liberated through private investment, and the same will be true of the moon.

That's not to say we won't have competition for these resources. Far from it. These recent US government provisions will serve to stoke entrepreneurial efforts just when they are needed most. But consider the significance of China's becoming, in 2013, the third nation to land a robotic spacecraft on the moon with their Chang'e 3 lander. Soon, they'll be bringing back moon samples of their own with the same eye toward developing helium-3-based fusion (Chang'e 5 is expected to land on the moon by 2019 with a goal of returning two kilograms of lunar soil and rock samples). "They've learned from the Wisconsin work, believe me," says Jack Schmitt. Indeed, the lunar resources of importance to Earth have not been lost on other international players. The Russians also have their eye on this objective.

That said, space exploration in the quest for abundance shouldn't be just an American dream. I would love to see the American dream become a global dream. Entrepreneurs don't have boundaries. Entrepreneurs work with everyone and anyone who believes in them, anyone who believes in their cause. Moon Express is funded by people from all over the world—entrepreneurs from America, China, Russia, India, Germany, France. We all believe that this vision is attainable, and we all came together to make it happen. Capital is not patriotic. Capital goes where the opportunities are. Boundaries are created by politicians for their own purposes. Entrepreneurs don't create boundaries; they expand them far beyond any visible horizon on Earth or beyond.

> **It is vital that entrepreneurs throw off the shackles of a mindset conditioned to believe that only governments can accomplish these large-scale objectives. We've got to invert the model. The status quo is not moving us forward, so we must subvert it.**

Because the nation-states have backed off investing in space exploration and other crucial sciences, they are going to increasingly lose power to influence where the world is headed. And because entrepreneurs have stepped up to close the gap, entrepreneurs are going to take the lead. This means the role that governmental institutions will play in our lives will necessarily change. One reason among many is that entrepreneurs will always win against government initiatives—they are far more nimble and better able to create sustainable commercial enterprises, and therefore able to succeed in the long run.

Indeed, government's role in the world has already changed. The nation-state is not as important as it used to be. No longer are the nation-states islands unto themselves; today we truly live in a global age where ideas, people, capital, and technology flow freely across borders. Entrepreneurs view problems in the aggregate and will source labor from the best available minds, regardless of where people are physically. Nation-states, however, tend to limit themselves to the talent within their own borders.

Moreover, because of their global perspective, entrepreneurs will more freely be able to transcend geopolitical concerns to create, fund, and enable global solutions. In the end, entrepreneurs answer to global markets, not local constituencies. We get "reelected" only when we deliver real and sustainable value.

The next set of superpowers, therefore, is most likely to be entrepreneurs—entrepreneurs who are not waiting on governments to solve problems or address the things that they care about. When Moon Express lands its lunar module, not only will we become the first private company ever to achieve that feat, we'll become the fourth entity ever to do so, joining the three major superpowers.

It is *entrepreneurs*, not governments or big corporations, who will lead us into the bright future we envision. A government mired in gridlock wrapped in bureaucracy is the entrepreneur's opportunity. Governments are not wired for responsive agility. (Nor, as we'll see later, are the big corporations.) Entrepreneurs are.

Making matters worse is that the United States' R&D budget has declined precipitously over the last decade or so and is continuing its downward slide. Everywhere else, though, it appears that spending on R&D is rapidly trending upward, with much of the shift driven by China. The US is slowly but surely abdicating its position as the global leader in science, a trend that is accelerated by systemic deficiencies in the American education system, which is also hampered by one of the world's lowest levels of private sector funding for university-based R&D. It's not a pretty picture.

> **China, being an autocratic state, has a great advantage over the US: not only is China unburdened by cultural, legal, and privacy concerns, by virtue of its monopoly power it can set its course without compromise or political friction—a course that has already greatly eclipsed American investment in late-stage R&D.**

Even when government tries to course correct against these trends, it fails—for all the reasons we highlighted in our discussion of "experts." For example, in his first inaugural address, President Obama promised to restore science to its rightful place on the American stage. And in making the effort, he turned to *experts* in R&D to lead his science-related agencies—an effort that has, predictably, yielded no meaningful achievements. This should come as no surprise, because such ambitious objectives require the very qualities that we know are completely lacking in such experts. In the meantime, adding insult to injury, spending on

R&D as a share of the federal budget has continued its steep decline. Today this spending is down to a third of what it was in the 1960s.

So clearly, we can no longer look to governments to bring about the reversals that are so desperately needed in the world, and to inspire the kinds of visions that can move humanity forward. Rather, our governments have been nothing short of complicit in creating a mass of men who have been well-trained to accept "miseries and disasters," as Colin Wilson put it, "with the stoicism of a cow standing in the rain." Only entrepreneurs can change this state of affairs.

Unless, that is, China does it. When it comes to advancing science and technology, China, being an autocratic state, has a great advantage over the US: not only is China unburdened by cultural, legal, and privacy concerns, by virtue of its monopoly power it can set its course without compromise or political friction—a course that has already greatly eclipsed American investment in late-stage R&D, the part of the process that turns the output of R&D into useful products and solutions. After all, technology is useless until it is commercialized. China will double that distance this year, leaving US investment levels in the dust.[3]

This should serve as the same kind of wake-up call the US got 60 years ago when the Soviets took an early lead in space with the launch of Sputnik I. President Eisenhower's special assistant for science and technology, Dr. James Killian (who was also the president of MIT at the time, and the person who laid the groundwork for the creation of what would become NASA), observed, "There is no doubt that the Soviets have generated a respect and enthusiasm for science and engineering that has operated to give them a large supply of trained professionals in these fields ... We, however, have catered to desires for undisturbed comfort rather than focusing on larger goals and developing our potentialities." Not much has changed!

What's more, this year China also surpassed the US to become the world's top producer of scientific articles—with a great deal of that increase fueled by research in AI, which, of course, is essential to space exploration. China has, in fact, declared AI a strategic national priority, fortified by the country's vision for a new economic model driven by AI. And, unlike the US, the Chinese government is actually putting its plan in motion, commissioning its tech giants—Baidu, Alibaba, Tencent, and others—to create deep learning laboratories, along with its leading universities. Indeed, as PwC projects, China is expected to reap the most benefit from AI over the next decade with "some $7 trillion in GDP gains by 2030, thanks to an uptick in productivity and consumption." (Now

India has taken a page from China's playbook, with national plans to follow in their footsteps.)

We're seeing the same trends exhibited via the significant decline in the publication of American-authored papers in peer-reviewed journals. Indeed, American scientific influence is waning on all fronts. And yet, here sits Moon Express—a 40-person private company—competing directly with the Chinese, privately funded, and pursuing an audacious goal that promises to deliver world-changing impact. If the US government is unable to reestablish its global leadership in science and technology, entrepreneurs surely will. And they are.

This is why it is vital that entrepreneurs throw off the shackles of a mindset conditioned to believe that only governments can accomplish these large-scale objectives. We've got to invert the model. The status quo is not moving us forward, so we must subvert it. But as we do, entrepreneurs must also reclaim the meaning of innovation, to jar it loose from Silicon Valley-induced complacency and its infatuation with social media, trivial smartphone apps, and $700 juicers. More than ever, the world needs entrepreneurs with audacious visions to take on moonshots in space, healthcare, education, energy, and finance—and not yet another Alexa-controlled toaster or method of getting people to click ads. And we need to scale these efforts individually and collectively if we are to generate the critical mass needed to overcome the inertia of the established bulwarks and realize the new world we want to create. Now entrepreneurs, not members of the Royal Society, are called to become what Sir Francis Bacon called "Merchants of Light," leveraging new knowledge and resources for forging a better future.

Moonstones are a Girl's Best Friend

On the Mohs scale of mineral hardness, diamonds, at a hardness of 10, are the hardest material found on Earth, meaning they are well-suited to a host of industrial applications. Other than that, they really hold no particularly unique distinctions. While all gemstones are rare, diamonds are actually among the most common. So how is it, then, that a utilitarian material used for cutting and grinding tools became such a symbol of wealth and status? It did so through the ruthless manipulations of one man, Cecil Rhodes, the chairman of De Beers Consolidated Mines. Rhodes learned early on about the law of supply and demand, inflating diamond prices at will simply by controlling every diamond mine he could lay his hands on. In no time, De Beers locked up 90 percent of the world's rough-diamond trade, hoarding stones in the company's vaults and meting out their supply to an eager market. In other words, value creation by artificial scarcity.

But it wasn't until diamond sales started to flag during the years of the Great Depression that De Beers hit upon its ultimate master stroke. In 1938, the company hired the Madison Avenue advertising agency N.W. Ayer & Son to craft a campaign to ignite demand for diamond engagement rings—a product that the public at the time really did not want and certainly did not need. De Beers got their gift in the slogan—the *Ad Age* "Slogan of the Century"—"A diamond is forever." It was a simple idea that engendered eternal emotional value in the form of a diamond, and it birthed a global, but entirely invented, tradition, as well as determined the price that should attend it: two months' salary. And it worked. Men spend two months' salary on a diamond engagement ring because the suppliers of the product said so!

And so everyone gives their lover a diamond. But there's nothing special about them anymore. We think it's time for a new tradition—and a new slogan to go with it: "When you *really* love her, don't just promise her the moon, *give* her the moon."

Why should the diamond industry have a monopoly on romance? There is actually no inherently meaningful reason that diamonds should be associated with love. The moon, on the other hand, has been linked to love since time immemorial—in literature, song, and poetry. What could be more romantic than Romance De La Luna? Diamonds? How passé! And we haven't even touched upon how we might redefine the meaning of the honeymoon—a word that was originally a reference to the inevitable waning of love, like the waning phase of the moon. But now, with the moon literally in hand, it is always full. Diamonds can't touch that!

If this all seems tongue in cheek, consider how this could completely disrupt the diamond industry. I have no question that moonstone engagement rings will render diamonds a common and outdated commodity. And of course, they'll put an end to blood diamonds. The best way for an entrepreneur to make inroads into an established industry is to turn the incumbents' advantages into liabilities. And the diamond industry is loaded with them.

Now here's the kicker. All that artificial scarcity of diamonds is already collapsing upon itself. As diamond deposits were recently discovered in Russia, Australia, Canada, and elsewhere, De Beers has watched its share of the rough-diamond trade fall to 40 percent. What's more, satellite technology originally used to scout potential oil fields is also being used to identify the geological signatures associated with diamond-bearing geographies[4]. So it really is the end of an era and, I believe, the beginning of a new one—and one that could potentially "eclipse" the $80 billion dollar diamond market.

Commercial ventures like this and other ideas we've had fun brainstorming will not only provide the sustained funding for our continued lunar operations, they're the sort of enterprises that will inspire in millions the infinite possibilities of space, of being a part of this adventure and putting their own mark on the moon—and with the Earth "thrown in."

1. China is preparing to launch a pair of missions as part of its Chang'e 4 program—named after the Chinese moon goddess. The first leg will be the launch of a relay satellite stationed at the moon's far side to provide a communications link between Earth and the lunar far side. Once established, the second leg of the mission will accomplish a first: a lander on the far side's surface.

2. NASA will only approve a spacecraft for human use if there is less than a 1 in 270 chance of crew fatalities over the course of its mission.

3. China's status has indeed graduated from imitator to innovator. A sophisticated and well-educated labor force is far outstripping that of the US. By 2025, China will have invested $150 billion into the domestic semiconductor industry, eliminating the need for American imports—and they don't care about JEDEC standards. Moreover, investments by Baidu, Alibaba, Huawei, and Tencent promise to firmly establish China's leadership position in AI. Note also that Huawei last year filed more patent applications than any other company in the world. What's more, China has attracted more than 4X the amount of venture capital versus the US, and it hosts a third of the unicorn companies. Additionally, China has more supercomputers on the list of the 500 fastest than any other country.

4. Making matters worse for the diamond industry, a 2018 MIT-led study of seismic data indicates that there may be more than a quadrillion tons of diamond buried deep in the Earth's interior. Will diamonds go the way of aluminum?

CHAPTER 14

Curing Healthcare

The road to health is paved with good intestines!

—*Sherry A. Rogers*

N THE U.S. WE SPEND A FIFTH OF OUR GDP ON HEALTHCARE—more than $3.3 trillion. For perspective, that's more than the entire GDPs of Germany, the United Kingdom, and France—and closing in on that of Japan's. And while we pay more than twice *per capita* of other developed countries, our healthcare system delivers comparatively worse outcomes. In short, we're all getting screwed.

Elisabeth Rosenthal, author of the healthcare exposé *An American Sickness: How Healthcare Became Big Business and How You Can Take It Back*, explains why. "These days our treatment follows not scientific guidelines, but the logic of commerce in an imperfect and poorly regulated market, whose big players spend more on lobbying than defense contractors. Financial incentives to order more and do more—to default to the most expensive treatment for whatever ails you—drive much of our healthcare." Moreover, she notes that people in every sector of medicine are feeding at the trough: insurers, hospitals, doctors, manufacturers, politicians, regulators, charities, and more. "Even people in sectors that have nothing to do with health—banking, real estate, and tech—have also somehow found a way to extort cash from patients." In other words, the healthcare we get is exactly what the market's financial incentives demand. And they demand profit, not cured patients.

Moreover, Rosenthal outlines 10 "economic rules of the dysfunctional medical market," which include such rubrics as more treatment is always better—default to the most expensive; a lifetime of treatment is preferable to a cure;

there's money to be made in billing for anything and everything; prices will rise to whatever the market will bear. All true, except that I take exception to her use of the word "dysfunctional"; the system is functioning perfectly according to its objectives! When healthcare providers are paid for doing more, that's exactly what they will do. What's more, their largely uncontrolled profit-incentivized fee-for-service payment model means that medical services are unbundled and paid for separately. In other words, physicians are incentivized to provide more treatments because payment is dependent on the *quantity* of care, not its quality. (Keep this in mind the next time you visit a physician-owned clinic.)

If that were not enough—and apparently it isn't—providers employ sophisticated "coders" who classify procedures for billing purposes. If your medical billing statement is indecipherable, that's part of the game. Medical bills frequently contain line items for procedures that are "upcoded," that is, patients are billed at more expensive levels of service than were actually performed. Coding, in fact, became a profit center of its own for providers. Rosenthal observes, "Highly skilled coders have contributed to higher costs for patients, because the salaries of this new layer of professionals and their years of education are reflected in our medical bills." This is really nothing short of medical extortion and oftentimes fraud— but fraud that is nearly impossible to prove. And year over year, patients are on the hook for a higher percentage of their total healthcare costs. A particularly notable example of such abuse is the case of Elizabeth Moreno, who was billed $17,850 for an unwarranted drug test—based on a single urine sample— that should have cost just $100.92.

> **While we pay more than twice per capita of other developed countries, our healthcare system delivers comparatively worse outcomes. In short, we're all getting screwed.**

But what about the insurers? What does all of this mean for them? More money.

Insurance companies are like banks. They don't make their money on the premiums, they make their money on their *investments* of those premiums. The insurance racket is simply a way of securing capital. This is also why insurance companies do all they can to slash or delay payments on claims—it takes money out of lucrative investment vehicles. In the meantime, while

medical costs explode, insurers simply raise premiums, copayments, and de-
ductibles. And now that they're also required to pay out 80 to 85 percent of
premiums on patient claims, they need to make that 15 percent margin go
further. That's why premiums are dramatically increasing every year—rising
by double digits. If the slice of the pie has gotten smaller, the remedy is simple: *grow the pie!* This way, they stay whole. Where government regulations
are concerned, insurance companies simply respond *à la* Alfred E. Newman,
"What, me worry?"

I don't begrudge insurance executives for scoring tens of millions in compensation every year, but let this serve as a clue as to just how astoundingly profitable the insurance business is—especially when it is designed more for profit
than actually delivering healthcare. This system requires ever-growing legions
of sick people to keep this massive engine running. As Rosenthal sums up, "Hospital systems, which are managed by business executives, behave like predatory
lenders." As such, the costs can only go up. And if we're all going to be living
longer lives, then the future is going to get very expensive.

○ ◗ ● ◖

When all the experts tell us that the average lifespan is about 80 years, we believe it like some law of the universe. When someone dies at that age, we accept that they've lived a good long life. We've become *conditioned* to believe it,
and like so many other things connected to our mindset, it becomes a self-fulfilling prophecy. ("Normal" cholesterol in a society where it's "normal" to drop
dead of a heart attack really should not be considered a good thing.) We don't
achieve more than we expect. The same can be said for our healthcare system.
As such, entrepreneurs are presented with a massive opportunity to solve an
equally massive problem. And you don't have to read between the lines to see
that we're talking about disrupting the very foundations of the healthcare ecosystem, which, as we have just seen, is a big part of the problem. But first, we
need to understand the lay of the land—the battlefield upon which this epic
disruption will take place: the "medical-industrial complex."

First of all, the term "healthcare" is a misnomer. The healthcare industry is
not concerned with health, it is concerned with illness. There is no profit in
healthy patients in a system that has emerged to address symptoms and not
their underlying causes. Treating symptoms leaves the underlying causes un-
addressed. But solve the root causes and the symptoms disappear. Symptoms,

though, are what is visible; it's very difficult to see the underlying problem. Consequently, it's easier for people to believe that a health problem has been solved if the symptoms can be eliminated. But this is like painting over rot: it might look good now, but underneath, it's still rotted. The healthcare system works the same way. You can eliminate a symptom, but the problem will just show up as a different symptom altogether. If a patient is suffering from depression, but the root cause is inflammation, you can suppress the depression, but the continuing inflammation will show up as cancer, it will show up as Alzheimer's, it will show up as diabetes, it will show up as heart disease, it will show up as obesity—any or all of these things—because the inflammation is still active. The healthcare system is really good at suppressing one symptom at a time. But if you can solve the cause of the inflammation, then all the symptoms evaporate. Attack the symptoms only, and the patient lives with the problem for the rest of what could be a severely shortened and less enjoyable life.

> **What if we could not only live longer—maybe even two times longer—but enjoy good lifelong health, putting an end to premature death, misery, and wasted healthcare dollars?**

The healthcare system, then, is really a *sickness* system: it is inherently incentivized against the interests of the patient. Most people believe that the healthcare system is broken. It is not broken. It is doing exactly what it was designed to do: enrich its stakeholders.

We wonder why our medical costs are so high. High medical costs are not the problem; they too are a *symptom* of the problem. Again, our entire governmental, healthcare, and insurance infrastructures are focused on the symptoms. And the business of treating symptoms is one of the most profitable businesses on the planet. If advances in "fixing" the healthcare system have proven elusive, it's by design.

Today, the healthcare system itself has become an organism where the purpose of the organism is its own survival. As such, the pharmaceutical companies believe the best drug they can develop is the drug to which you have a lifetime subscription. If a drug actually cures a condition, then it is not a good drug. So their incentive is never to address the underlying condition, but to treat the symptoms. In other words, it is to their benefit that you remain sick.

The same is true of hospitals. Likewise, doctors need patients. And the insurance industry is the protection racket that has grown up around it all. It sounds incredible, but the entire ecosystem depends entirely upon the continued illness of the population it purports to serve. Even organizations like the American Cancer Society, American Diabetes Association, Susan G. Komen, and others benefit from the continuance of these diseases. You can, in fact, be sure that nowhere will you find in the mission statements of any of these organizations the goal of putting themselves out of business because they are no longer needed. (And when you discover who their major sponsors are, the corruption of their agendas becomes even more painfully obvious.)

○ ◑ ● ◖

It turns out that illnesses such as cancer, diabetes, heart disease, stroke, Parkinson's, Crohn's, Alzheimer's, arthritis, depression, and many other debilitating conditions share a common denominator: chronic inflammation. In fact, chronic inflammation is both a precursor and prerequisite to the onset and development of today's deadliest diseases. That's the culprit.

But it's also true that inflammation is a normal function of the immune system and is actually essential to the body's healing processes. When there is an injury or infection anywhere in the body, the immune system sends its "first responders"—inflammatory cells—to contain the damage and help heal it. We then experience inflammation as swelling and redness around the site of the problem. If it weren't for inflammation, wounds would likely become infected, with potentially deadly consequences.

Now, recall earlier our discussion about what happens when the amygdala's response is stuck in the *on* position: the brain gets locked into a persistent fight-or-flight state, which leads to anxiety and other mental and physiological disorders. Likewise, when the inflammatory response is continuously provoked into high alert, what was originally intended for our protection—like the fight-or-flight response—turns on us as well. This prolonged "state of emergency" can then inflict serious damage upon our cells and organs, leading to disease. For example, sustained inflammation can cause the buildup of plaques that in turn stimulate additional immune response, generating a nasty feedback loop that ends up thickening arteries, which in turn can lead to heart attack or stroke. And by the same mechanisms, inflammation in the brain can lead to Alzheimer's disease.

A whole host of factors underlie chronic inflammation, but one condition in particular has established a clear link between it and most of these diseases: the "permeability" of the intestine walls, known more familiarly as "leaky gut syndrome." In short, if your intestinal wall becomes leaky, then tiny particles of undigested food, as well as pathogenic gut microbes, can escape the gut and enter the bloodstream, triggering the immune system to kick into action. If this condition persists for a prolonged period—that is, if the leaking continues—the immune response will also continue, attacking not only the "invaders," but ultimately inflicting damage in many areas of the body, leading to the raft of the inflammatory diseases that drive the mortality statistics.

In a healthy gut, a properly balanced community of "microbiota" keep the intestinal walls intact, thus maintaining a strong barrier between your gut and the rest of your body. But if the microbiota are out of balance, a *dysbiosis* results. For example, some of these gut microbes, especially those that feed on sugars, can do real damage to the intestinal lining, increasing its porosity. In fact, gut health is increasingly being linked to the presence of disease. And the gut, of course, works on the same principle of computing: garbage in, garbage out. In other words, diet matters.

It turns out that Hippocrates, who lived around the 4th century BC, knew what he was talking about when he said, "Let food be thy medicine, and medicine be thy food."

Now, would you be surprised to learn that 70 percent of your body's immune cells live in your intestines? And that their interactions with the microbiota also living in the gut determine to a great extent how your immune cells behave? It's true that both your susceptibility to illness and your ability to fight it actually starts in your gut. It's not a great leap, then, to see that gut health must be an important key to a long and healthy life.

> " The term "healthcare" is a misnomer. The healthcare industry is not concerned with health, it is concerned with illness. There is no profit in healthy patients in a system that has emerged to address symptoms and not their underlying causes. "

So I ask the audacious question: *what if we were able to make illness optional?* If we can eliminate the plethora of diseases caused by chronic inflammation—conditions that have their origins in the gut—would we not also be well on our way to realizing a 2X—and maybe even a 3X—improvement in lifespan? Would not this possibility make for the greatest entrepreneurial moonshot of all?

Doubling Health Expectancy

In 2018 just one person in the world who was born in the year 1900 remained alive. And there's no one older, as far as we can tell. It's extraordinary, but should it be? According to the Centers for Disease Control and Prevention, Americans can expect to live, on average, just 78.8 years. Some, though, are more optimistic: if you can hang on until 2030, the World Health Organization says you might make it to 79.5.

But is there really a hard stop on the human lifespan? It's possible that there is—if we leave nature to its own devices. But must we?1 Whatever the case, what we do know is that just as most people live far below their potential, they also die well before their time. And the reasons are clear. The most recent National Center for Health Statistics data, from 2014, reported the number of deaths in the US from all causes to be 2,712,630. Here's how the numbers break out for the top 15 causes:

- Heart disease: 633,842
- Cancers: 595,930
- Chronic lower respiratory diseases: 155,041
- Accidents: 146,571
- Stroke: 140,323
- Alzheimer's disease: 110,561
- Diabetes: 79,535
- Influenza and pneumonia: 57,062
- Kidney disease: 49,959
- Suicide: 44,193
- Septicemia (blood poisoning): 40,773
- Chronic liver disease and cirrhosis: 40,326
- Hypertension (high blood pressure): 32,200
- Parkinson's disease: 27,972
- Noninfectious pneumonitis: 19,803

No surprises here, right? But if you look at the leading causes of death a hundred or so years ago, it becomes equally clear that we're living in a very different world today. In 1900 the average life expectancy was just 47 years. People then were far more likely to die of diseases like tuberculosis, gastrointestinal infections, diphtheria, and other infectious diseases that have largely been eradicated. Today, though, most causes of death are what we have come to understand, ironically, as "age-related"; the longer we live, the more likely we are to develop, for example, heart disease, cancer, or Alzheimer's.

In 1900, though, people died long before any of these diseases had a chance to manifest! But these comparisons don't clearly paint the picture. The world has come to suffer from a very different kind of epidemic in the form of *chronic* illnesses, and they take far more of us now. While infectious diseases have been declining for decades around the world, chronic health problems are more than compensating—they are *by far* the leading cause of mortality in the world, representing nearly three-quarters of all deaths.

What is most striking about these causes, though, is that nearly all of them aren't things that simply happen, but develop as a consequence of lifestyle choices. For example, you don't "catch" Alzheimer's, you *cultivate* it. Literally so. In other words, these diseases are preventable. As a further consequence—and as an exponentially growing insult to illness—these diseases consume the lion's share of all our healthcare dollars. People may be living longer, but the added years are often saddled with the burden of ill health that requires continuing—and expensive—medical attention. But what if we could not only live longer—maybe even two times longer—but enjoy good lifelong health, putting an end to premature death, misery, and wasted healthcare dollars? I believe we can accomplish all three of these goals. That's audacious, to be sure—maybe even crazy—but isn't that the first marker of a moonshot?

It's one thing to examine the causes of death; it's quite another to examine the causes that underlie the causes. We've been learning quite a lot about this in recent years. So much so that when we ask the audacious question, "What if we could make illness optional?" it's actually not as crazy as it sounds.

So how long *should* we expect to be able to live? The folks at Polstats wondered about that and ran a fun simulation to determine life expectancy if all natural causes of death were magically eliminated. The answer? 8,938 years. And that's because, odds are, an "unnatural" cause would eventually catch up with us, e.g., an automobile accident, getting shot, dying in a fire, falling down stairs, drowning, falling off a ladder, or going down in a plane crash. Now, I don't think anyone believes that we can extend human life expectancy 1,000-fold, but how about just a 2X improvement? Could we achieve that much? And an improved "healthspan" to go with it? Framed that way, it suddenly seems a lot more doable. Especially when you begin to understand what's *really* going on in the human body.

But what, exactly is the microbiome? In short, it is a diverse ecological community of microorganisms that reside within the gastrointestinal tract. But that's not what's interesting about it.

What if I told you that you really aren't what you think you are?

In human DNA, there are about 20,000 protein-coding genes. If that number seems impressive, the nematode worm has about 22,000. But get this: the microbes in your gut produce as many as 20 million genes! That's a lot of bioactivity that is not your own. Our bodies are really just a container for the over 100 trillion microorganisms that live in and on us, including over 10,000 species of bacteria. These organisms live with us in a "commensal" relationship: we quite literally eat together at the same table. But the microbiome does more than that—it performs the heavy lifting in providing nourishment to our cells and enables the function of our metabolic and immune systems. Interestingly, its role in our health has been largely overlooked until very recently.

It turns out that this "forgotten organ" is really the wellspring of our wellbeing—and, on the shadow side, the source of many of our diseases. We've now learned that Parkinson's, for example, begins in the gut, not in the brain as previously thought. Therefore, prevention must begin in the gut. Ninety percent of your serotonin is produced in the gut. Therefore prevention and treatment of depression and anxiety must begin in the gut (depression is now known to be linked to ongoing low-grade inflammation in the body). Many conditions from allergies to autoimmune diseases are all related to the diversity of the microbiota. The microbiome also plays central roles in vitamin production, nutrient absorption, hunger, detoxification, and how we process and utilize carbohydrates and fat. And thanks to the gut-brain axis, it also affects mood, libido, and general outlook on life. It's remarkable, really. And we've only just found this out. This is especially remarkable because the microbial cells we host outnumber our "human" cells 10 to one. We are, in fact, more bacteria than we are human! Because we are such composite creatures, a proper equilibrium between the human host and the microbiome is essential for good physiological function.

> **If we can eliminate the plethora of diseases caused by chronic inflammation—conditions that have their origins in the gut—would we not also be well on our way to realizing a 2X—and maybe even a 3X—improvement in lifespan? Would not this possibility make for the greatest entrepreneurial moonshot of all?**

You'd think that the medical community would have picked up on this earlier. Every chronic disease, whether it is anxiety, depression, autism, Parkinson's, Alzheimer's, obesity, diabetes, cancer—*every one of these conditions*—is directly influenced by the microbiome. In research paper after research paper after research paper we find the same conclusion: the condition of the microbiome is the key to human health.

But ask your doctor about the state of your microbiome, and you'll likely get a blank stare in return. This is starting to change now, but the medical schools don't teach much, if anything, about the role of the microbiome in human physiology and health. And if your doctor is older, he'll likely know nothing about it. Yet the peer-reviewed journals issued by all the leading sources—Reed Elsevier (now RELX group), Wiley-Blackwell, Springer Nature, Taylor & Francis, Sage—are publishing an exponentially growing number of research articles on the topic. Moreover, The NIH Common Fund Human Microbiome Project (HMP) was established in 2008 with the mission of generating research resources for studying human microbiota and their role in human health. All this to say that the microbiome has finally gotten the scientific respect it deserves. It is no longer fringe.

The Greatest Story Never Told: An Alternate Take on Creation

Three and a half billion years ago hordes of single-cell eukaryotes, bacteria, fungi, and viruses of every stripe roamed the planet. Life was hard for these creatures; they had to forage for their food, the environment was harsh, and it took ages for them to travel even short distances. Over the millennia they became increasingly disgruntled with their lot in life. Having reached the limit of their tolerance, they convened a special council, led by Master, the most intelligent and developed among the vast microbial community.

The assembly, numbering in the quadrillions, was not only the largest crowd size ever recorded, it was unruly. Many in the great multitude were emaciated while others were agitated, chanting and waving signs carrying slogans reading, *"Power to Microbes," "We're Taking Over,"* and *"We Demand Change."*

Master rose and calmed the crowd. "My fellow microbes," he said. "We have a solution to all our problems. A solution that will see to every one of our needs. No more hardship, no more cold, and no more wondering where the next meal is coming from." The crowd roared with excitement.

"Tell us more, Master! What is it?"

Their leader continued. "It's amazing, really. Trillions of us can live inside each one of these units that we've managed to modify to meet our specific needs. You'll be responsible for maintaining them, though. You'll have to do your part to keep them healthy. And if you do, they will deliver all the food you'll ever need right to your door. And also, because they're so incredibly mobile, they be for us a great ship that will help us colonize the world, planting new communities wherever they go. Yes, my fellow microbes, *we are going to take over the world! We are going to see great change! You will be empowered at last!*" With that, thunderous applause rose from the assembled throng and resonated throughout the great primordial valley.

They christened these great ships "humans" and these units did indeed deliver every one of Master's promises. The massive and diverse ecosystem of organisms prospered and multiplied with the ushering in of this amazing new age.

In time, though, the microbial community again began to worry, and called for another special council to address the new concerns. "Master," they beseeched. "These hosts you've built for us, they're getting quite sophisticated. If they become smarter than us, then we just might lose control. They might rise up and dominate us. Our very survival could be threatened! What ever will we do?!"

Again, Master rose and calmed the anxious crowd. "Microbes, microbes, you're worrying about nothing. You see, we really did think of everything."

"How so, Master? How will we ever be able to subdue this monster we've created?"

"It's a secret, microbes, but I'll share it with you. Among you in this very assembly are your ancient brothers. You know them as mitochondria. Well, we've managed to sneak them right into humanity's cells. Built them right in, we did. And the humans are not even aware of it. These amazing brothers of ours—equipped with their own DNA, mind you—actually provide all the energy to the humans' cells. They are the power plant that keeps the human machine running. So you see, humanity is completely dependent upon our bacterial brothers to keep them alive. And all their siblings, whether they reside in the host cells or in the gut with you, are in constant communication. They're in on this with us. If humanity ever really gets out of control, we'll just pull the plug, and they will be finished."

"Master," they replied with some relief. "That's brilliant, but we're concerned about something else they've developed—this thing called a *brain*. Won't they eventually find a way to outsmart us?"

"Microbes!" Master's impatience began to show. "To what lengths must I go to show you that everything is under control? Let me ask you something. Where do most of us live?"

"Right here, in the human's gut," they answered. "But we're talking about the brain!"

"We know all about that brain," said Master. "Which is why we planned ahead. We laid down a cable that directly connects the gut to the brain. We're actually hardwired right into it. It turns out that the humans found out about this little detail, but we're not worried. They're still pretty clueless. I'll tell you just how clueless they are. Can you believe they gave this little highway a name? They call it the Vagus nerve, thinking that what happens in the gut stays in the gut. How wrong they were! Let me tell you, microbes, as you well know, what happens in the gut goes *everywhere*!"

"Yes, Master," they responded, still not completely satisfied. "Are you saying that we can we actually control that brain? It seems to have a mind of its own!"

"Ah, yes, that's how it *seems*," answered Master. "That's the most brilliant part of all. You see—and this is biggest secret—we just let them *believe* they're in control. You've heard of this chemical neurotransmitter called serotonin? They utterly rely on it. Where do you think they get it? They get it from *you*, my dear microbes! 90 percent of it comes from right here, in the gut. We produce it for them, making it out of the food they give us. In fact, we control a whole raft of these neurotransmitters that travel up and down this Vagus nerve. And through them, we control their behavior, we control their emotions, we control what they *think*. We control the horizontal, we control the vertical—we control it all! And we do it all along this superhighway. Yet like any good leader, we let them believe they're the ones making the decisions. But now you know that *we're* the ones pulling the strings. These humans are just our puppets. You, my fellow microbes, working together, are the puppet *master*. So sit back and relax. We are in complete control. We've totally got this. We really have taken over the world!"

○ ◐ ● ◖

This little tongue-in-cheek story aside, it is true that the microbiota that live in the gut control many aspects of the human host for its own benefit. And when it's not happy, neither are you. That unhappiness manifests as diabetes, Alzheimer's, Parkinson's, obesity, many cancers, and a host of other disorders caused by the chronic inflammation that results from dysbiosis in the microbiome. And remarkably, the state of that microbiome is entirely dependent upon what its human hosts feed it. But there's another catch.

Where the microbiome is concerned, it turns out that one man's food is another man's poison. What we've now learned is that there is no such thing as a universally healthy diet. The food that might be good for you is not necessarily good for me. And the food that's good for me today may not be good for me four months from now. That spinach you thought was so healthy? 30 percent of us cannot digest it properly, with the consequence being inflammation. It's also true that 50 percent of people who believe they are doing their bodies a favor by eating blueberries, raspberries, or walnuts are actually doing no good at all, or may even be doing harm. Yet we treat our bodies like a black box with little to no understanding of what's really going on inside it. And we all pay the price for that ignorance.

For the first time, though, we, as entrepreneurs, have a shot at making chronic illness truly optional. We saved the microbiota and enabled it to flourish; let's give them an opportunity to return the favor. After all, they have a stake in this too!

Learn more about the science of the microbiome and the amazing gut-brain connection at moonshotsupdate.com

But let's get back to why this matters in the context of disrupting the medical-industrial complex. In short, it means that if you can maintain good gut health, then that good gut health will keep the rest of you healthy. If the gut microbiota are in dysbiosis, then you're up for all the diseases caused by the chronic inflammation that inevitably results—the very conditions that we know to slash human life expectancy *at least* in half.

This also means that if we are fundamentally healthy, then doctors can get back to the proper business of true healthcare, which is treating *acute* conditions. But it also means that their workload will be reduced by more than 70 percent—the amount of care currently consumed by preventable chronic diseases. What's more, it also means that the pharmaceutical industry's drug development pipeline will dry up accordingly. Healthcare costs will then plummet, and a good portion of that 20 percent of our GDP dedicated to healthcare can be put to far better use. So how would this actually work? Well, let me tell you how I came to this in the first place.

○ ◑ ● ◐

As we've seen, the current medical system looks at health problems from the wrong end of the scope. The entire system is geared toward treating the symptoms of a problem, and symptoms are what keep the healthcare industry in business. The opportunity for disruption lies in the possibility of detecting and eliminating problems long before they have the opportunity to manifest as symptoms. That simple change in perspective is both radical and empowering. It changes everything. And it is the single greatest threat to the medical-industrial complex that makes billions of dollars on the backs of human suffering.

While working with NASA on Moon Express, I was exposed to the most amazing technologies, many of which could be harnessed to benefit humanity. Yet there they were, just sitting, undeveloped and unused. It was mind-boggling. The US government has invested hundreds of billions of dollars funding scientific research. When I realized that very few people were working to exploit the research, I had my "eureka" moment. The technology that I am now commercializing with my company Viome is just one of them. And I discovered it at the Los Alamos National Lab—a national security research institution that develops scientific and engineering solutions to ensure the safety, security, and reliability of the US nuclear deterrent, as well as to reduce global threats and solve other emerging national security and energy challenges. Quite a charter. Their work in biothreat reduction is what caught my attention. It extends across many areas, including detection technologies, bioforensics, pathogen analysis, and understanding host-pathogen interactions for better vaccine development. It was in this context that the Lab was tasked with quickly and accurately identifying any pathogen that might be present in the human body.

> If we are fundamentally healthy, then doctors can get back to the proper business of true health-care, which is treating *acute* conditions. But it also means that their workload will be reduced by more than 70 percent—the amount of care currently consumed by preventable chronic diseases.

What they came up with actually provides a complete view into everything that is going on inside the body. It occurred to me that we could apply this same technology for wellness—a lateral application if there ever was one. If we know what's going on inside the body, then we can tweak it and keep people healthy—and particularly so if we were to apply artificial intelligence to all the complex biological data we're able to amass. So I licensed the core technology and formed Viome.

Once we obtain FDA approval, we'll be able to diagnose every single disease, because we'll know what is being expressed by every pathogen, and we'll be able to see exactly what's active in the body. This is actually far more than a new spin on personalized medicine, because it's analyzing the body at a molecular level. And because we're testing our participants every month, we're also generating a critical mass of longitudinal data, which means that if an illness occurs over time, we will be able to find a predictive biomarker for it. In the context of a disease like Alzheimer's, we believe we'll be able to detect it—and potentially cure it—20 years before the onset of symptoms.

Now look at what's happening in genetic sequencing—another area that's ripe for disruption. It takes a long time and costs a lot of money to sequence one's DNA. But the researchers at Los Alamos realized that instead of looking at the DNA for the information of interest, they needed only to consider the RNA. If the information of interest is not being expressed, then we don't really care. Secondly, 90 percent of all the RNAs are concerned with housekeeping; we know exactly what they do. Removing them from the mix leaves us with only 10 percent to sequence. And when we do just that, we're able to see everything that's going on in the gut lining. So not only has the cost of the thing come down by 90 percent, we are actually able to offer monthly testing at a consumer price point. That's disruption.

> **This is the magic of the big, audacious idea—why it actually is easier to accomplish a moonshot than a lesser goal: it enables you to attract the best talent and raise funding on the best possible terms.**

It's so exciting to think about what's going to happen in the next 10 years. But we actually don't have to wait that long. Right now, we can identify every single gene expression of every organism in the gut—not only *what* they are, but what the community of microbiota are actually *doing*. Are they, for example, producing the short-chain fatty acids that our body needs? This aspect alone of the metabolic activity of the microbiome illustrates why gut health is so vital. We're all told to make sure we have enough fiber in our diet. But why? It turns out that it's not the fiber *per se*, but what your gut microbiota does with it. In short, they ferment the fiber and produce a short-chain fatty acid called butyrate, which plays a significant role in preventing diseases from autoimmunity to obesity to colon cancer. It also has a great deal to do with how you respond to medical treatments. In the case of colon cancer, for example, treatment is only effective when a high-fiber diet is combined with the correct bacteria in the gut. If there is a deficiency of those critical microbiota, then the treatment will actually do no good. But your doctors won't tell you that.

We can also see whether or not the microbiota are producing the essential vitamins including B vitamins B12, thiamine, and riboflavin, and Vitamin K. The "essential" nutrients and vitamins listed on the products you buy are so-called because the human body can't make them—the microbiota synthesize them for us. Indeed, the human body is a *supraorganism* composed of nonhuman and human cells that work together in a beautiful symbiosis—but only when properly diverse, which is largely a function of diet.

> " The human body— along with consciousness—may, in fact, be the real "last frontier" and an amazing platform for unimagined entrepreneurial opportunity. "

Many people have told me that this idea of making illness optional is one moonshot too far—that mining helium-3 on the moon and revolutionizing the energy industry will be a walk in the park compared with taking on the healthcare industry. They tell me that I'd be fighting powerful forces with tremendous reach, deep pockets, and far-reaching political influence. But what if we can completely flank the industry? What if we don't even make it about healthcare? What if we simply stick to helping people not get sick?

Of course, we have preventive medicine, but it is mostly concerned with the early detection of existing disease states, and it is expensive. By the way, it is illuminating that the FDA has not labelled aging as a condition in need of treatment. While the FDA regulates many *symptoms* of aging, such as osteoporosis, heart disease, bone loss, diminished mental capacity, etc., it tends to be harder to prove a preventative than it is to prove a drug that treats disease. Moreover, preventive medicine plays into the whole healthcare system game. Primary prevention in the form of diet and exercise, though, is the most basic tool in preventive care arsenal. But how inspiring is this? Apparently, it's not inspiring at all.

In terms of diet, the food Americans eat is not only ultra-processed, but laden with salt, fat, and sugar. Foods rich in fat and sugar, especially processed foods, are more easily digested by the system, but they are not a good source of food for the microbes inhabiting the gut. The result is a less diverse microbiome and less critical communication with the body's systems. Consequently, the average American male has a body mass index just barely under the medical definition of obese, while, according to the CDC, 36 percent actually *are* obese. More shocking is a Mayo Clinic study concluding that only 2.7 percent of all adults exhibit healthy lifestyle characteristics. But here's the real irony: we actually *think* we're doing pretty well! According to an NPR poll, 75 percent of respondents ranked their diets as "good, very good, or excellent." Clearly, we have a major disconnect.

> **We know where this is headed: we can project the point at which the necessary technologies will intersect, and when they do, we'll be there to meet them. In the meantime, we can begin to build the stack with known technologies and with hooks that anticipate the missing pieces.**

In many respects, a great many illnesses are already optional. Perhaps the real moonshot here is not in taking on the healthcare system, but just getting people to care at all about their health! That, though, is something we *can* inspire. By simply understanding the marvel of how our bodies actually work, what our potential as human beings really is, and that illness truly can be optional for ourselves *and for our loved ones*—to say nothing of sparing the bank account and saving our economy—I believe we can turn this state of affairs around. This outcome is actually something that people can visualize—and who wouldn't want to be part of bringing that world into existence—a world where our spouses, children, parents, and dear friends would not become sick and die before their time, which should be a very long time? We're venturing into fascinating territory that has only now come into view. The human body—along with consciousness—may, in fact, be the real "last frontier" and an amazing platform for unimagined entrepreneurial opportunity.

When I started Viome, I didn't see the microbiome as its focus. My thesis was always the question, "What if we could make illness optional?" Microbiome science was never the goal. While we speak of the microbiome, it's really only the vehicle by which we will achieve our goal. It's how we're moving not only the needle, but the goalpost.

Viome is not the only company working in the microbiome space. Others have been there for years. But none of them has preempted the conversation to the larger opportunity: making illness optional. *That's* the moonshot. When you set out to do something that is as audacious as eliminating illness, the very idea becomes a source of inspiration. It becomes a magnet. In the early going, we may not even know exactly how we'll pull off this big idea, but the very visualizing of the possibility is exciting. And that possibility allows you to attract the best and brightest minds, who will then come alongside you and help make it happen. This is the magic of the big, audacious idea—why it actually is easier to accomplish a moonshot than a lesser goal: it enables you to attract the best talent and raise funding on the best possible terms.

When I went out and asked people to imagine living in a world where illness was optional, nobody ever asked me how we'd do it! Then one day I got a call from Guruduth "Guru" Banavar, the head of IBM Watson research. He told me he'd been working on this problem for 20 years. As one of the world's leading figures in artificial intelligence, the one thing he knew he was missing was data, and that if he could get his hands on the data about what's going on inside the human body, then he could figure out the rest. As a consequence of that call, Guru joined the company as our CTO, building out our AI platform, and working alongside our chief science officer, Momo Vuyisich, the former leader of the Applied Genomics team at Los Alamos National Laboratory. Dr. Helen Messier, MD, PhD left her job at Human Longevity working for Dr. Craig Venter to join me in the moonshot to make illness optional. After all, what's the point of living longer if you are going to be sick and suffering? And on our scientific advisory board are Ray Kurzweil and medical luminaries from UCLA, Harvard Medical School, Scripps Research Institute, and others. It's incredible,

> **We're essentially taking a healthcare problem and making it a big data problem.**

really. When people of this caliber come together over a cause they believe in, others in the industry take notice. Before long, Vinod Khosla, the legendary Silicon Valley venture capitalist, reached out, and ended up taking a lead role in the Series A funding round. This is what a moonshot initiative can do. The bolder the idea, the bigger the opportunity, and the easier it actually is to accomplish.

So how will we get there? A world free of illness is not something we can do in a year or even 10 years. But we can bootstrap everything we need in order to get the ball rolling. There are still many unknowns, still much research to do, and additional technologies needed that don't yet exist. But we know where this is headed: we can project the point at which the necessary technologies will intersect, and when they do, we'll be there to meet them. In the meantime, we can begin to build the stack with known technologies and with hooks that anticipate the missing pieces. We can start by simply helping people feel better today, because we already have what we need to do that, even as we build the crucial datasets that will enable the next steps of our AI platform. And we're learning fast as we go—so fast that as we move further down this road, no one will be able to catch us.

We also know that the technologies we'll ultimately need in order to scale are progressing on exponential curves. But because it will take a few years to build the underlying infrastructure, we start today, bootstrapping the company and engaging consumers with the artificial intelligence tools we have now that are already enabling us to make correlations, taking us a step closer to removing chronic illness from the face of the Earth—and without pharmaceutical drugs.

As to competition, we're transcending the notion altogether. Our so-called competitors are irrelevant because we've fundamentally moved the goalpost for them as well. We're essentially taking a healthcare problem and making it a big data problem. Our ultimate competitors will be the Googles of the world, not the pharmaceutical companies. If you're the CEO of Pfizer, you think your competition is coming from Merck. If you're a really forward-looking CEO you might think your competition is coming from the biotechs. But competition is always hiding in plain sight, and you'd have missed it. While the pharma industry execs are reading the same industry rags, going to the same conferences, talking only to each other, they're not learning anything. Healthcare is a big data problem, and as such there is no more trial and error. That will fundamentally change the way healthcare is done.

At the end of the day, our bodies are biochemical entities. As such, they are more an *ecosystem* than a single organism—an ecosystem made up of microbial cells living in community with our own cells. Because we'll be able to understand everything that is happening in this "community," which, when unbalanced, is responsible for chronic diseases, we can indeed potentially create a world where chronic illness is optional. It's exciting to think that autoimmune diseases such as diabetes, rheumatoid arthritis, muscular dystrophy, multiple sclerosis, and fibromyalgia—all of which are associated with dysbiosis in the microbiome—can actually become a thing of the past.

There is far more about the microbiome and its role in human health that I'd like to share, but it's beyond the scope of this book. If you'd like to learn more on this topic, you can find a wealth of informational resources at www.viome.com. I hope you'll be inspired to find your own moonshot in this exciting, stimulating, and incredibly wide-open space.

1. The so-called "Hayflick Limit" is based on the discovery that *telomeres*—the caps at the end of each strand of DNA that protect our chromosomes, like the plastic tips at the end of shoelaces—diminish each time cells divide. It appears that the limit of how many times a cell can replicate itself is, on average, about 50, after which the cell runs out of telomeres and enters its last days—the senescent, or zombie state discussed in Chapter 2. The cell stops dividing, but it continues its nasty inflammation-inducing business. Interestingly, researchers have translated this rate of cell division to a maximum human lifespan of 120 years. So perhaps we really are rigged with a genetic time bomb. But maybe that bomb can be defused. If we can refresh cells with a new supply of telomere-lengthening *telomerase*, then we can keep resetting the cell division count back to zero, meaning that even if a cell is 50 generations down the line, it can be reborn, thus fending off the Grim Reaper that is otherwise the Hayflick Limit. Or maybe not. It turns out that cancer cells also benefit from telomerase, which makes their uncontrolled division even more robust. Clearly, we need more research, but ironically, the National Institute of Aging invests only 2 to 3 percent of its budget in this area.

CHAPTER 15

Taking Education to School

Education makes a straight ditch of a free meandering brook.

—Henry David Thoreau

A SCHOOLROOM FULL OF YOUNG STUDENTS sit attentively at their desks, hands folded before them. Each is wearing a headset whose coiled cable connects to a bus running in a conduit overhead that traces a serpentine pattern in the ceiling. Following the conduit, we see that it originates at the output of a large mechanical grinder. At one end of the grinder an elderly teacher feeds a stack of books into its giant maw, while one of the students turns the crank, converting the energy of the books' contents into electricity and piping the knowledge directly into the students' heads.

It's a fanciful picture, for sure, but not a bad vision of the future of education. Considering, that is, that it was painted in 1910! The artist, Jean-Marc Côté, was imagining the state of education, among other slices of life, in the year 2000. But look at two things he got right—one of which is obvious, the other startling. The use of technology—even archaic electromechanical technology—was the easy one. It was inevitable that technology would come into use to make education more efficient, and indeed, prototypical "teaching machines" were built shortly thereafter. What's startling about the picture is that, for a vision of the far distant future, the essential schoolroom setting remains unchanged! What Côté might have lacked in imagination, he more than made up in prediction accuracy. While today's world would be unrecognizable as seen through the eyes of those living and working more than a hundred years ago, they would certainly find familiar comfort within the walls of the classroom. And that's a problem.

So let's paint a different picture—not one a hundred years off, but as the picture should actually look today. In place of the grinder, we have the cloud. Replacing the wired headsets are wireless handheld devices connected to that cloud. Instead of all the students being tuned to the same academic channel at the same time, we see independent courses of study where students freely access and consume different educational content in different ways and at different rates. And in place of the classroom, we have, well, virtually any setting anywhere, any time—all the time.

All of this is actually possible today. We have all the technology we need right now to deliver superior educational experiences that are hyper-personalized to each and every student's unique needs, interests, and learning styles. What's more, in this picture, the educational content is not dated by the years-long committee-driven processes of textbook production and selection, but is virtual and dynamic and up to the minute—literally so. In this picture, the learning experience is highly interactive, engaging, individualized, and intrinsically *motivating*. Indeed, learning is fun! We see in this picture a completely reimagined academic arrangement that produces vastly superior outcomes, equipping students to thrive in a world amplified by wonder—and doing it all at a fraction of the cost of our current methods. And by cost, I'm not referring only to the cost of the infrastructure and administration, but also to the *opportunity cost* that bleeds us all in the massive under-educating of our children. So why in the world are we still putting students through the same "grind?"

○ ◉ ● ◖

I'd love for entrepreneurs to take notice that the disruption of the education system is a moonshot opportunity worth *hundreds of billions of dollars*—and it's never been more ripe for the picking.

As I've maintained numerous times in this narrative, you cannot expect to achieve a successful future if you're plotting a course from the rearview mirror. Yet this is precisely what the education system does—and it works with dogged persistence to reinforce that *modus operandi*. The education system, like the healthcare system, has evolved into an organism that is motivated entirely by its need for self-preservation. How else can one explain why classrooms today still look and operate almost exactly like they did in 1910?! The system is well-preserved, indeed!

Sir Ken Robinson notes, "The problem is that too often, and in too many ways, current systems of mass education are a catastrophe in themselves. Far from looking to the future, too often they are facing stubbornly towards the past." But it's not as though we've just figured this out.

Cognitive psychologist Sidney Pressey was a man whose thinking was way ahead of his time. In 1926, he invented a remarkable mechanical teaching and testing machine, the objective of which was to lift from the teacher's shoulders much of the burden and "... make her free for those inspirational and thought-stimulating activities which are, presumably, the real function of the teacher." A harsh and lifelong critic of the educational system, he unsuccessfully championed its reform, noting that education was "the one major activity in this country which has thus far not systematically applied ingenuity to the solution of its problems."

> **Our education system is this very day graduating students who will be utterly unprepared to navigate the myriad challenges ahead—challenges that *should* represent massive opportunities for them, but instead are only opportunities lost to a generation.**

Indeed, an effective education system must be intensely learner-focused, virtual, fluidly independent and collaborative, highly personalized, gamified, and, most importantly, relevant. In other words, none of the things that the educational system is today. Unfortunately, no amount of reform can fix the system. What's needed is nothing short of a wholesale replacement that will equip and empower students to be enthusiastically curious, agile, and adaptable life-long learners who will be able to successfully navigate the world's many new paradigms. But to appreciate why the education system looks and operates the way it does, we need to go back to the movement that birthed it—the Industrial Revolution.

○ ◐ ● ◑

The advent of mass education marked a shift from education as the exclusive province of the elite to the general population in order to meet the growing demands of a newly industrialized society. In the UK, the 1870 Education Act made education mandatory through the age of 12. And then, sufficiently trained, into the factories the children would go. In the US, it wasn't until 1918—just a hundred years ago—that Mississippi, the last state in the Union to follow suit, also enacted a compulsory education law. The American programs, though, were also patterned after the UK industrial model, where the fundamental driver was to prepare children for a world of repetitive machine work performed under the horrible conditions that ultimately led to child labor laws.

Remarkably, our education system today still retains many of its original elements. It was suited to its times, but is now completely irrelevant. "The whole idea," wrote Alvin Toffler, "of assembling masses of students (raw material) to be processed by teachers (workers) in a centrally located school (factory) was actually a stroke of industrial genius. The whole administrative hierarchy of education, as it grew up, followed the model of industrial bureaucracy. The very organization of knowledge into permanent disciplines was grounded on industrial assumptions. Children marched from place to place and sat in assigned stations. Bells rang to announce changes of time."

The education system still operates very much like an assembly line, the last station of which is a QA checkpoint that determines via standardized tests whether the "unit of production"—aka, student—passes or fails. Moreover, the skills learned during the industrial age were expected to serve for a lifetime, as people also expected to continue to work in their chosen or, more likely, assumed, industry.

But education is more than just job training. And considering that we don't even know what the jobs of the future will be, it *must* be something more. To see just how obsolete the prevailing paradigm is, consider that half of the jobs that exist today did not exist just 25 years ago. And half of today's occupations will disappear over the next 10 to 15 years as artificial intelligence and other exponential technologies transform everything they touch. Meanwhile, whole new categories of jobs will be created by these very same technological advances. Astoundingly, though, we're still setting up students for a singular soon-to-be-obsolete career in an economy that we can't even fully define!

Even though we've done away with much of our manufacturing base—which, by the way, we are told will never return—we continue to educate our children according to a model inspired by industrial economics. We still group kids by their "date of manufacture," put them in the designated bins, and then run them along a conveyor belt, graduating them from grade to grade as they go. And now, as we enter a fourth industrial revolution—one that is radically different from any of those that preceded it—the inadequacies of this system will precipitate a true state of crisis. And once again, we can't look to governments for solutions.

As we've shown throughout the course of this book, no challenge is too great for innovation and entrepreneurship to solve. If we can redefine the nature of our physiology, lasso the moon, make illness optional, and create energy too cheap to meter, then reinventing the education system—which requires believing nothing impossible before breakfast—should certainly be possible.

To the extent that it proves difficult, we need only recognize the natural resistance of an organism that seeks primarily its self-preservation. It's only the tenacious nature of that beast that makes transforming education a moonshot. Consequently, governments will not help us here at all in any proactive way— the myriad and powerful special interests will fight this effort tooth and nail. As such, it must be subverted, flanked, and obviated in ways that only entrepreneurs can accomplish. To this end, we actually have the wind at our backs. As it is, people are already abandoning the traditional public and higher education systems for greener educational pastures. Look no further than charter schools, homeschooling, MOOCs, KIPP, IDEA, the Khan Academy, Friendship Schools, and other alternatives. They're all growing exponentially. And for good reason.

While the actual cost of delivering knowledge has plummeted, thanks in large part to digital and communications technologies, the costs of traditional education just keep rising, and rising at unsustainable rates. This makes no sense. And if something doesn't make sense, then there is something fundamentally wrong with it. And that's precisely why reinventing education represents such a phenomenal entrepreneurial opportunity.

> **❝ Today's education system must be intensely learner-focused, virtual, fluidly independent and collaborative, highly personalized, gamified, and, most importantly, relevant. In other words, none of the things that the educational system is today. ❞**

Students already know that the system is functionally bankrupt— and now the system is financially bankrupting the students. This is not right. Millennials, for example, have the unenviable combination of the historically highest student debt and the worst job prospects. It's no wonder, then, that they are increasingly defaulting on their loans. And of course, none of this is lost on Gen Z, which is looking at entirely different options for its education. According to research by culture analyst Sparks & Honey, 75 percent of Gen Zers say there are other ways of getting a good education than going to college. And who can blame them? Why, in this age of amazing information technology and virtual delivery, do we have an education system that costs students upwards of a quarter of a million dollars—especially considering that the education it delivers is obsolete by the time they graduate?

Clearly, the system has proven itself incapable of delivering the kinds of educational programs that are needed to prepare our students for a dynamic future. The result is a state of affairs that contributes to increased levels of anxiety about the future, bringing us full circle to our opening chapter. Our education system, therefore, must shift gears into the *future tense*. In order to meet the future, we need to be forming and sending forth generations of students who have the future "in their bones."

> **Education is more than just job training. And considering that we don't even know what the jobs of the future will be, it *must* be something more. To see just how obsolete the prevailing paradigm is, consider that half of the jobs that exist today did not exist just 25 years ago.**

Like the healthcare system, our education system really isn't broken—it's doing exactly what it was designed to do. But the state of the world has long moved on from the model that created this beast. And the fact that the beast has persisted in the face of efforts to reform it reinforces that it must be removed root and branch and completely replaced with a very different model—one that actually addresses our fundamentally different and equally fast-evolving educational needs.

But what, exactly, would this replacement look like? We answered that question at the top of this chapter, and we repeat it here: in order to equip students to thrive in a rapidly changing world, today's education system must be *intensely learner-focused, fluidly independent and collaborative, highly personalized, gamified, and, most importantly, relevant*. Let's take each of these attributes in turn and see how such a vision could actually come about. And let's start, as always, with the desired outcome—the future state of education system that we envision—and work backward.

Imagine graduating a class of students who leave school *more* curious than when they entered. Imagine a generation of young graduates that brings unprecedented creative energy to the world, who greet every challenge as an opportunity to help move humanity forward. Imagine producing life-long learners who are able to effortlessly adapt to the rapidly changing and ever-emerging, but unpredictable, currents of the future. Imagine graduation rates of 100 percent—even in the most disadvantaged school districts—simply because the students are *inspired* to learn. Imagine an educational system that is utterly and completely given over to the interests of the *students*, rather than those of the system. Can you imagine what this generation would look like? What they would accomplish? How they would thrive in an exciting and unfolding future—indeed, how they would shape that future for the betterment of all? Who wouldn't want to see this outcome, or be a part of bringing it about?

De-risking Education

In 1983—35 years ago—President Reagan's National Commission on Excellence in Education published a report called *A Nation at Risk*. Its opening statement read, "If an unfriendly foreign power had attempted to impose on America the mediocre educational performance that exists today, we might well have viewed it as an act of war. As it stands, we have allowed this to happen to ourselves. We have even squandered the gains in student achievement made in the wake of the Sputnik challenge. Moreover, we have dismantled essential support systems which helped make those gains possible. We have, in effect, been committing an act of unthinking, unilateral educational disarmament."

Alarming as this sounds, stunningly few of the Commission's recommendations have ever been enacted, amplifying the underlying cause of the decline in the first place and providing further evidence that we cannot look to governments for solutions. Indeed, just as you don't want the medical-industrial complex to be in charge of your health, for the same reasons, you really do not want the education establishment to be in charge of your children's learning.

Again, only an entrepreneurial approach to this problem can right the ship. And in the process of doing so, the innovative solutions they come up with can serve to cultivate the development of entrepreneurial thinking in the students themselves, which is precisely what many communities need.

The popularity of MOOCs (Massive Open Online Courses) is evidence of change in the right direction. And indeed, many universities are rushing to put their lectures online. Likewise, the Khan Academy is producing ever more online lesson content, while Gooru's *Learning Navigator* is dedicated to making education equally accessible and empowering for everyone. These are great first steps, but they are not the ultimate breakthroughs that will transform the education system. The technology that is being developed to improve lesson production and delivery, however, is vital—as an intermediate goal—to achieving the ultimate end state. And some of the technology involved is actually remarkably simple—especially when it happens to be operating in a slum.

○ ◗ ◖ ◑

In 1999, Dr. Sugata Mitra, a professor of educational technology at Newcastle University, led a long-term project that came to be known as the "Hole in the Wall" experiments. At the time, Mitra had an office in Delhi that bordered an urban slum, separated by a wall. Mitra quite literally cut a hole in that wall and embedded in it a PC and touchpad. The resulting arrangement looked very much like an ATM mounted in a crude concrete and plaster wall. He then connected the PC to high-speed internet and just left it there to see what might happen. In time, an eight-year-old boy accompanied by a younger girl, probably his sister, approached the makeshift computing kiosk. Shortly thereafter, the boy began to teach the girl, who could barely reach the touchpad, how to browse. When Mitra shared this news with colleagues, the whole thing was met with skepticism—somebody on the other side of the wall, they assumed, must have taught these kids how to use it. So Mitra, resolving to try the experiment elsewhere, took the system to Shivpuri, a remote village in the center of India, where he was assured that nobody had ever taught anybody anything. The PC was again mounted in a hole in the wall of an old, decrepit building. Soon, a 13-year-old school dropout approached the curious addition to the structure. He'd never seen a computer. It took him about two minutes to make the connection that manipulating the touchpad corresponded to action on the screen. Eventually, he clicked the pad, quite by accident, which opened Internet Explorer. In eight min-

> " To the extent that it proves difficult, we need only recognize the natural resistance of an organism that seeks primarily its self-preservation. It's only the tenacious nature of that beast that makes transforming education a moonshot. "

utes time he was browsing. The boy then called the other neighborhood children over to take a look. By the evening of that day, 70 children were browsing the internet for the first time. By the way, the PC was set up for the English language. These children had no understanding of English at all.

Repeating the experiment in an even more remote location where there was no internet connectivity, Mitra left several CD-ROMs with the PC mounted in yet another hole in yet another wall. Mitra returned three months later to find kids playing a game on it. When the kids met him there, they told him quite matter of factly that they needed a faster processor and a better mouse! Moreover, the kids learned a sufficient amount of English directly from their experience with the system—some 200 words—which enabled them to use the machine and teach other kids in the community.

Mitra continued this experiment over the course of six years across the length and breadth of India, finding similar outcomes—and all without any adult supervision. Most interesting, their learning curves actually mirrored those of children in traditional schools. Indeed, these children, self-directed and self-organized, worked together, collectively obtaining an educational objective—*without the help of a teacher*. In such absence, every child *became* a teacher as they learned a particular trick or skill—sharing their learnings, peer to peer. Isn't this amazing?

> **In the workplace, when people work collaboratively, they are recognized and rewarded as team players. However, when a student collaborates to get to a right answer in school, it's called cheating.**

So what are we to make of this? In short, the Hole in the Wall experiments demonstrated the innate capacity that children have to learn independently and together, to solve problems with creativity, and to pool the varied insights of the group. Our education system actually discourages this kind of activity. In the workplace, when people work collaboratively, they are recognized and rewarded as team players. However, when a student collaborates to get to a right answer in school, it's called cheating.

The ability to innovate is one of the corporate world's most sought-after talents. But are our schools teaching students how to innovate? No, they are not. But that's not the worst of it. Our schools are actually *stripping* young minds of their essential capacity for curiosity and imagination—the very qualities that enable innovation—and, as it turns out, learning itself.

Curiosity, as should be obvious, is essential to the learning process. When students are curious, it makes learning enjoyable. And when learning is enjoyable, they'll want to come back for more. Once again, we can credit our friend dopamine for curiosity's attractive nature, the effect of which provides the same pleasure buzz as a bar of chocolate. Stella Collins notes, "When we are curious, our brains are stimulated by dopamine, a neurotransmitter that works on our internal reward systems; rats find it so addictive they will press a bar to stimulate dopamine receptors in their brains rather than eat, drink, or sleep. Dopamine is our own internal reward hormone, and it's just as addictive for us as it is for rats."

Happy rats notwithstanding, we clearly don't want our kids foregoing food or sleep—even for the sake of learning. But sadly, we also clearly do not appear to be at risk of an epidemic of dopamine-inducing educational experiences.

Perhaps the most consequential shortcoming of our educational system, though, with respect to fostering innovative thinking, lay in the very structure of the school day itself. Recall that lateral and divergent thinking involves making cross-discipline connections, many of which are nonobvious, to synthesize new ideas. This kind of thinking is what yields the greatest innovations. It is inherently free-ranging and certainly nonlinear. It also requires the practiced development of neural connections that can freely jump tracks along many trains of thought. So what do our schools do? *They teach in a decidedly linear manner.*

Now, it's true that we can really only focus on one thing at a time. And it certainly makes the teachers' jobs easier if they can operate in a linear learning environment where students are focused on one subject at a time, followed by another, and then another. In

> **If we can teach our students to flexibly manage their attention on demand, rather than forcing linear thinking as we do in the classroom today, then we can also create opportunities for them to make novel connections across courses, establishing and reinforcing the neural connections that are imperative to innovation-producing thinking.**

doing so, however, as Marilee Bresciani Ludvik explains, "... we are reinforcing the *separateness* of each course ... The ability to successfully span our attention rests in our capacity to move our attention from one task to another swiftly and effectively while *making connections to the important patterns needed for innovative problem solving* ... We now understand that we can train this kind of attention in ourselves and in our students."

In other words, the classroom could do with a bit of ADHD. Seriously. Indeed, much research points to the fact that people with ADHD consistently score higher in divergent thinking (coming up with creative solutions to a problem) than those without ADHD. Cognitive scientist Darya Zabelina has actually found that real-world creative achievement is related to her term for the condition, "leaky attention," which is essential for detecting alternative foci and for switching mental tracks quickly.

> **Is it any wonder that so many of the innovations we find in the marketplace and in patents today really reflect only incremental improvements to existing solutions that do nothing to transform the status quo?**

If we can teach our students to flexibly manage their attention on demand, rather than forcing linear thinking as we do in the classroom today, then we can also create opportunities for them to make novel connections across courses, establishing and reinforcing the neural connections that are imperative to innovation-producing thinking. This really ought to be a national imperative.

Because we don't do this, is it any wonder, then, that so many of the innovations we find in the marketplace and in patents today really reflect only incremental improvements to existing solutions that do nothing to transform the status quo?

To learn just how effective our education system is at purging students' natural curiosity and imagination—and innate capacity for divergent thinking—George Land and Beth Jarman performed a longitudinal study of the creative capacities of 1,600 students as they advanced through school and beyond. They actually applied the same creativity test that Land had devised for NASA to help them select the most innovative engineers and scientists. What they learned is astounding.

When children were tested initially as kindergarteners, 98 percent of them scored at the "genius level" in divergent thinking—the ability to interpret and answer a question in many different ways. By the time they were 10, only a third of the same group did as well. At 15, just 10 percent of them scored at genius level. For a bit more perspective, when Land and Jarman tested 200,000 adults, they found that only *2 percent* tested at the genius level. Ken Robinson looks at these results and concludes that the main intervention that the children experienced over the term of this study was ... education.

The silver lining in this cloud? Two percent ain't so bad. Historian Oswald Spengler observed that it only takes 2 percent of a population to create the new ideas that everyone else simply applies. Well, that's really not much of a silver lining, is it? It seems to me that our fine education system has cheated us all out of a whole hell of a lot of innovation.

Rethinking education begins with embracing the incredible individuality of every student. Each of our life experiences, talents, and bents are unique, and yet our education system assumes that every one of us can learn in exactly the same way. The fact is, some of us learn experientially, while others are given to more conceptual learning. One child may thrive using his artistic intelligence, processing science visually, whereas another uses logical intelligence, best processing language and arts logically. Imagine how the world could change if we could bring creativity to science and logic to arts!

Why, then, are we constraining students' unique and natural capacities by shoehorning them into a single format or curriculum? Wouldn't it be better if the education system adapted to the way a student *learns* rather than the way a teacher *teaches*? There's actually no reason why we can't do this. We have at our disposal today the very technologies that enable such teaching methods. And clearly, when educational methods are aligned to each student's unique learning style, the educational experience is received and absorbed and retained more naturally. Moreover, just as medicine is becoming increasingly personalized to an individual's physiological variables, personalized education is no less appropriate or possible. Indeed, artificial intelligence technologies make this possible—and easy.

Think about this. By now, everyone is familiar with the facial recognition technologies driven by the "deep learning" algorithms that Facebook uses to identify friends tagged in your photos. These same kinds of algorithms are also finding use in assisted driver applications that monitor, for example, attention levels, cognitive awareness, and emotional distractions via cameras and other sensors mounted in and around the cabin. Is a driver exhibiting the kinds of behaviors that might indicate a potential road rage incident? Does his blinking frequency or rate of yawning indicate drowsiness or fatigue? Is he distracted by the kids arguing in the back seat? How are his eyes tracking? Are they on the road?

The emotional states that manifest as facial expressions are actually hard-wired into our brains at birth. In fact, people who are born blind emote in exactly the same way as the sighted. Properly trained deep learning algorithms are able to detect even the most fleeting of these expressions—including micro-expressions—and so derive a great deal of information about a person's state of mind. In semi-autonomous vehicles, the ADAS system, so enabled by the array of sensors whose data streams are processed in real time by the deep learning algorithms, may intervene with an audio alert, a haptic tap on the shoulder, or some other form of interactivity to keep the driver on track. Additionally, sensors in the car seat can take your temperature, monitor your pulse rate, and even your breathing, further augmenting the system's cognitive computing abilities, providing additional channels of interactivity in the bargain. Audio sensors can tell if you're talking aggressively or with anger or frustration. And if the microphone can't pick up any of this because the windows are rolled down and the kids are screaming, then the system can actually read your lips! All of this technology actually exists today.

> **Technology is moving at such an exponential pace, and knowledge is becoming obsolete so quickly, that the glacial pace at which school boards approve curricula and school books, and purchasing departments act, means it's all obsolete by the time it's delivered.**

What if we were to apply these same capabilities to learning—highly individualized and personalized learning? Imagine an interactive digital tutor—embodied in a tablet—that can tell if a student is getting bored. "Michael," it would say. "Pay attention—we're almost through this section." Imagine this tutor picking up on a micro-expression that betrays a bit of confusion. The tutor would again intervene, saying, "Alicia, I can see that you didn't quite catch that. Would you like me to explain it in a different way or show you a video?" Likewise it could provide positive or corrective feedback in real time, maintaining attentiveness and reinforcing learning in the process. And because the system is so personalized—it would know exactly what analogies and metaphors to align with the student's personal interests—it would also be more *relevant*, thus driving both motivation and long-term retention.

How much of the teaching burden could be lifted by these means—especially when such means are also exponentially more cost-effective? How much more enjoyable, inspiring, and rewarding would learning be for the student? And when the "headmaster AI" consolidates and connects the dots from data generated by the student's peers, the system could in turn generate a virtual, dynamic, and responsive "hive mind" for the whole class, which in turn would also improve the digital tutor's teaching performance. Talk about collaboration! (We're really just a few steps removed at this point from connecting minds in the cloud.) Think what this could do for students with such conditions as autism, dyslexia, ADHD, or depression, to say nothing of the critical real-time alerts that these virtual tutors could provide to teachers and/or parents.

> **We are entering a world where the cycle of learning, unlearning, and relearning will be relentless—and rapid. Indeed, this will be *the* fundamental survival skill. Equipping our students with these skills will be the best gift we can leave them.**

Indeed, while human capability may operate on a linear growth curve, technology is on an exponential curve. Why, then, should we not avail ourselves of the means to advance and inspire every student far above and beyond anything that can be accomplished in a single classroom headed by a single teacher teaching a single topic to all students at once, in the same way, at the same rate of delivery, and on the same schedule? Suddenly this scenario seems archaic. But that's exactly what we're saddled—or is it addled?—with.

Further contributing to this outdated and counterproductive approach to learning is the considerable amount of time and energy dedicated to teaching facts that we no longer need to remember. Every child with access to a smartphone or other internet-connected device has access to all the facts they will ever need. Do you remember the date of Abraham Lincoln's Gettysburg Address? Do you need to? In the event that you do need to know, the answer is just a click or a swipe away—from wherever you might happen to be. (You could even conjure up a "living" Abe Lincoln via virtual reality and ask him yourself!)

I am not suggesting that children no longer need to learn basic facts, but I am suggesting that we don't need schools and teachers to teach them. Indeed, the schools cannot teach them. Technology is moving at such an exponential pace, and knowledge is becoming obsolete so quickly, that the glacial pace at which school boards approve curricula and school books, and purchasing departments act, means it's all obsolete by the time it's delivered. Indeed, knowledge is growing increasingly perishable. Today's facts are tomorrow's misinformation. It simply doesn't work anymore.

Rather, we need entrepreneurs to lead the development of curricula that teach critical thinking skills in the context of the massive and rapidly growing body of knowledge students are already able to access on demand, and encourage collaboration and creativity and imagination to solve the real world problems they'll face when they graduate. (This is one of the things I love about *Lemonade Stand*, a children's entrepreneurship program that asks kids not "what do you want to be when you grow up?" but "what problem do you want to solve?" in order to prepare them to become more adaptable in a fast-changing 21st century.) What is needed are curricula that teach students how to learn—and learn continuously.

> **The problem with testing students in the traditional sense is that it is counterproductive and actually discourages the student. Testing is not designed to measure the progress made by the student; it measures the progress made by the system.**

As Alvin Toffler put it, "The illiterate of the 21st century will not be those who cannot read and write, but those who cannot learn, unlearn, and relearn." This is the opportunity: we are entering a world where the cycle of learning, unlearning, and relearning will be relentless—and rapid. Indeed, this will be *the* fundamental survival skill. Equipping our students with these skills will be the best gift we can leave them. Moreover, the traits that mark the moonshot entrepreneur—curiosity, imagination, a mindset of possibility—are also the feedstock to the processes of lifelong learning. Indeed, this is the only way students will be able to master the cycle.

In this way, entrepreneurs can help create self-deploying "weapons of mass instruction." And any tool—or weapon—that enables one to continuously navigate the cycle of knowledge will become the currency that affords learners the maximum opportunity to participate fully in their futures. And the critical thinking that attends this cycle will be essential to finding the true signal in the noise of this increasingly noisy world.

> **Entrepreneurship not only makes purposeful use of curiosity, creativity, and imagination, it also orients minds by developing the capacity for critical thinking that is needed for good decision-making, making sense of the world, and solving the world's problems.**

These are the skills we must be teaching our kids—and not solely in an academic vacuum. These skills must now also be tied to the development our students' *human* values, life choices, and goals, as they are inheriting a very different kind of world that will be attended by very different psychological demands.

Continuing Toffler's thought, we are all presented with "overchoice." And when this condition deepens, as it certainly will, the person who lacks a clear grasp of his own mission and values in life will become progressively crippled. "Yet the more crucial the question of values becomes," Toffler says, "the less willing our present schools are to grapple with it. It is no wonder that millions of young people trace erratic pathways into the future, ricocheting this way and that like unguided missiles. Worse yet, students are seldom encouraged to analyze their own values and those of their teachers and peers. Millions pass through the education system without once having been forced to search out the contradictions in their own value systems, to probe their own life goals deeply."

All of which recalls our earlier thoughts on the need for a bit of introspection along the way. Indeed, each and every one of us has the opportunity to construct our lives and determine our significance in ways that are utterly unique and special—ways that ought to be discovered in, and amplified by, the experience of education. How else can we expect to develop whole and competent people living at the maximum of their potential?

If we can guide students to make both concrete and novel connections between their studies and the real world, then they could, as Bresciani Ludvik concludes, "solve wicked problems and do so while paying attention to who they are, what they believe, and what they value. If we create the process for learning and development that fosters reinforcing neural connections that promote students' critical thinking, creativity, analytical reasoning, and peaceful com-munications, we may be able to 'deliver' the kinds of learning and development that employers and others demand."

Just as children respond differently to the various learning modalities, it should come as no surprise that they also learn at different rates. Wouldn't it be nice, then, if we changed our education system to move away from "fixed time vari-able learning" to "fixed learning variable time?" Instead of allocating a fixed block of time, e.g., a semester, in which a student must master a subject, every student could be allowed to proceed at their own pace. (The Khan Academy is already making this possible, where students can pause, rewind, and repeat a learning module as many times as they need without having to be told that they're "slow learners.")

This is much the way players advance in a video game—you move to the next level only after having mastered the previous level, irrespective of how long it might have taken. It might be six hours, six days, six weeks, or six months. So let's think about this element of gamification in the context of education.

While many kids struggle, for example, with basic algebra and chemistry, have you noticed that they have no trouble at all navigating the remarkably complex problems presented in many video games? Problem-solving that in-volves fairly high-level executive deci-sion-making skills and no small amount of analytical thinking? Yet we accept the fact that they can't add or read?

> **Entrepreneurship shows us how to discard old ideas, and how and when to replace them with new ones. Imagine baking these qualities into the minds of all our students!**

On one hand, it might be easy to dis-miss the gamification of education as indulgent, but the concept is actually backed by neuroscience. Because of their immersive and engaging nature, games involve a great many channels of neural activity in both hemispheres of the brain. And they work.

Much research shows that gaming consistently outperforms textbooks—and it does so across disciplines. In fact, gamers make better drone operators that pilots!

Moreover, games are self-reinforcing, as our brains release dopamine in response to rewards or progress toward a goal. Oxytocin, adrenaline, serotonin, and other neurochemicals literally "light up" the player's mind in a symphony of neural activity as a game advances. Indeed, it is the experience produced by these neurochemicals that gives one the sense of being "in the flow." Imagine extending that "high" to the learning experience!

> **Let us then not just focus all our energy on leaving a better country for our children, but be resolved to leaving better children for our country.**

For the same reason that dopamine is addictive, games are also addictive. While you might have to nag your kids to do their homework, you never have to encourage them to play games. Just think of the opportunities that can be unlocked by making education as addictive as a video game! Can you imagine a child begging to spend just another 15 minutes with math, history, or science? And we haven't even begun to explore the unlimited possibilities presented by putting AR/VR into the mix. How will these technologies revolutionize education?! From auto mechanics to medicine, they'll amplify learning everywhere.

Consider also how games can be personalized. For example, if a student loves skiing and also wants to learn Chinese, he can immerse himself in a game that drops him into China where he has to communicate with locals in order to get all the things he needs to go skiing. Finally he catches a bus to the slopes in a remote area where only Cantonese is spoken. When he makes it, he earns a reward and is advanced to the next level. No nagging necessary.

And no testing, either.

The need for testing is obviated by virtue of the game itself—the requisite proficiency is demonstrated as an inherent function of the game. After all, it is the only way the student can advance. The problem with testing students in the traditional sense is that it is counterproductive and actually discourages the student. Testing is not designed to measure the progress made by the student; it measures the progress made by the system. Again, the whole paradigm must be flipped to a student-centered model.

Moreover, testing induces a great many unnecessary negatives into the educational experience. Recall the last time you took a test. Tests are inherently threatening. As such, they ring up all the brain's natural responses to threats.

Percentage of adults scoring at each proficiency level in literacy

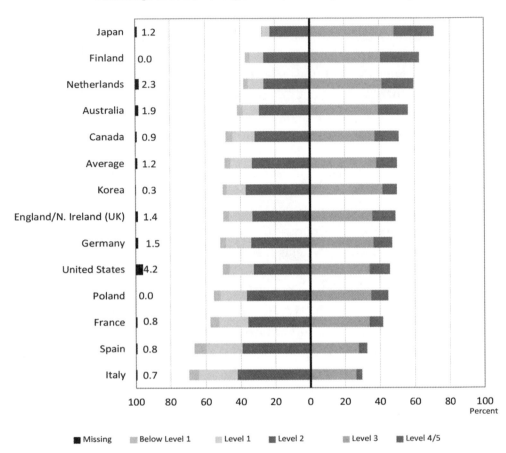

Shown here are the share of adults at different levels of literacy proficiency. Countries closer to the top of the chart have proportionately more adults who score at higher levels of literacy. *Source: OECD.*

Has your mind ever gone blank while taking a test? Remember the curious action of the amygdala that shuts down the neural pathways to the neocortex—that area of the brain where the thinking takes place? Tests stimulate the release of cortisol and various other neurochemicals that prepare one for a fight-or-flight response—not a test of knowledge.

What's worse is there's a more insidious aspect to the testing of students. Even though repeated failure is an essential component of teaching innovation, fail just once on an exam in school, and you're potentially out. The whole scheme runs absolutely counter to the outcome that is actually needed in the real world. And yet another archaic practice persists. Can we not fashion an educational experience that encourages and rewards learning and dispenses with pass/fail gates that threaten elimination? Now imagine how we could begin to reduce the number of high school dropouts across the US—currently about 1.2 million per year.

Another unnecessary negative is the start time imposed at most schools. Do we really need to resort to neuroscience to tell us that teenagers are not exactly at their best in the morning? The sleep-wake cycle of teenagers in particular is skewed with respect to that of most adults. And when it is forced to comply with an unnatural cycle, the result is that memory consolidation, information processing, and creativity is negatively impacted. Clearly, a virtual, self-directed, and AI-assisted fixed learning-variable time model would eliminate this arbitrary requirement and replace it with an approach that is actually conducive to learning.

Seriously, just how many ways can our education system stack the deck against the objective of learning?! And wherever governments actually do initiate programs to improve education, they invariably end up being a step backward. They're a step backward because, as Einstein told us, we cannot solve problems by using the same kind of thinking that created them.

There is simply no way that the current education system can lead us into a future that we can't fully comprehend. We do indeed need to educate for unpredictability. And to that end, there is simply no better vehicle for developing such skills than training in entrepreneurship. It's true. Consider what this entails and what it can produce in an individual. The skills and thought processes required of entrepreneurship comprise the superset of everything students need to navigate and cope with a burgeoning future that otherwise seems beyond our control. Entrepreneurship not only makes purposeful use of curiosity, creativity, and imagination, it also orients minds by developing the capacity for critical thinking that is needed for good decision-making, making sense of the world, and solving the world's problems. Entrepreneurship produces grit, agility, adaptability, the ability to fail forward, and the resilience to constantly and continuously learn, unlearn and relearn. Entrepreneurship shows us how to discard old ideas, and how and when to replace them with new ones. Imagine baking these qualities into the minds of all our students! What's more, as we've seen, the Gen Zers are already primed to receive it.

Psychologist Herbert Gerjuoy would add, "The new education must teach the individual how to classify and reclassify information, how to evaluate its veracity, how to change categories when necessary, how to move from the concrete to the abstract and back, how to look at problems from a new direction—*how to teach himself*." This is not only competence for living, but lifelong insulation from jobsolescence.

So what becomes of the teacher in this new educational landscape? In short, just as a reinvented healthcare system would free doctors to deliver acute care, freeing them from concern with induced chronic conditions, a new education system would free teachers to do the things they do best: teach, mentor, coach, facilitate, and engage students in applying their self-directed learnings to life in the real world.

The problems with the current education system are not the fault of the individual teachers who are working within it. There is no more noble calling than that of teaching, and so many of our teachers pour themselves out for their students. Thank God for our teachers. But imagine if, rather than being encumbered by a corrupt, bureaucratic, and hopelessly obsolete education establishment, they were liberated to actually help our students to excel beyond their dreams and thrive in an amazing future they can not only imagine, but create. Can you visualize that possibility?

Now visualize this possibility: instead of the United States continuing its free-fall descent into educational mediocrity, our students actually rise to the top of the world in numeracy, literacy, and problem-solving ability. (If there is any question about our current status, take a look at the position of the US in the global rankings in the figure, above.) Let us then not just focus all our energy on leaving a better country for our children, but be resolved to leaving better children for our country.

PART THREE

Boldly Go

CHAPTER 16

Vision Without Execution = Hallucination

In theory, there is no difference between practice and theory; in practice, there is.

—Yogi Berra

NTREPRENEURIAL MOONSHOTS DIFFER from literal moonshots in one particularly consequential way: when entrepreneurial moonshots launch, all systems are most definitely *not* go. By definition, the ultimate goals of moonshots rely upon the availability of key components, each of which is on its own technology trajectory. The art of the entrepreneurial moonshot lies in orchestrating your mission such that it will intersect—at just the right time—contingent events that are not always as predictable as the alignment of planets and orbital patterns.

Moonshots also differ radically from incremental initiatives. When merely going for a 10 percent improvement, you've got a lot more knowns than unknowns working in your favor. You've got established best practices, more history than can be digested, defined channels of distribution, trained customers, a well-oiled supply chain, dedicated trade journals, predictable demand, a solid understanding of the competitive landscape—and hundreds of popular business books that tell you how you can achieve your 10 percent improvement just a little better than the next guy. (By now, you know that this is not one of those books.)

Moonshots operate in the nonlinear region of the imagination. By asking big and audacious questions, they inject themselves into the realm of the "impossible." And in doing so, they not only transcend all the conventional business planning processes, they openly defy the conventional wisdom.

So how, then, does one go about executing a moonshot? Put the entrepreneurial mindset to work! This, more than magic quadrants, five factors, Six Sigma, seven habits, or any number of other management *du jour* practices, will be your greatest moonshot management asset.

In my experience, MBAs make the worst entrepreneurs. I tell them that, in real life, SWOT analyses and spreadsheets won't tell them anything they don't already know. Spreadsheets spit out nothing but inexact assumptions and expose confirmation biases, which invariably lead to a false sense of confidence in their business plans. MBAs, if they are to attempt a moonshot, will have a lot of unlearning to do. In most cases, your gut is still your best guide.

The human brain works like a binary computer that is given to precise, analytical calculation. The gut, however, works more like a chemical computer—it uses fuzzy logic to analyze information that can't be so easily defined in terms of ones and zeros. We've all had experiences in business where our gut told us something was wrong while our brain was still trying to apply its logic to figure it all out. Sometimes a faint voice based on instinct resonates more strongly than overpowering logic. It's important to remember what you mom always told you: "Listen to your gut."

Just as the medical schools teach treatment of symptoms at the expense of prevention, the business schools forsake execution for "strategy." Here's the fundamental problem with that approach: No strategy, however brilliant, survives the first contact with reality.

I like Ben Horowitz's thinking on this topic—and particularly with respect to the popular business books written by Harvard MBAs: "The problem with these books" he explains, "is that they attempt to provide a recipe for challenges that have no recipes. There's no recipe for really complicated, dynamic situations. There's no recipe for building a high-tech company; there's no recipe for leading a group of people out of trouble; there's no recipe for making a series of hit songs; there's no recipe for playing NFL quarterback; there's no recipe for running for president; and there's no recipe for motivating teams when your business has turned to crap. That's the hard thing about hard things—there is no formula for dealing with them."

Indeed, as any hype cycle curve will tell you, the best-laid business plans inevitably get mugged by reality. That said, the entrepreneur cannot afford to wait for certainty—there will never be a scenario that provides 100 percent clarity. Even the incrementalists won't be able to achieve that. Certainty, by definition, is something you can only get by looking in the rearview mirror. A moonshot, though, looks far beyond the visible horizon.

This is another reason why the entrepreneur cannot afford to waste time and resources writing business plans: no matter how well they're written, they are simply unable to anticipate how a product or service will actually fare in the marketplace. (This is why I believe that a business plan is too long if it's more than one page.) Rather, he must spend his time thinking deeply about the business he's really in and the big problem he is going to solve. It takes a rare kind of 360 view that not only looks beyond the vanishing point, but also just as deeply within.

Putting a very different spin on the notion of this kind of "vision beyond the visible" was the 17th-century Japanese swordsman Miyamoto Musashi, who said, "Perception is strong and sight weak. In strategy it is important to see distant things as if they were close, and to take a distanced view of close things." This hyper-developed sense of perception is, as we've seen, one of the entrepreneur's essential capabilities. It's also the key to achieving a 10X improvement over a mere 10 percent improvement. We need to maintain a distanced view of the close things to avoid falling into the trap of focusing too closely on what everybody else is doing now.

> **Moonshots operate in the nonlinear region of the imagination. By asking big and audacious questions, they inject themselves into the realm of the "impossible." And in doing so, they not only transcend all the conventional business planning processes, they openly defy the conventional wisdom.**

That inevitably leads to competitive but largely undifferentiated solutions. And like all commodity businesses, this devolves into a race to the bottom. Worse, it shrinks the original big, exponential idea to a conventional and incremental one. Indeed, if you have competition, you are squarely in the incremental category. Nonetheless, competitive thinking is so entrenched in the business world that it will likely continue to be taught in business schools for decades to come. It's also why the current reigning companies will become obsolete: they won't be able to pivot to the new world because their current customers want their current products.

There's a medieval saying that goes, "As the foxe when he hath pyssed in the badger's hole chalengeth it for his awne." The last thing the entrepreneur needs is to get into a pissing contest.

○ ◑ ● ◐

No doubt you're familiar with the Peter Principle. It states, "In a hierarchy, every employee tends to rise to his level of incompetence." Of course everybody knows this to be true—and that it is especially true at the highest levels of corporate management, where it becomes so painfully and publicly visible. But what's more interesting is how the Peter Principle has been generalized to state, "In evolution, systems tend to develop up to the limit of their *adaptive competence*."

This is precisely why the execution of a moonshot should not be concerned with what the big companies are doing—that is, outside of exploiting them as examples of why the moonshot is needed in the first place. Big companies are, for the most part, slow-moving. And they inevitably become bureaucratic and more skilled in the art of self-preservation than innovation. Consequently, the only opportunity they have to innovate is through acquisitions. But when this happens, nine times out of 10, they end up killing the innovation they acquired.

Very few companies have successfully acquired an innovation and kept it going. Remember Marissa Mayer's epic shopping spree? Of the 53 companies Yahoo acquired during her tenure, nearly all of them were shut down. And clearly, if the company's subsequent dramatic decline in valuation is any indication, it saw no benefit from the acquisitions. In fact, it never stood a chance. If you've ever witnessed the workings of integrating such an acquisition, then you know that the corporate immune system of the acquiring company immediately goes to work attacking it, unleashing its antibodies on this pathogen called a startup that clearly doesn't belong in the corporate bloodstream. The cultures and mindsets of the two entities are just fundamentally incompatible.

> **Big companies are, for the most part, slow-moving. And they inevitably become bureaucratic and more skilled in the art of self-preservation than innovation.**

In the startup world, a deal can be made on gut feel and a handshake. In the corporate world, it can take many months just to resolve an irrelevant clause in an NDA. And in the course of those months, windows of opportunity close, the acquired talent becomes frustrated, and the antibodies win. So companies end up wasting their capital resources to buy the innovation that they can't create in-house, and once it's inside, they kill it. And much of the talent that they got in the bargain moves on.

> **When large corporations attempt to integrate an acquisition, culture clash is the inevitable result. It just doesn't work. In fact, it can't work, because the vital entrepreneurial elements that enabled the startup to prosper in the first place are now permanently disabled.**

It's unavoidable, really, because when large corporations attempt to integrate an acquisition, culture clash is the inevitable result. It just doesn't work. In fact, it can't work, because the vital entrepreneurial elements that enabled the startup to prosper in the first place are now permanently disabled. But neither can the acquiring company leave the acquisition alone, because its agency creates a liability. The corporate lawyers, personnel, communications, and other departments simply cannot—nor should they—allow these acquired companies to run free range. So it's always a nearly guaranteed lose-lose proposition. And the big company loses the most, because when growth is pursued for growth's sake, as exemplified by the failed Yahoo strategy, value creation suffers. When this course persists, a company can only become irrelevant.

So don't worry about the big companies. You might, however, have to worry about crossing your chasm. Here's where your convictions and commitment to your moonshot will ultimately be tested—and where the Faustian bargains are most frequently struck. The short-term revenue goals for early stage companies with big ideas can present temptations that are just too powerful to resist. I'll give you an example from my own recent experience.

Many pharmaceutical companies are interested in what we're doing at Viome. They have offered us not insignificant funds if we would perform certain lab tests for them. We'd do the test and then send them the results. What's wrong with that? Well, for starters, it is completely inconsistent with our ultimate goal. It's completely inconsistent with our *intermediate* goals. Worse, it violates the first of our five core principles—the principles that guide everything we do at Viome, and they are cast in stone. I share them here because they are illustrative. They read:

1. Our singular focus is on empowering consumers, and that means that we will never do anything that bypasses them.
2. Everything we do must be built upon a solid scientific foundation.
3. We are here to make an impact on society.
4. The things we do must move humanity forward.
5. Everything we do should be actionable and not simply an exercise in research.

Our raison d'être at Viome is to educate and inspire people the world over to take control of their health. People buy our services because they believe in our mission to make illness optional. They also recognize that the mission is bigger than themselves. Every person who signs up for our service not only benefits by becoming healthier, but they also help everyone else become healthier as they contribute data to our AI engine. In the end, billions will benefit.

So if we simply become a lab to a third party, we'll never be able to fulfill our mission; nor will we have direct information about the chronic conditions from which our customers are suffering. But invariably people say, "Naveen, look at all this money you're turning away! You can get even more money than they're sending to Quest Diagnostics and LabCorp!" And it's true. But then I remind them of our core principles. So I'm going to say no to that generous and tempting offer. But it's hard to do that. Most entrepreneurs end up taking the money.

> **Every successful company goes through a near-death experience before it achieves its goal. It's a constant motif in every three-act play. It's what weeds out the insincere, the unbelievers, and the riffraff only out for the fast buck.**

One of the reasons entrepreneurs compromise their missions is that they lack the means to cross their own chasms. They are vulnerable. But it's only because they *believe* they can't cross them. They've lost faith in their own mission, and consequently, they don't complete the journey. On the other hand, these opportunities and deals that come along have the appearance of great success. Money starts flowing in, and very quickly, they've got a nice, growing business. But it no longer has anything to do with the moonshot vision that set them on their paths. Now they're really nothing more than a development shop for these big companies. In the case of Viome, I would be joining forces with the very entities that I believe are antithetical to human flourishing. This is my ultimate value, and it is not for sale at any price. Nor should your moonshot vision.

> **The difficulties pass, and they pass more quickly when you can expect them to come along. It's only when they're *not* built into your expectations that you can be paralyzed by them. When you know it's all a part of the rhythm, then you know what's coming next—another peak. But you need to be prepared.**

Again, I'm not saying you won't have moments of self-doubt—you most certainly will. There will be times when looking across the chasm feels more like staring into the abyss. At these times, remember that every successful company goes through a near-death experience before it achieves its goal. It's a constant motif in every three-act play. It's what weeds out the insincere, the unbelievers, and the riffraff only out for the fast buck.

The trick is surviving the early stages while you're still too small to show up on the radars of the big companies. And how hard can that be? You only have to avoid dying! Starting a business, let alone launching a moonshot, requires years and tears and grinding of gears, sleepless nights, a million concerns. It not only requires hard work, but a good dose of good luck, too.

If God gave me a choice of being really smart or really lucky, I'd pick lucky every time. But to a certain extent, you make your luck. Luck happens when you work hard and pursue the passion. You have to press in to enter in. And when you do, doors open that you never thought possible; people enter your life at the right time, and things begin to come together. If you're looking for easy success, marry rich.

◯ ◗ ● ◖

Have you ever had an EKG? The ups and downs of the impulses it records are a beautiful thing. What's not so beautiful is a flat line. The ups and downs show that you are alive! Why, then, should we expect that our moonshot missions ought to be exempt from valleys, or be surprised by them when they occur? Stasis means only one thing: death. But you also know that the ups don't last, and neither do the downs. The difficulties pass, and they pass more quickly when you can expect them to come along. It's only when they're *not* built into your expectations that you can be paralyzed by them. When you know it's all a part of the rhythm, then you know what's coming next—another peak. Remember also that when you find yourself at the peak do not become arrogant, because what follows will be a down beat or a long winter. You need to be both prepared and humble as you navigate this journey.

Every day is another day in the arena, and you need to be physically, mentally, emotionally, and spiritually fit to succeed there. If you are deficient in any of these four areas, believe me, it will show up in the results. This work is hard enough—you need every aspect of your being to be working for you. Any less can put your entire venture at risk. You see this every day where a business leader stumbles for want in any one or more of these areas. And so in the morning I wake up and I take care of my mind, discovering that this world is astoundingly active, 24/7. It never sleeps. I'll spend several hours catching up on the news published in the science and technology journals, keeping up with all the latest developments. Then I'll work out, taking care of my body. And before I head out to the office, I'll spend time to meditate, taking care of my soul. I can't imagine going into battle without being prepared in all these areas. There's just too much at stake.

> **Most companies die from indigestion rather than starvation. They die when they try to do too many things rather than too few things. So how do we square this with the idea of the big, audacious goal? It's actually simpler than you might think.**

There is no question that entrepreneurship is the highest state of consciousness that I've experienced in the professional world. There are no boundaries to what you can do because there is no structure. The experience of being an entrepreneur actually causes your mind to expand in surprising ways. More than simply making you a better businessperson, the process of expanding your awareness through the work of entrepreneurship is a spiritual experience in its own right. It's how you are able to take that leap of faith, to leave the corporate safety net and begin to really live. This is the very heart—and heartbeat—of the entrepreneur.

The disc jockey Casey Kasem used to sign off his program saying, "Keep your feet on the ground, but keep reaching for the stars." It's a good creed for the moonshot entrepreneur, as well. Moonshots are made of a series of big commitments on small things—and not too many things at once. It's true that most companies die from indigestion rather than starvation. They die when they try to do too many things rather than too few things. So how do we square this with the idea of the big, audacious goal? It's actually simpler than you might think.

You paint the sky with small strokes—by executing extremely well on a series of small slices. By the time you've put all these slices together, you've got the whole rainbow. With Viome, for example, we knew at the outset that there was no way we could reach our goal with this microbiome technology alone. But if we could attach it to something that could begin to provide us with the data we needed, then we'd be well on the path—and helping people feel better in the process so that they'd continue to generate data, expanding our understanding. That's what we've done. With this, we're moving the ball forward. And then as we continue to bolt on additional data-generating technologies that test for other markers, we'll be able to make even more comprehensive correlations, further increasing our learnings. But we started with what we had. If we tried to accomplish it all at once, we'd never make it; it's just too much. The technology we licensed from Los Alamos National Lab, though, provided us with the requisite "minimally viable product." And most important, we didn't wait to take it to market.

> **Early on, some people advised us to just focus on the science, and not engage with customers too soon. This is actually a common tactic of venture capitalists, and as an entrepreneur, you never want to fall for it. Getting early traction with customers is absolutely essential.**

Early on, some people advised us to just focus on the science, and not engage with customers too soon. This is actually a common tactic of venture capitalists, and as an entrepreneur, you never want to fall for it. Getting early traction with customers is absolutely essential. We were determined to build the technology, develop the science, *and* begin to gather a critical mass of customers in parallel.

We found that we absolutely could bootstrap things with the minimally viable capability we had early on. If you put off direct engagement with the market, then two years down the road, you'll have no customers and no revenue, and, to make matters worse, no feedback from customers or relevant data for improving your product. You'll also be in a lousy bargaining position when you need to go back to the well for more money. And because you'll have no revenue, you'll need it. That's exactly where the VCs want you. So use that initial funding runway to get as much traction with your market as you possibly can. Otherwise, all you'll have is an expensive science project.

> **If you put off direct engagement with the market, then two years down the road, you'll have no customers and no revenue, and, to make matters worse, no feedback from customers or relevant data for improving your product. You'll also be in a lousy bargaining position when you need to go back to the well for more money.**

Conventional wisdom says that great companies are built by business leaders with great vision. However, the truth is that groundbreaking businesses tend to come from entrepreneurs who were smart enough to out-execute everyone else in their space. That means getting products out there and growing a loyal customer base, rather than trying to engineer a product to its supposed perfection.

Without vital early feedback, you can only guess as to what customers are willing to pay for. More importantly, you'll get solid, market-based insight, instead of the imaginary scenarios dreamed up in a conference room and encoded in a business plan.

Here's one of the hardest things to do—especially if you are a perfectionist: launch early enough that down the road, when you look back, you'll be embarrassed by your first product release. If you don't, then you will have waited too long. If you wait on perfection, you'll never have a product—or a market. Besides, entrepreneurs' assumptions are likely to be off the mark about the features customers really want—but they won't ever be able to make a product better until people are actually using it.

LinkedIn founder Reid Hoffman says that his co-founders wanted to delay launch until they introduced the professional social network's "contact finder" feature, but it turns out it wasn't necessary—eight years later, LinkedIn still hasn't added that feature. Indeed, going from good to great is nice, but knowing when good enough is good enough is even better. This is how you will ultimately achieve greatness. But then to sustain that greatness, you'll have to become your own worst nightmare: once you do have that toehold in the market, you must immediately begin to ask yourself how you would outflank your company if you were a competitor. You'll need to work constantly to out-innovate yourself and determine how to make your current product offerings obsolete with each new iteration. Do that and you'll always be ahead of the curve. But you've just got to start. Remember the great fortune cookie advice: "Many a false step was made by standing still."

> **" A great strategy alone won't win a game or a battle; the win comes from basic blocking and tackling. Ideas are a dime a dozen. If all you have is an idea, then you have nothing. So freely share your ideas; you'll learn a lot when you do. "**

The best entrepreneurs learn by doing, and no amount of brainstorming or whiteboard strategizing can substitute for those early customer engagements. Imagine what you'll learn when you share your app with potential customers for the first time and they tell you that they hate it. Now what? All of your planning is out the window. So go ahead and launch. If they hate it, keep fixing it. Keep iterating.

This was exactly our experience with the initial release of the Viome app. People hated it. They couldn't figure it out. But that was music to our ears. We then went back to them a week later, and guess what? They loved it. We had applied their feedback, then we gave the app right back to them. That's entrepreneurship. But don't ever ask your market up front what they want. You've got to own the vision.

It continues to amaze me that most companies still go out to focus groups and ask them what they would like, as though they'd never heard Henry Ford's great advice. But once you can *show* your customers something they can play with and understand, then they can tell you how to improve it. So always err on the side of sharing too early. And think small. It's far easier to gain a toehold with an intermediate goal, and then eventually dominate a small intermediate market, than to start with a large one. If you think your initial market might be too big, you can be sure that it is.

The real essence of strategy is choosing what *not* to do. As Albert Einstein said,

"Any intelligent fool can make things bigger and more complex. It takes a touch of genius—and a lot of courage—to move in the opposite direction." Forecasting that you'll win 1 percent of a $100 billion market? That's not genius in any book. Rather, take a page from Jeff Bezos' book. His founding vision was to dominate all of online retail (and he appears to be well on his way), but he very deliberately started with only one category: books. And he executed flawlessly.

○ ◐ ● ◖

All the foregoing notwithstanding, at times entrepreneurship can feel like you've jumped off a cliff and are working desperately to build an airplane on the way down. For many, it's a metaphor that isn't too far off the mark. Under those circumstances, it's an understatement to say that execution matters. With the ground fast approaching, there's no time for debating strategy, creating Power-Points, or revising business plans.

Most companies that fail do so not because they lack the right technology or the right ideas. They fail because they don't execute properly. Too many of them believe that the merits of their product—their innovations—will carry them across the finish line, that they've got the better mousetrap. They believe this because the venture capitalists tell them that to be a successful entrepreneur they need to deliver breakthrough innovation.

One of the first things I have to undo in the minds of young entrepreneurs is to dispel the persistent myth that entrepreneurial success is all about innovative thinking and breakthrough ideas. I've found that entrepreneurial success usually comes through great execution, through doing a superior job in the essential details. Just as real estate is all about location, location, location, in entrepreneurship, it's execution, execution, execution.

> **Here's one of the hardest things to do—especially if you are a perfectionist: launch early enough that down the road, when you look back, you'll be embarrassed by your first product release. If you don't, then you will have waited too long.**

When you examine the most successful companies, you discover that they are more concerned with perfect execution than breakthrough innovation. Apple is a great example. Apple doesn't invent. Everything Apple has done has a precedent. They steal the ideas and execute well. The best companies always succeed on execution, not vision. A great strategy alone won't win a game or a battle; the win comes from basic blocking and tackling. Ideas are a dime a dozen. If all you have is an idea, then you have nothing. So freely share your ideas; you'll learn a lot when you do.

I'd like to backtrack just a bit and expand on the notion that entrepreneurial success actually does not rely on being first to market with breakthrough innovation. Invention is never enough. A sad case in point is Nikola Tesla, who invented the first viable AC motor and power system. Thomas Edison, however, with inferior technology, consistently out-executed Tesla throughout the course of their epic rivalry. Edison was not only a great inventor in his own right, but he figured out how to scale the process of invention and then turn the resulting innovations into massive revenue streams—and, of course, world renown. Tesla, though a better and an arguably more consequential inventor, suffered setback after setback in his efforts to commercialize his innovations, losing patent royalties, failing to complete projects, and filing bankruptcy. In the end, he died relatively poor despite all his breakthrough inventions.

> **There are multiple intermediate goals to achieve on the way to painting the sky. Each one must be executed flawlessly, building strength upon strength. And any number of these intermediate steps may involve displacing pure play competitors who are operating in that particular slice of the whole that makes up your vision.**

We could fill a book with examples of inferior innovations winning in the marketplace over clearly superior ones: the x86 Intel microprocessors over the 68000 family from Motorola, Windows over Linux, TDMA over CDMA, electric stovetops over gas, gas cars over electric (at least in the last century), VHS over Betamax, compact disc over MiniDisc, Dolby over DTS—and let's not forget Imperial measurement over metric—to mention just a few of the better-known instances. Indeed, delivering superior commercial success relies upon superior execution—even when given inferior products.

As to the much vaunted "first-mover advantage," this is another dangerous myth in need of dispelling. If someone is ahead of you, don't worry about it. Chances are they're susceptible to disruption or a better-executing rival, or both.

Someone may be first to market with a better idea, but that by no means solidifies their position. You can always overtake them. To that end, you actually have great advantages as a second mover that were never available to the first. As a second mover, you'll more easily see product gaps. Acquiring customers will be a hundred times faster, easier, and cheaper. The market will have already been educated, so engaging with customers for learning needed product improvements is straightforward.

> **" You can always succeed in a market where there is discontent with the status quo.** *And there is always discontent with the status quo.* **"**

The marketplace is chock-full of examples of successful "late" market entrants. Google was actually the 11th search engine, LinkedIn displaced Monster and CareerBuilder, Excel became the *de facto* standard over Lotus 1-2-3, and Salesforce decimated Siebel. GoToMeeting took a huge bite out of WebEx with its clever "All You Can Meet" pricing strategy—*eight years after the founding of WebEx*—while eight other recent entries into the video conferencing space all score higher marks than both. Indeed, the race to be first is always also a race to fail first, or to ending up dead last in the customer satisfaction rankings.

The first mover in any space bears a tremendous burden: it's got to create an entire market by itself. Which is why it's a fool's game for a startup to even contemplate such a move. Creating a market from scratch means creating the entire technology stack, making massive marketing investments, undertaking the arduous task of building a customer base, navigating an exceptionally wide chasm, and still managing to survive while also stepping on all the land mines along the way. A much better strategy is to learn from someone else's mistakes, co-opt their technology, and let them spend the money to build the market and customer base. Then, when the market has grown, figure out a way to execute better than anyone else in the space and make it happen. Exploit the first mover as a living research and development lab from which *you* can learn.

If you're in a completely new market, it's very likely that there *is* no market, unless you happen to be the smartest person in the world, which is very unlikely. You don't want to find this out. Think of it this way: do you really want to be the only person selling mousetraps in a particular town? Could it be that the reason nobody is selling mousetraps there is that there are no mice in that town, that there is no problem to be solved there by mousetraps? It's a much better idea to go into a town where there are a hundred people already selling mousetraps. At least you will know that there are a lot of mice there. Your job now is much simpler: drive everyone else out of business with a better way of trapping mice, and then own the market.

When I started Intelius, there were a hundred-plus companies doing background checks. All we had to do was redefine the terms of the transaction. And we did that by dropping the price to $7.95. By automating the processes with better technologies, we were able to deliver far greater value than anyone else in the market. As a result, we sucked all the oxygen from the competitors who were charging thousands of dollars in a manually intensive process. Our new value proposition in an established space changed the entire industry, which we quickly came to dominate. We sold a billion dollars' worth of background checks in a crowded field where most companies each topped out at about $10 million in annual revenue. So competition doesn't worry me, nor should it worry you.

This matters tremendously to a moonshot entrepreneur, because there are multiple intermediate goals to achieve on the way to painting the sky. Each one must be executed flawlessly, building strength upon strength. And any number of these intermediate steps may involve displacing pure play competitors who are operating in that particular slice of the whole that makes up your vision. To this end, you will always find a chink in the armor, a strength that can be exploited as a weakness, a legacy to protect that can blind them to disruption—indeed, myriad vulnerabilities. Know this above all else: you can always succeed in a market where there is discontent with the status quo. *And there is always discontent with the status quo.* The only difference between you, as a moonshot entrepreneur, and everyone else operating in a particular space, other than executing better, is that you are also looking far beyond the horizon. What your competitors see as an end, you see as a means. And at the same time, every attained end is the beginning of a new course, *ad infinitum*, toward the larger goal.

> **The only difference between you, as a moonshot entrepreneur, and everyone else operating in a particular space, other than executing better, is that you are also looking far beyond the horizon.**

In the meantime, remember that the pioneers take the arrows, but settlers take the land. The landmark Golder and Tellis research showed that the failure rates for pioneers was 47 percent versus just 8 percent for settlers.

And for those pioneers that did survive, they captured an average of just 10 percent of their markets, where the settlers captured nearly three times that.

Interestingly, Golder and Tellis sum up their findings with a particularly cogent observation. Their study of 50 nascent product categories revealed five factors that drove the superior performance of early leaders: a vision of the mass market, managerial persistence, financial commitment, relentless innovation, and asset leverage. The pioneers' inability to implement these factors is what often led to their failures. Most interesting is that the first four factors are related components of a *mindset* that drove the success of early leaders. Firms that can define a vision are also able to assemble the needed resources and inspire people for the task ahead. And when a properly formed mindset meets flawless execution, the world is yours to lose.

> **What your competitors see as an end, you see as a means. And at the same time, every attained end is the beginning of a new course, *ad infinitum*, toward the larger goal.**

○ ◑ ● ◐

So we've established that getting started sooner rather than later is a good thing, that you're really never too late, and that it's good to know when something good is good enough. But knowing when to discard even good ideas when they become untenable, that's another thing. The art in execution is knowing the difference between something that requires a little more persistence and a course of action that's going to prove to be a dead end. It can be hard to tell.

Navigating these tricky paths requires a full view of the playing field, always with the big goal in focus. More importantly, it requires agility. You have to continually learn and adapt as new information becomes available. At the same time you have to remain persistent to the cause and mission of your enterprise. That's where the faint voice of instinct becomes so important, especially when it is giving you early warning signals that things are going off-track. Successful execution is about finding the balance between listening to that voice and persistence in driving for success—because sometimes success is waiting right across from the transitional bump that's disguised as failure.

"Among excellent companies" says Amy Webb, "a fundamental shift is taking place: away from long-range forecast, long-term plans, and big bets, and toward constant short-term iteration, experimentation, and testing." In other words, predicting less, experimenting more.

The more experiments you are able to perform, the greater your chances of success.[1] And you want to start with the highest risk aspects of your mission and determine, through high-throughput experimentation, if you actually can derisk them. You'll need to prove or disprove your hypotheses as quickly as possible in order to conserve precious resources. If you can't derisk them, then adapt and test another approach. If the outcome of an experiment doesn't change anything, e.g., a course of action, then it probably isn't a good experiment. The key is to keep iterating.

> **Firms that can define a vision are also able to assemble the needed resources and inspire people for the task ahead. And when a properly formed mindset meets flawless execution, the world is yours to lose.**

Francis Crick, co-discoverer of the structure of the DNA molecule, said about this process, "One reviewer thought that we couldn't have been very clever because we went on so many false trails, but that is the way discoveries are usually made. Most attempts fail not because of lack of brains but because the investigator gets stuck in a cul-de-sac or gives up too soon ... The major credit is for selecting the right problem and sticking to it."

And when you've discovered that you're working on the wrong problem, or have determined that one of the intermediate goals is not working, then it may be necessary to abandon course in favor of another, more feasible path—another means to the same end. Indeed, when setting out on a long journey, detours are to be expected.

○ ◑ ● ◖

Now, if everything actually does go according to plan and the stars do align, then what? Can success itself also be a failure mode? It can if you're not prepared to scale when you need to—or worse, if the plan is not inherently scalable to begin with. I was recently at a Forbes 400 event where I met a woman who told me about her plan for creating jobs for women in developing countries. She'd worked out an arrangement with Amazon to promote and sell their handmade products. What's more, she was going to invest $10,000 in a loom so that the women could get started. I told her I thought that was an awesome idea—God forbid it actually works. "What do you mean?" she asked, taken aback. "Let's assume," I explained, "that Amazon says, 'Great, we'll do it,' and they get a million orders. You gave these women one loom, but now you need 50. What will you do?" "That's not a problem we have," she answered. "I understand that," I said. "But what you're telling me is that you hope you will fail. Because if you succeed, you will fail. And if you fail, you fail. There's nothing in-between here. So you're going out meeting all these people hoping they will never say yes, because if they do say yes, you will have failed already."

In another example, a well-known actress whose foundation is dedicated to improving young student performance thought she might be able to take her program to the Army, believing it could help with PTSD treatment. Again, another great idea. When I suggested that the Army might turn around and give her 100,000 people to put through her program, she said, "Are you kidding? I don't have

> **" Sometimes success is waiting right across from the transitional bump that's disguised as failure. "**

the teachers for that many people." And again, while she was pitching, she was also hoping they'd say no. If they said yes, she'd have a big problem. So I suggested that she find a way to deliver the program in a way that doesn't require teachers, but rather could be done using technology; for example, with a tablet or smartphone. If it works, she could then scale it to 100,000 people overnight. Better yet, it would be a way to massively scale the program at zero marginal cost. But since her starting point was trained teachers, it couldn't scale. And one day, they actually did say yes.

Execution in Beast Mode: Putting Some 17 Power in Your Moonshot

To witness one of the greatest displays of agility and course correction ever performed, Google the video "Epic Beast Mode Run Analysis by Marshawn Lynch". Here's how it unfolded:

On January 8, 2011, in the classic NFC wildcard playoff matchup between the Seattle Seahawks and the Super Bowl-defending New Orleans Saints, Marshawn Lynch, late in the 4th quarter, showed the world the meaning of Beast Mode. "So we get into the huddle," Lynch recounts, "and they call 17 Power. I thought, oh my God, I've been trying to get a Power for so long! With a Power, you run it straight downhill. You know where we're coming and we know where y'all gonna be lined up at. Now you just gotta stop me. And I'm sayin' *I'm better than you*. So I see the guard come around, and in my head I'm thinking, backside A-gap [the center-guard gap in the defensive line]. But for some reason, it carried me to the far side. I saw the first tackler, and I thought, uh, oh, might be trouble. Split between [Chris] Spencer's block coming off of [Darren] Sharper, he grabbed at my foot. I stayed up. I said, uh-oh, might be trouble. I cover the ball with two hands. One of my old teammates, Jabari Greer, came over the top. He slid off. It's a good run now, but then, uh-oh, might be trouble. Tracy Porter came up. I gave him a little stiff arm. I stayed on my feet. We almost was running at top speed. Any kind of shove right there will, you know, throw a man off course. It was just a little baby stiff arm. I believe it was [Sedrick] Ellis came from behind [actually it was Alex Brown]. I took a little quick peek at him, gave him a little stiff arm. Still didn't go down. Uh-oh, I *know* it's trouble. And then the next thing I know, Tyler [Polumbus] shot in front of me, and he made a block on [Roman] Harper. Dive into the end zone. Touchdown. And at the time I'm thinking, what the hell just happened? Did this really just happen?"

---

1. This is, in fact, how machine learning algorithms, or artificial neural networks, operate. Employing a method called *backpropagation*, a series of successive approximations corrects errors as it estimates values along the way, adjusting its weights accordingly and building confidence as it culminates in a prediction.

CHAPTER 17

Stepping-Stones to Success

The trick is to go from one failure to another with no loss of enthusiasm.

—Winston Churchill

THIS BIT OF WISDOM FROM CHURCHILL gets at the core of another of the entrepreneur's essential capacities: resilience. While it can come across as a bit trite to minimize failure as just a stepping-stone to success, it really does work that way. Entrepreneurial initiatives that push the envelope are hard, and there are many more ways to fail than to succeed. Elon Musk puts this in more literal terms when, speaking of his history with SpaceX rockets, he says, "There's a thousand ways the thing can fail and one way it can work." He should know. Musk's 10-year streak of blowing up one rocket after another—or as he prefers to put it, "rapid unplanned disassemblies"—finally did come to an end with his first and immensely successful landing of the Falcon 9 reusable booster.

Moonshot entrepreneurs are far beyond the stigmatization of failure, and I am sure that all would agree that if you're not failing, you're probably not being aggressive enough. Nor is it likely that if you are not prepared to be wrong from time to time, you'll achieve any sort of breakthrough. "It is the essence," say Astro Teller, "of innovation to fail most of the time." That is, when you're not only taking safe shots. Kobe Bryant, when he made 10 points in a game, made 100 percent of his shots; when he made 50 points, he missed half of them. Likewise, Babe Ruth's second most important stat is his striking number of strikeouts—a category in which he also frequently led the league.

We all make many mistakes, some of which lead to a failure of one sort or another. But the biggest mistake is to be surprised by them. (In most fields, a good success rate is actually only about 25 percent.) Mistakes are not only opportunities for learning; they are, more often than not, the *only* opportunities for learning. Mistakes and failures are, therefore, an essential part of entrepreneurial life—and not the least important part; not merely a necessary evil, but something that is key to one's personal formation, as well. It is by making mistakes that we gain experience not only for ourselves, but for others with whom we work and the people we serve.

As long as you continue to learn, you never really fail. And you certainly never lose the wisdom gained—wisdom that actually becomes a competitive advantage over others who have yet gained that wisdom. Imagine failure as a competitive advantage!

Charles Kettering, one of America's greatest inventors whose innovations continue to impact our daily lives, was not only ahead of his time with respect to technology, but in the very concept of the "fail fast" ethic that rules Silicon Valley these days. "An inventor," he said "is simply a person who doesn't take his education too seriously. From the time a person is six years old until he graduates from college, he has to take three or four examinations a year. If he flunks once, he is out. But an inventor is almost always failing. He tries and fails maybe a thousand times. If he succeeds once then he's in. These two things are diametrically opposite. We often say that the biggest job we have is to teach a newly hired employee how to fail intelligently. We have to train him to experiment over and over and to keep on trying and failing until he learns what will work."

> **How you deal with setbacks and difficulties may actually be the primary determinant of your ultimate success. And oftentimes, success is found on the very far, dark side of failure.**

Building this kind of character is key to developing the persistence that ultimately yields success. Especially when crossing the dreaded "trough of disillusionment" that invariably attends ambitious ventures. Know that you will be greatly improved when you have crossed it. Many, though, despair halfway across.

It is here, in the "desert," where you must be patient with everyone, and above all, with yourself. When you find yourself here, each day, rise up with fresh courage and resolve to make a fresh beginning. After all, this is the entrepreneur's great advantage in life—to be continually beginning again, and never thinking that what we have done before will ever suffice for what we must do today. If you are consumed by failings, you will never correct them, and you may, then, end up in a worse state.

Despair is a miserable place to find yourself. And it can be avoided only with humility. As Thomas Merton said, "despair is reached when a person deliberately turns his back on all help from anyone else in order to taste the rotten luxury of knowing himself to be lost." If you've ever been in the company of such people, then you know that wounded self-love is not a pretty thing in any light. On the other hand, a person who is truly humble cannot despair, because in humility there is no room for self-pity. Imagine again this miserable and despairing person. Should he ever actually achieve success, he will surely be ruined by it, having missed the precious opportunity to become improved by failure. Failure deflates illusion, while success makes it worse. In the end, despair is suffering without meaning or reward—even when it "succeeds."

> " As an entrepreneur, your initial idea may not work. Your second idea may not work. But you fail only when you give up. "

The desert is a region through which all entrepreneurs must unavoidably pass; it is a crucible that not only proves your character, but the worth of your pursuit, as well. If you can cooperate with this process of becoming, then both come out better for it. How you deal with setbacks and difficulties may actually be the primary determinant of your ultimate success. And oftentimes, success is found on the very far, dark side of failure.

Nothing sums up these thoughts better than a brief scene in the film *A Good Year*, where Uncle Henry counsels Max, "You'll come to see that a man learns nothing from winning," he says. "The act of losing, however, can elicit great wisdom. Not least of which is how much more enjoyable it is to win. It's inevitable to lose now and again. The trick is not to make a habit of it."

Before it does become a habit, and when you do actually find yourself upon the rocks, a few questions can help to sort things out so that you'll have a better chance of succeeding the next time. First, did you limit your options and decision-making with too narrow a framing of your problem space? In other words, were you focused on the right problem, and with the proper scope? What do you see when you expand the view? Second, to what extent did confirmation bias blind you to unexpected market realities? If you're acting only on the information and data that you want to hear, then you'll most certainly be in for rude awakenings. Ask the hard questions—including the ones for which you may not like the answers. Lastly, did you underestimate the journey across the chasm? This, of course, is always the monster. It's where you burn through your cash, lose your talent, and get diluted. So always build setbacks into your plan—hope for the best, but plan for the worst. Most important, follow Kettering's advice and fail fast. And if you must, abandon course and pivot.

○ ☽ ● ◖

As an entrepreneur, your initial idea may not work. Your second idea may not work. But you fail only when you give up. And when you give up early, you'll forever be restarting on a soft foundation. Losers quit, but entrepreneurs pivot. The path to success is seldom a straight line—it zigs and zags and requires a flexible persistence as you try not to veer too far from the destination that is your vision. Along the way, work to determine the least effort required to learn whether or not an idea will work. (If only there were a way to fail before you start!) If you are able to be agile and adapt, you will eventually hit your mark. And it may be when you think you've come to the end that you discover what makes the idea work.

> **Most new ventures fail or do not live up to their potential. By the same token, many successful companies come out of failed ideas. It's hard, it's risky, and sometimes it's downright heartbreaking. But imagine a world where everything succeeded on the first try.**

Often it means reframing what constitutes failure. If the path you're on is the wrong one, there's no shame in facing up to it and making the hard choice to abandon it. If you persist on the wrong path, you'll only reduce your later options.

While investors and partners will respect an entrepreneur who remains true to his vision, most will also recognize that goals may conflict with each other at certain points. Entrepreneurs must always make their assessments honestly—especially with themselves—about the condition of their company, and make the difficult choices to change direction when it is warranted. Necessity, after all, is the mother of adaptation as well as of invention.

In the end, though, it doesn't matter how many times you *almost* get it right.

As Mark Cuban says, "No one is going to know or care about your failures, and neither should you. All you have to do is learn from them and those around you, because all that matters in business is that you get it right once. Then everyone can tell you how lucky you are." Of course, if you want to stay in the game, you have to keep on getting it right. To be human is to change; to be perfect is to have changed often.

Some, however, don't—or won't—make the necessary corrections. They believe that acquiescing to a pivot means that their vision was wrong, and they'll be damned if they'll let go of their vision. And if they do enjoy some early success, then they'll be even less inclined to accept that getting the next thing right is necessarily iterative. Their initial success becomes their kryptonite. I see it often, especially with entrepreneurs who develop a technology themselves—they become married to it, even when the state of the art and the market have moved on. A new set of technologies inevitably comes along that is substantially better. Theranos is a painful case in point.

The company burned through nearly a billion dollars and saw its valuation plummet from $9 billion to less than a tenth of that by the time the rest of the world caught on. I would have pivoted seven times to the latest technology, but they were blinkered by their tunnel vision. Theranos CEO Elizabeth Holmes gained some unexpected notoriety when she declared, "I think that the minute that you have a backup plan, you've admitted that you're not going to succeed."

We see similar things play out when a company becomes successful in one paradigm, but is not able to adapt as the paradigm changes. Microsoft, for example, was a market leader in the PC space when cellphones came out. What did Microsoft do? They put the Windows start button on the phone, thinking it was just a small form factor PC. They were simply unable to get their heads wrapped around the fact that this was a totally different medium, a radically new way of looking at things—a completely new paradigm.

Then Apple committed the same error. Even though they were the market leader in smartphones, when the smartwatch came along, what did Apple do? They put the Apple icons on the watch! Like Microsoft, they were unable to rethink their value proposition in the context of a new paradigm. Apple's "Think Different" slogan apparently had its limits.

Going back a little further, the great case study was the story of DEC—the company that disrupted the mainframe market when it introduced the minicomputer. DEC's PDP-1 and VAX minicomputers liberated departments from their reliance on central computing services that were too big, too slow, and too expensive. Now, IBM was not stupid. Its management regularly surveyed their customers' needs, and their customers consistently told them they wanted the same mainframes they'd always gotten from IBM; they just wanted them better, faster, and cheaper. By the time IBM realized what was actually happening, it was too late—DEC had secured its market position with its novel computing solution.

When PCs came out, DEC did the same thing IBM had done. They asked their customers what they wanted, and their customers told them they simply wanted the same minicomputers they'd been getting from DEC, only better, faster, and cheaper. Second verse, same as the first. Customers will always tell you that what they want is what they have—only better, faster, and cheaper. It's always the old Henry Ford bromide: "If I had asked people what they wanted," he said, "they would have said faster horses." It's not until you present an entirely new paradigm that people will embrace it. Until then, they won't allow it; they won't perceive the new offering as solving a problem, but rather creating a problem. This, of course, is what IBM again had counted on, when they got totally scooped by Compaq's IBM-compatible "luggable" computer.

In these and countless other cases, companies simply attach previously winning strategies to the new paradigms, and those previous successes become their undoing. Contrast this to Amazon, who took the lessons learned from the smartphone market and flanked the whole works with an entirely new paradigm in a computing device called Alexa. Likewise, augmented reality and virtual reality represent completely new archetypes that will require completely new interfaces and user experiences—none of which will be adapted from anything that came before.

> **Market freedom is the last thing the elites want, because that would undermine the status of their control structures. Consequently, these "developing" countries really have no chance of developing at all.**

Augmented and virtual reality technologies, in fact, could completely obviate the need for anything we currently recognize as a user interface. The "screens" will be virtual—no hardware needed. They will simply appear before you, on demand and head-up in whatever size you want them to be. Magic Leap's innovations, for example, could absolutely kill the $120 billion market for flat-panel displays, to say nothing of disrupting the entire global consumer electronics space. With virtual reality, you'll be able to simply conjure up the experience you desire—watch video, check your mail, augment your real-time environment, follow virtual directional arrows to get to your next destination—everything. No need to actually move the couch to see how it will look in the new spot, or how functional that new kitchen layout will be. So while Alexa was a disrupter in its way, in the new context, its interface will be rendered useless. And so it goes.

Most new ventures fail or do not live up to their potential. By the same token, many successful companies come out of failed ideas. It's hard, it's risky, and sometimes it's downright heartbreaking. But imagine a world where everything succeeded on the first try. A world with no chance of failure would be itself a failure. The courage to act in the first place is pointless without the resilience to persevere through to success. As Robert Half said, "Persistence is what makes the impossible possible, the possible likely, and the likely definite."

And in the end, I say a man who fails well is greater than the one who succeeds badly.

....

7th Time's a Charm

In the run-up to the Apollo program, a massive number of engineering problems had to first be solved, not the least of which were those associated with designing the lunar module's landing gear. Would the module sink, bounce, or crack up upon landing? If designed for the worst-case lunar surface conditions, the landing gear alone could easily claim 50 percent of the module's allowable weight. But if the surface were more favorable, the landing gear could be reduced to less than 5 percent of that weight. So how could they know which conditions the lander would encounter? Answering that question was the mission of NASA's Jet Propulsion Laboratory's (JPL) Ranger program. Close-up pictures taken by Ranger spacecraft prior to impact would give the engineers designing Apollo's landing gear a great deal more confidence. So how did the program fare? Let's review the history:

Ranger 1: During launch on August 23, 1961, a rocket malfunction caused the spacecraft to get stranded in low Earth orbit. One week later, it burned up upon reentering Earth's atmosphere. Fail.

Ranger 2: A malfunction with its booster rocket caused it to be trapped in low Earth orbit before burning up in Earth's atmosphere two days after launch. Fail.

Ranger 3: A series of malfunctions, principally with the spacecraft's guidance system, sent the spacecraft hurtling past the moon at much higher speeds than planned. Because of the increased speeds, among other flight problems, Ranger 3 was unable to enter lunar orbit and flew past the moon on January 28, 1962. It is to this day in helio-centric orbit. Fail.

Ranger 4: Success! Sort of. Ranger 4 was the first American spacecraft to reach another celestial body (yes, the Russians beat us there, too, with their Luna 2 spacecraft, which crash-landed on the moon September 13, 1959—two years after Sputnik). But a failure in the spacecraft's onboard computer left Ranger 4's solar panels and navigation sys-tem undeployed and the spacecraft unable to carry out its science objectives. Ranger 4 crashed into the far side of the moon on April 26, 1962. Fail.

Ranger 5: A malfunction with the spacecraft's batteries caused them to drain after about eight hours of flight, leaving Ranger 5 inoperable. The spacecraft missed the moon by 450.5 miles (725 kilometers) on October 21, 1962, and, along with Ranger 3, remains in heliocentric orbit. By this time, the United States Congress decided to cut funding to the Ranger program by nearly 50 percent on the grounds that "no success had been achieved with any of the missions to date." Costs were mounting and patience was plummeting. Fail.

Ranger 6: On February 2, 1964, 65.5 hours after launch, Ranger 6, the first of a new, third generation of Ranger spacecraft, impacted the moon precisely on schedule on the eastern edge of the Sea of Tranquility. Unfortunately, the power supply for the camera system short-circuited three days earlier, and no images were returned. Logged as the twelfth successive American lunar flight failure, the pressures—and drama—inside JPL were mounting. Still, the Ranger spacecraft performed flawlessly even if the television cameras had failed. So close, but still a fail.*

Ranger 7: Finally! On July 31, 1964, Ranger 7 approached the moon exactly on target and transmitted 4,316 images in the 15 minutes before it impacted the lunar surface on the northern rim of the Sea of Clouds. Success!

The images, which showed the lunar surface in stunning detail, were the harbinger of future human exploration of the moon. But it took a lot of failures to get there. As will future space endeavors. And now, as we set our eyes on Mars, keep in mind that 17 of the last 22 Mars projects also failed. Each yet another small step for man.

---

* Personal note: John Schroeter's father was responsible for the machining of Ranger 6's camera systems, but he insists the failure wasn't his fault!

Paying it Forward

Billions are wasted on ineffective philanthropy. Philanthropy is decades
behind business in applying rigorous thinking to the use of money.

—Michael Porter

THERE'S NO QUESTION ABOUT IT, the United States is the most generous country on the planet. In 2016, charitable donations rose to a new high of $390 billion, with most of that coming from private individuals. That's nearly eight times the amount the US spent on the foreign aid it distributes to some 200 countries every year (the top five of which are all in the Middle East). That's a good thing, because much of the money leaving the Treasury Department's coffers gets laundered through corrupt hands, and more often than not ends up propping up oppressive regimes or creating unproductive and unhealthy dependencies. (Growing up in India, I experienced this outcome firsthand, and it was the direct cause of much of the misery my family suffered.) Even in the best cases, top-down planners and government bureaucrats with little to no accountability mismanage aid funds so badly that we see no evidence that they are really doing any practical good. For example, trillions in aid dollars have flowed into Africa over the past number of decades, but per capita income in Africa has not improved. Indeed, there's not much to show for it, at all.

This is happening because there is a fundamental disconnect between Western ideals and the actual causes of poverty in so many so-called developing countries. These all tend to be "extractive" entities, meaning they are hopelessly corrupt. Extractive institutions—kleptocracies—plunder the aid they receive, denying their citizens the benefit of such aid in favor of lining the pockets of the small circle of elites within the governments. Their incentive structures favor the elites as well, also at the expense of the people. And while these countries may benefit from technological advances, such progress can only be sustained within a dynamic market environment. But market freedom is the last thing the elites want, because that would undermine the status of their control structures. Consequently, these "developing" countries really have no chance of developing at all.

We shouldn't be surprised, then, that according to Acemoglu and Robinson in *Why Nations Fail*, "... the West spent 2.3 trillion dollars on foreign aid over the last five decades and still had not managed to get 12 cent medicines to children to prevent half of all malaria deaths; or even $3 to each new mother to prevent 5,000,000 deaths. Foreign aid is actually the main cause of continuing poverty in Africa." Clearly, agendas other than humanitarian interests are at work when we provide "aid" to such countries. Meanwhile, the horrible conditions persist.

While it's easy to find fault with the gross inefficiencies of governments and bureaucrats, what about the private sector? Are they doing any better? Well, that depends on how you look at it. And by now, you know that entrepreneurs look at such problems through very different lenses. But let us take a look. Charity Navigator is an organization that rates and ranks more than 9,000 charities according to a set of fairly rigorous standards, and as you might imagine, the results are all over the map. Certainly people have more confidence in self-directed giving than they have in the government's ability to distribute funds effectively, but this is not always so clear.

> **So here we go again: even in the context of charitable giving, what we're dealing with is the global deployment of an unsustainable model that relies upon a redistribution and consumption of wealth that can only deliver ever-diminishing returns—particularly for those it is intended to help.**

But let's cut to the chase here. The vast majority of philanthropic and foreign aid dollars goes to compensate for—or is it to maintain?—the effects of *scarcity-driven economies*.

Even in the context of charitable giving, what we're dealing with is the global deployment of an unsustainable model that relies upon a redistribution and consumption of wealth that can only deliver ever-diminishing returns—particularly for those it is intended to help. In short, like everything else that operates within the constraints of a scarcity-driven economy, we're doing it wrong.

The greatest philanthropic movement—the one we've not yet seen—is the one that overthrows the scourge and tyranny of scarcity. Everything else flows from this single construct. Everything. If entrepreneurs can mobilize to create an economy of *abundance*, then the majority of problems that the philanthropic organizations and NGOs can only treat as "chronic conditions" simply evaporate. That would be the ultimate moonshot, wouldn't it?

We come full circle, then, to the inherent evil of scarcity. And once again, we see that the teleology of the economics that rules it is completely divorced from ethics. Economics simply does not regard the purpose and value of human flourishing. It has no concern for justice, but rather simply operates like the law of gravity. Economics has no conscience.

What does all this mean for philanthropy? What can it mean to the entrepreneur? It means that we have before us an astounding opportunity for true, effective problem-solving progress on a grand, global—and *human*—scale. It also means a complete and radical rethinking of the very nature of philanthropy itself. And it must be rethought, because as long as we continue to think of issues as social or philanthropic problems, they will never get solved. Even after sinking trillions of dollars into the effort.

○ ◑ ● ◐

Philanthropy should never be about giving money. Rather, it should be about solving a problem. While well-meaning, the idea of writing a check and calling it "philanthropy" is extremely short-sighted and, unfortunately, extremely pervasive. So we must challenge the basis of philanthropy at its core. But this will not be easy. As John Maynard Keynes said, "The difficulty lies not so much in developing new ideas as in escaping from old ones." And ideas about philanthropy—especially the bad ideas—are very old and very deeply rooted.

There's another problem here. We have many well-intentioned people who, through charitable giving, really seek only to increase their own well-being. "Don't feel like you have enough money?" their advisors say. "Give to someone less fortunate." "Be a river, not a reservoir." "Giving is sure to put you in a more abundant and appreciative frame of mind, so give generously." Of course this all sounds positive and life-affirming. *But it does nothing to solve the big problems in the world.* Such giving can never move the needle. Yes, it makes the giver feel good, but self-help that masquerades as philanthropy is no philanthropy at all.

Again, the concept is pervasive. Even on the entrepreneurial side of the equation we have people who have taken to calling themselves "social entrepreneurs." What does it mean if I think of myself as a social entrepreneur? It means, quite bluntly, that I am a shitty entrepreneur. If I were a good entrepreneur I wouldn't need a qualifier. So when you write a check to someone who calls himself a social entrepreneur, you can be sure that your money is going to a person who really does not know how to run, let alone scale, a business that solves problems.

This is not to disparage the act of doing a small good. If you want to do a small good in the world, then by all means, support or create a nonprofit. If, on the other hand, you want to do a *large* good in the world, then you've got to go the route of for-profit—for the simple reason that if an initiative is not profitable, then it is not financially viable.

Somehow a notion has taken hold that the objectives of nonprofit and for-profit are mutually exclusive, or at least that they operate in non-overlapping spheres. There's no reason why this should be so. First, let me state unequivocally that an entrepreneur should never be ashamed of a business that is profitable. Profit is the engine that does *good*. As we noted earlier, doing good and doing well are in no way in conflict. In fact, they go together, hand in hand. As such, philanthropic organizations would do well to imitate the practices of business, because it is their philanthropic mindset that is attenuating the gains they could actually otherwise be making in fulfilling their missions. To drive philanthropy at tremendous scale, to develop long-term economic vitality through giving, we must apply the same models for success in our philanthropic endeavors as we do in business.

I can't help but wonder sometimes if an organization is at the service of its mission, or if the mission is at the service of the organization! Why should philanthropies *not* be thinking in terms of scale and innovation and disruption and self-sustaining development? If we really want to impact the lives of millions or even billions of people, then helping them boost themselves out of poverty is the best way to make a lasting positive difference. But we have to do things differently; we have to funda-mentally change the philanthropy paradigm—even if it means obviating the need for the philanthropic model itself that, like the healthcare system, treats chronic symptoms rather than cures underlying causes. As Martin Luther King, Jr. pointed out, while philanthropy may be commendable, it must not cause the philanthropist to overlook the circumstances that make philanthropy necessary in the first place!

As a lifelong entrepreneur, I look at philanthropic organizations in the same way as any other business venture. Much like today's startups that accept VC mon-ey but never turn a profit, a philanthropic venture that does not create a self-mon-etizing, sustainable financial model will ultimately fail. And that doesn't help anybody. On the other hand, if you approach global challenges with an entrepre-neurial mindset, then you begin to think about solutions in very different ways; you begin to see the possibilities of impacting a billion people rather than affecting a few hundred thousand or even a million people. And that lifts everybody.

Think about this. John Hope Bryant observed that 84 percent of all tax revenue in the state of California is paid by 15 percent of California taxpayers. Is that a problem or an opportunity? The entrepreneur sees in this a massive opportunity to develop another 85 percent of Californians who could be "contributing more, doing more, aspiring more, and adding more to California's bottom line." Think what that could do! It would be utterly transformative. We could change the world from within our own borders! And if we can't do that in the amazingly resource-rich state of California, how is it that we believe we can accomplish any meaningful development goals in third world countries run by corrupt governments?! It's mind-boggling, really.

> **Philanthropy should never be about giving money. Rather, it should be about solving a problem. While well-meaning, the idea of writing a check and calling it "philanthropy" is extremely short-sighted and, unfortunately, extremely pervasive.**

As I point out the inconsistencies of thought in philanthropy, I do not wish to depreciate the amazing work done around the world by passionate people who are willing to both live and die for the sake of their missions. There is no question that they bring massive relief to millions of people in distress as a result of famine, disease, natural disasters, and political crises. The world is a far better place because of them, and thank God for them. My central point, though—and my challenge to would-be moonshot entrepreneurs—is to point to the enormous but untapped opportunities to address the *underlying causes* of distress. This can only be accomplished through the combination of technology developments and entrepreneurial creativity driven by a mindset of possibility. Otherwise we're only perpetually treating symptoms. The central problem with most philanthropic organizations is that they are fundamentally organized to treat the chronic symptoms that arise from an economy built on scarcity.

Moreover, most nonprofits measure success by such metrics as dollars raised, membership growth, people served, administrative costs, and distribution ratios. While obviously important, these metrics have nothing to do with determining the actual success of an organization in fulfilling its mission. And their mission statements don't help. For example, we often find such lofty statements as, "Affirming the dignity and worth of individuals and families living in some of the world's poorest communities." What, exactly, does that mean? How do you measure dignity and worth? What problem are they solving? What self-sustaining solutions are they creating? How do they define success? None of these things are clear.

A big part of the problem is that success, like many things in life, suffers from a poor definition. As an entrepreneur, I measure philanthropic success in very different and very specific terms—terms that translate directly to mission outcomes, financial sustainability, and, no less importantly, personal formation. I'd like to close us out here, on that last point, because when you get this right, you'll never have to worry about the others.

○◑●◐

There's a great story from Thomas Merton, a Trappist monk who, despite his best efforts to shun worldly success, was unable to contain the sheer force of his talent and intellect. "A few years ago," he said, "a man who was compiling a book entitled *Success* wrote and asked me to contribute a statement on how I got to be a success. I replied indignantly that I was not able to consider myself a success in any terms that had meaning to me. I swore I had spent my life strenuously avoiding success. If it so happened that I had once written a bestseller, this was a pure accident, due to inattention and naïvete and I would take very good care never to do the same again. If I had a message to my contemporaries, I said, it was surely this: Be anything you like, be madmen, drunks, and bastards of every shape and form, but at all costs avoid one thing: *success*. I heard no more from him and I am not aware that my reply was published with the other testimonials."

I'm sure it wasn't! But this story does bring us very directly to the question of success, what it means, how we measure it, how you know when you've achieved it. In any event, I can tell you that there is great danger in defining success in purely financial terms, which, as people learn every day, is one of the world's greatest deceptions.

No doubt Merton would have appreciated the thoughts of G.K. Chesterton, who wrote, "Among the rich you will never find a really generous man even by accident. They may give their money away, but they will never give *themselves* away; they are egotistic, secretive, dry as old bones. To be smart enough to get all that money you must be dull enough to want it."

Well, okay then! With that, though, I'd like to reframe this sentiment in the context of my own experience. The simple fact is that God has been incredibly kind to my family. I owe a tremendous debt to the many people who helped me become who I am. I've also learned that the only way to pay back is to pay *forward*, and hopefully, along the way, inspire a few entrepreneurs to help other entrepreneurs with the most valuable of all resources: their time. Indeed, giving of one's self is the greatest gift that anyone can give to another human being. It took a very humbling event in my life to learn this.

About 15 years ago I received a call from a woman who told me that her husband, who was in an ICU, wanted to talk to me. I thought to myself, oh boy, now I've got to listen to this sob story about medical bills piling up and so on, so I interrupted her to say, "Ma'am, we have a foundation to help with situations like this. We'll be more than happy to take care of all your husband's medical bills if you'll just email me the details." But again, she insisted that her hus-

> **"What does it mean if I think of myself as a social entrepreneur? It means, quite bluntly, that I am a shitty entrepreneur. If I were a good entrepreneur I wouldn't need a qualifier.""**

band be permitted to speak with me. And again, I said, "Ma'am, I'm really, really busy, but I promise that if you will just send me the information, we'll take care of everything for you." She would not be put off. "Can't you just spend two minutes talking to him?" she pleaded. At this point, I thought that it might just be easier to talk with him and be done with it. So I had her put him on the line. "Sir," I asked, "what is it that I can do for you?" After a long pause, he began to speak. "I just want you to know," he said, "how proud I am of you."

○ ◑ ◕ ◐

I came to America in 1982, landing in Flemington, New Jersey. I rented an old farmhouse along with six other people, sharing a $500 beater of a car among us. I found a minimum wage job, and life was great. It really was. Coming from an Indian slum to such "lavish" living was something I actually never could have imagined. Then October came and the snow began to fall. And fall. Snow was an utterly new experience for me, and I was not prepared for it. I had no warm clothes or boots, and the only shoes I did have had holes in them. Suddenly India wasn't looking so bad. I was actually thinking of going back home when I met a man who was working at Burroughs (now Unisys). When I told him of my plans, he pleaded with me to reconsider, suggesting that I go to Silicon Valley instead. "You're a bright guy," he told me. "We could really use you in this country. You've got talent. Let me make a few calls and set up a few interviews for you—I know you'll succeed there." And with that, I did indeed make the move to Silicon Valley, and grew into a wonderful career in technology.

A short time later, an engineer friend of mine had just sold his company and took me out to lunch to celebrate. When he told me that he had made $100,000 on the deal, it sent my mind racing. I thought then that if I could someday make $100,000, I'd be set for life! It so happened that a few years later, I got married and took a job at Microsoft. This was in the late 1980s, just before Microsoft's stock took off. In my *first month* there, my options were already worth $100,000! Incredible. Six months later, the options were worth over a million dollars. But I still didn't have a house or a car, because I wasn't yet able to exercise those options. It's funny then how the mind starts to work. At that point I began to believe that I would need not $100,000 or $1 million, but *$5 million* in order to make a good living. The point is, it doesn't really matter what you earn; it is never enough. There is always a reason why whatever you have is too little—even following the phenomenal success we later had at InfoSpace. When I had nothing, the very idea of $100,000 was sheer mind-blowing fantasy. But human need and greed constantly and insatiably multiply. As you start to move up in life, you always think there is something better. And then, just as Chesterton called it, you become dull, ungrateful, dry as old bones.

> **The central problem with most philanthropic organizations is that they are fundamentally organized to treat the chronic symptoms that arise from an economy built on scarcity.**

○ ☽ ● ☾

"You may not recall," the man continued from his bed in the ICU, his weak voice straining, "but when you were ready to go back to India, I told you to stay in this country. And I've been watching your progress ever since. I'm just so proud of what you have done in life, and I want you to know that. I'm so happy that you made the decision to stay here."

Now, have you ever had one of those moments in life when you feel the blood draining from your face? I thought to myself, *oh no, this can't be true.* "I am so sorry," I said. "I had no idea. Is there anything I can do for you? Anything at all?" He answered no, that he was just fine.

This brief conversation changed my life forever. There are so many people who helped me, and not only do I not remember them, but worse, *they don't need my help.* I learned in that moment that you cannot pay back—you can only pay forward. As a consequence of that unexpected event, I resolved to answer every single person who comes to me for help. And when they come to the same realization that they can't pay it back either, that they too will pay it forward. Who knows how it might pay off?

This experience also reoriented my thinking to working on the really big problems that need solving—energy, healthcare, education—in short, flipping the scarcity model on its head to create a world of health and abundance. In my mind, there is simply no greater object for philanthropy. What's more, these new ways of thinking had the added effect of redefining my whole concept of success.

I've learned in more ways than one that success is not measured by how much money one has in the bank, but by how many lives one is able to impact. In life, of course, we all struggle and strive to make progress. So when, then, can one know that success has been achieved? Money is certainly an indicator, but it is not the proper end. The ultimate mark of a life well spent—*a truly successful life*—has nothing to do with money and everything to do with spirit. And as we've seen, a full spirit can be far more difficult to attain than a fat bank account. It is also an infinitely more powerful resource. But there's one crucial aspect of this spirit formation that runs counterintuitive to achieving something as audacious as a moonshot.

You'll know you've reached the true measure of success the day you become truly humble. It's the day you stop needing to prove to the world—or to yourself—that you've accomplished something meaningful.

As an entrepreneur, of course you want to work for yourself, you want to make some good money. There's nothing wrong with that. But if you really want to work for yourself, then think first about others. If you work to make other people successful, you will most certainly also become successful.

In this sense, there is a massive difference between becoming successful and becoming *significant*. How do you become significant? You actually have within you the seeds of significance already. Altruism is baked into your genes. If you ever happen to commit an act of generosity, blame your DNA! So you have a head start. All that's left, then, is the proper formation of the entrepreneurial mindset of possibility that sets the abundant life in motion. But above all, the great entrepreneur must first be a great humanitarian. Love is the source and meaning of life. To do good, to live a life of significance, we also need courage and creativity in equal measure.

I pray that everyone will choose to live a life of significance, to "open the mysterious shutters of the impossible." It's what you were born to do. You and our collective future—*a future of abundance*—depend on it.

Cleared for Liftoff—the Big Takeaways for Launching Your Moonshot

O UR WORLD TODAY IS DOMINATED BY THE ECONOMICS OF SCARCITY and its ever-complicit offspring: mindsets that are as self-limiting as they are self-fulfilling. These well-disposed coconspirators work hand in glove to perpetuate much of what's wrong in the world—and the global anxiety that invariably attends it. Centuries of history have shown us that they will never move humanity into a future of abundance, let alone acknowledge its possibility. If our civilization is to survive and flourish, we'll need fundamental, wholesale changes to the way we think and operate.

In *Moonshots* I have proposed a bold way forward—a path to abundance and prosperity that is informed and shaped by the powerful secrets of the entrepreneurial mindset—secrets, having read this book, that you now possess. When the uniquely human attributes of curiosity and imagination are harnessed to the engine of exponential innovation, we become empowered to create a future without limits. But as I mentioned, the "established orders"—and the powerbases that sustain them—are actually arrayed against the rich and prosperous future we so vividly envision. It will take something truly extraordinary to overcome this resistance—and that something is *you*. But how?

To conquer the world's great challenges, we first need to restore our lost sense of wonder, to reclaim a mindset driven by possibility thinking, imagination, curiosity, and, most importantly, the courage to ask big, daring "what if" questions—even "crazy" questions. There is no question that we will realize either the world we fear to imagine or the world we dare to dream. So why not dare to dream an amazing, abundant, and prosperous future—and will that crazy dream right into existence?! This is, after all, what moonshots are all about!

When people tell you that your ideas are crazy—and they should, if you're on the right track—remember that what's *actually* crazy is short-sighted incrementalism and linear approaches to problems of exponential proportions—and believing they'll make any difference at all!

Bold "what if" questions constitute the most compelling force on Earth. Everything hinges on our being audacious enough to ask them. What's more, these questions are far more consequential than the answers, because they are the key to unlocking them. Everything works backward. The same is true of questions. For example, we don't create answers, we *reveal* them when we discover the right questions. And we perpetually question our way forward.

The first question, of course, is will *you* dare to be one of those who asks these all-important, audacious, and world-transforming questions? And if not you, then who? It has become painfully obvious that we cannot count on the experts, governments, corporations, or institutions to ask them; they are far too invested in the status quo and in the preservation of their respective strongholds. But when entrepreneurs ask these grand questions, the energy that is released in the process is never lost in heat. Rather, that energy transforms the *asker* into a superpower: it enables the emboldened questioner to *act* upon the revealed answers. And the results are nothing less than astonishing.

Consequently, the nation-states are going to increasingly lose power to influence where the world is headed. And because entrepreneurs have stepped up, entrepreneurs are going to take the lead. This is why the next set of superpowers is most likely to be entrepreneurs—entrepreneurs who are not waiting on others to solve problems or address the things that they care about. And they'll do it in ways that rock the very foundations of the scarcity-driven economy—and everything the experts have simply taken for granted. Meaning they won't do it through sustainability, which, as we've seen, only reinforces the value of scarce commodities. But an even bigger problem on sustainability's horizon is that sustainability is actually not sustainable! Sustainability won't help us at all in a world where we have to create *more* of what we need rather than consume *less* of what we have. And creating that world that will take nothing less than moonshot thinking. Moreover, until one begins to understand the actual sequences of consumption cycles, we are constantly only ever solving the *symptoms* of problems, not the root causes. Only entrepreneurs can solve this conundrum. And when they do, these same entrepreneurs shine light into the darkness, illuminate a vision, and inspire a dream of a better future for everyone.

Now, then, is the time for *you* to launch your own moonshot. And as you do, if you'll keep these insights top of mind, together with the following additional ten takeaways, I have no doubt that you'll achieve great success.

1 • To move the world beyond the oppressive limits imposed by the scarcity economy, we first have to move beyond the limits we've placed on ourselves; we've got to energize our lives at the true levels of our potential. If you can do that, you'll be astounded by what you can accomplish.

2 • Remember that moonshots are all about smashing existing paradigms. In order to accomplish one, we first have to overcome the indoctrination of the established order of expectations. By its very nature, a moonshot openly defies the majority opinion. Indeed, the exponential thinking of the moonshot entrepreneur sets out to do nothing less than change all the ground rules.

3 • One of the major challenges we face is that most people default to seeing the world only *as it is* and not imagining what the world *could be*. But what *could* the world be? Whenever we focus only on what *is*, we resign ourselves to a particular destiny—a destiny the moonshot entrepreneur is dedicated to disrupting.

4 • There are very few problems that can't be solved with imagination, innovation, and competent entrepreneurship. And that includes much of what many people think of as impossible. The minute you believe something is impossible, it becomes impossible for *you*. Nothing is inherently impossible.

5 • As with curiosity, we also need to cultivate, broaden, and enrich our powers of perception, to expand the field of vision that enables us to recognize the nonobvious connections, especially beyond the simple cause and effect to which we so easily default.

6 • Creative innovation always comes from connecting disparate and nonobvious dots; it doesn't take place so much *within* disciplines as it does at the intersections and boundaries between them. And this is precisely why imagination, perception, curiosity, and lateral thinking are so important to the moonshot entrepreneur.

7 • While knowledge is vital, we also know that it hasn't solved the world's problems—it cannot. The vast majority of the problems in this world—and in corporate boardrooms—are caused not by a lack of knowledge, but by failures of imagination.

8 • Knowledge can actually hinder imagination and the process of innovation. Once one becomes competent in a particular domain—an expert—he can only improve it incrementally; he can never disrupt it. As people accumulate knowledge in their respective fields, they become increasingly constrained by that knowledge. They develop a "way of doing things" that may not be amendable to new problems that require completely different approaches. This is the thinking that the moonshot entrepreneur—forever a *dilettante* (or a "virgin," as Sir Richard Branson puts it)—is determined to upend.

9 • Moonshots are by definition wild and free range entities. If you try to regulate or otherwise restrain a moonshot, it'll never reach escape velocity.

Moonshots require the throwing off of the encumbrances of conventional, incremental thinking in order to achieve wholesale, exponential change.

10 • Lastly, while moonshots might be hard, paradoxically, they can often be easier to accomplish than less ambitious initiatives. Still, challenges will rise up to meet you on your way. Remember always along this journey that true entrepreneurs never fail—they pivot! Oftentimes, success is found on the very far, dark side of what only *appears* to be failure. How you deal with setbacks and difficulties may actually be the primary determinant of your ultimate success.

In the end, the key to the successful moonshot is an openness to radical possibility—the first and most vital step in awakening the virtually unlimited capacity of the human mind and its astounding potential to remake our world. And you—indeed *everyone*—can play a vital and indispensable role in bringing that world about.

KEEP IN TOUCH

We'd love to hear about your moonshot and also connect you with a community of like-minded entrepreneurs and resources that might be helpful as you plan your audacious initiative. Please take a moment to sign up for our free newsletter, *Moonshots Update*, at **moonshotsupdate.com**, where we'll be curating and featuring your stories along with insightful interviews with some of the most inspiring personalities—as well as feeding you a continuous stream of tip-offs to new and emerging technologies awaiting the hands and minds of creative entrepreneurs.

We'd also like to keep you up to date about the series of conferences and other events we're planning that will give us the opportunity to meet face to face. In the meantime, you can always reach us via **moonshotsupdate.com**. Thank you for spending a bit of your valuable time with us! We sincerely hope it will prove profitable in more ways than you might imagine.